—

Green
Politics
One

—

EDITOR
WOLFGANG RÜDIG

—

Green
Politics One

1990

—

SOUTHERN ILLINOIS UNIVERSITY PRESS
Carbondale and Edwardsville

Published in the United States,
its dependencies, Canada, and the Phillipine Islands by
Southern Illinois University Press,
P.O. Box 3697
Carbondale, IL 62902-3697

© Edinburgh University Press 1990
22 George Square, Edinburgh

Set in Linotron Joanna
by Koinonia Ltd, Bury, and
printed in Great Britain by
Page Bros. Ltd, Norwich

ISBN 0-8093-1734-6

ISSN #1052-5335 : GREEN POLITICS ONE 1990

Editorial

WOLFGANG RÜDIG

Green politics is taking off, not only politically but also academically. Green Politics One is the inaugural issue of a periodical publication which seeks to provide a forum for the new academic research field of green politics. Green Politics One takes the form of a Yearbook, and further yearbooks are planned with Green Politics Two due out in 1991 and Green Politics Three in 1992.

Anybody embarking on a project like this must have some confidence that the subject matter of such a yearly publication will not disappear quickly. In many ways, the green euphoria of 1989 must instil some scepticism. Have we not seen all of this before? In all too many ways, the issues raised in 1989 are just the same as those, say, in 1970 when Earth Day galvanized environmental concern in the United States, or in 1972 when the 'Blueprint for Survival' spelled out the practical implications of the environmental crisis to a startled British audience. Certainly, the issues vary a little. It was the population bomb in the late 1960s, the depletion of resources in the early 1970s, and it is the greenhouse effect today. The details may vary, but the type of doomsday scenario predicting global disaster is not that dissimilar. Nor is, arguably, the response: politicians then as now confirm the seriousness of the situation but prefer to appeal to the individual to change his/her ways rather than contemplating any major shift in policy or a more fundamental change in economic, social or political structures.

Have we thus not seen everything before, and will the issue not again fade into the background before long, at the latest when we approach the next national elections? Will the real issues of jobs, inflation, mortgage rates and economic growth then not dominate the headlines again?

The reawakening, or redramatization, of environmental concern in the late 1980s, sparked off by dramatic incidents such as Chernobyl and the Exxon Valdez disaster, can also be interpreted as a sign of the endurance of a concern which long ago has lost the innocence of a 'single issue'. Issue attention cycles apply most of all to the behaviour of the media and,while we live in an age in which the definition of social reality through the media is progressing faster than ever, the periodic changes in attention to the environment are mere surface reflections of a phenomenon which is more enduring, far more enduring, than most commentators in the late 1960s and early 1970s would have dreamt of. Environmental issues are here to stay; they are not just going to fade away so long as serious environmental problems remain unsolved. More profoundly, these are arguably not simply issues any more, they reflect a more fundamental conflict which is concerned with the very nature of the future development of society as a whole.

Whatever one's view of environmentalism, ecology, greens, and assorted phenomena, even the most ardent protagonist of industrial development cannot deny that the 'greens' have become a major influence and cannot be reduced to some marginal phenomenon of minority groups populated by hippies, nut-cases, and utopian leftists. What has changed between 1970 and 1990, particularly in Europe, is that radical ecology now has an organized voice; the environment is represented, not just by docile single-issue pressure groups but by a new range of organizations which have set out to challenge the dominant paradigm of industrial society.The fortunes of these new representatives of radical political ecology may fluctuate, their organizational form may change, they may split up or join new alliances, they may change strategy, disappear and reemerge in a new guise. But, in whatever form, they are here, and staying here, to represent the enduring concern with a fundamental problem of the society we live in.

Why, some readers may now ask, are we only talking so far about 'the environment'? Is 'green politics' not much more than that; is it not the epitomization of a new breed of radical politics which embraces not just environmentalism but also peace, social equality, feminism and alternative ways of living?

Green politics is, indeed, many things to many people. Everybody likes to be green nowadays, and, not surprisingly, the inflation of greenness abounds. It is not that long ago that the colour 'green' was universally recognized as a 'new' political colour with no connection to Irish politics. When the German Greens introduced the term to an international mass audience in the early 1980s, 'green' stood for a radical environmental and anti-nuclear stance which embraced many of the 'New Left' concerns of the 1960s student movements. With the success of the German Greens, other, initially less successful, parties, such as the British Ecology Party, also moved to adopt the new label. However, this did not imply a transformation of 'green politics' throughout Europe according to the German model; it broadened the political meaning of 'greenness' to include a wide variety of green outlooks. With the success of green parties throughout Europe, spearheaded by Britain in 1989, the use of the term 'green' has come full circle: while it was first used to characterize the politically most 'advanced' and radical form of ecological and anti-nuclear concern, sharply divided from conservation and reformist environmentalism,now any conservation or environmental activity, attitude or other inclination is bound to be dubbed 'green' with little regard for the finer differences in political outlook.

Given this ubiquitous confusion about 'green politics', where does this Yearbook stand? The use or misuse of the term 'green' in political discourse, advertisements, and the media generally may well be one topic of analysis but the core area of our concern lies in the manifestation of greenness in terms of social movements and political parties. It is through their choice of labelling themselves as 'green' that the field of 'green politics' has been defined. The prime function of this Yearbook is thus to provide a forum for academic discussion on the social scientific analysis of all aspects of green social movements and green political parties.

Green Politics is not a partisan publication; it does intend to propagate any particular view of green politics. Neither is Green Politics a 'movement' publication in which activists can read about the next conference or the latest policy resolutions. Beyond a basic assumption that 'green politics' is an important political innovation which is worthy of serious academic study, all points of view including those critical of green politics are admitted.

Green Politics seeks to fill a gap in the literature which is felt even more profoundly in face of the recent media bally-hoo: a forum for academic debate on green politics, reporting social scientific research to provide a basis for a more profound understanding about the nature of green politics in its many forms.

Such a forum is all the more necessary in view of the fragmented and dissipated nature of research. Green politics spans a number of disciplines. In Britain, environmental issues have traditionally been the domain of geographers and planners, with the new environmental studies discipline chipping in occasionally. For various reasons, British sociologists and political scientists played no or very scant attention to environmentalism. The rise of green politics on the continent added to this problem: Area studies specialists were one of the first in Britain to take an interest in this phenomenon. Most of the studies of the German and French ecology movements have thus been conducted by academics specializing in French and German culture and language rather than political scientists or sociologists. In the USA and in continental Europe, sociologists and political scientists did take an earlier interest. Within each of these disciplines, green politics has, however, remained a fairly marginal affair.

It is noticeable that it is particularly postgraduate researchers and junior faculty at the beginning of their careers who are developing a strong interest in green politics and who find that their publishing opportunities are often blocked by the less than enthusiastic attitude of their peers about the subject matter of green politics.

It must also be said, however, that much of the published material on green politics has been of dubious quality. The book market has been flooded with 'green' books but few of them contain any significant material of an empirical or theoretical nature which any more rigorous social scientists would be happy with.

It is these shortcomings which Green Politics sets out to overcome. First, Green Politics will be an interdisciplinary publication in which representatives of all social science disciplines making a contribution to the study of green politics are welcome. It is conceived as an explicit attempt the bridge the gaps between the disciplines and to stimulate an exchange of views between them.

Second, Green Politics will rigorously follow the highest academic standards and only publish material which is the result of original scientific research. It is not a ghetto in which sub-standard articles which do not stand a chance to be published in mainstream academic journals are dumped. To the contrary, Green Politics offers the chance to publish substantial contributions which are too voluminous for most academic periodicals.

And third, Green Politics is an international enterprise in which authors from all corners of the world publish articles on aspects of green politics covering a wide range of countries and regions.

This first volume seeks to live up to all three of these far-reaching aims which we set for the Yearbook. To take the last aim first, the contributions to Green Politics One provide up-to-date analysis of developments in a wide range of countries, coming from a truly international authorship. In some cases, the volume provides information on some of the smaller European countries,such as Belgium, Italy and Ireland, which are rarely covered in the literature. The geographical focus of this first volume is decidedly European, partly reflecting the topical upsurge of green voting in 1989 throughout Europe, but in future volumes, developments outside Western Europe will also be covered.

All of the articles in this volume report the result of original social scientific research. In many cases, results of major empirical work are reported for the first time. It is a clear sign of the increasing sophistication of social science work on green politics that a substantial amount of data on green voters and members of green parties can now be reported, and that quantitative methodologies are used by most of the contributors.

Thirdly, the authorship of this first volume is an interdisciplinary one, bringing together members of sociology, political science, business studies, and modern languages departments. In future volumes, these will be joined by geographers, planners and environmental studies specialists.

What has the first volume of *Green Politics* to offer to the reader? We begin with an article on perhaps the most startling green political event of 1989, the staggering success of the British Greens in the European Elections which is analysed by Gene Frankland. After more than 16 years in the political wilderness, the British Greens polled 15% in June 1989. As Frankland can show, the signs for a major upsurge of green concern were, however, already there earlier in the year. What does this unexpected success mean for other small green movements across the Atlantic? Frankland looks at the USA and Canada and sees if one unexpected success could be repeated elsewhere.

In the second paper, the rather different problems of a well-established German Green Party are discussed by Thomas Poguntke. Sweeping electoral successes have been hard to come by recently for the German Greens. With some of the original momentum gone, can the Party maintain its level of support among members and voters, or is the world's best-known green party destined for decline and marginality?

The internal structure of two green parties is analysed by Herbert Kitschelt who seeks to confront the Belgian experience of grassroots democracy with the 'iron law of oligarchy', the principle established by Roberto Michels at the beginning of the century when he looked at another party which had a movement character at that time, the Social Democrats. Can the Greens combine their commitment to direct forms of internal party democracy with the stringent demands of political operation in a parliamentary system? Kitschelt looks at the two Belgian parties Agalev and Ecolo to find out.

Anthony Affigne looks at the specific influence of the Chernobyl accident on the development of the Swedish Green Party. He can show some remarkable links between the degree of direct impact of the Chernobyl fallout on individual regions and their inclination to move towards the Greens at election time.

The further articles in this volume concentrate somewhat less on party political manifestations of green politics. Susan Baker provides a thorough historical account of the development of the Irish ecology movement. Mario Diani seeks to interpret the particular experience of the Italian ecology movement, a process of moderation rather than radicalization, within a broader framework of European social movement development. And Brendan Prendiville and Tony Chafer look at the membership and ideology of the French Green Party in the context of the specifically French movement culture as it has emerged in the ecology field since the early

1970s. The volume is concluded by a review essay in which Andrew McCulloch has a look at the flood of British green books of the 1980s, and a number of book reviews covering some important new theoretical issues in the field.

Green Politics One gives some indication of the type of subject area which will be covered in this Yearbook, but it only covers one part, if a major part, of the area. We have already indicated the desired extension of the geographical focus: Future yearbooks will contain contributions on green politics in Eastern Europe, the USA and Japan, as well as the 'Third World'. Also, we are interested in substantial contributions on green political theory. This is one area which has been given particularly scant attention by social scientists and has been virtually ignored by the traditional political theorists. Finally, we are also interested in the analysis of green policy making in terms of the policies pursued by green parties which have gained some form of governmental responsibility, and in the form of analyses of the policy impact of green movements and parties generally. However, is not intended to publish general articles on environmental policy in the Yearbook as there are already a number of periodicals and other well-established publication outlets for this type of material.

It lies in the character of a Yearbook that it does not present a homogeneous view of its subject matter.On the contrary, one of its crucial functions is to stimulate debate, to rouse controversy, to provide a forum for discussion. The contributions to the first volume reflect a number of different theoretical approaches, methodologies, perceptions of green politics. Future volumes will also reflect the multitude of views in this area, but, it is hoped will bring them together in a form which will stimulate discussion and move the debate on green politics forward to a new level.

1. Does Green Politics have a Future in Britain? An American Perspective

E. GENE FRANKLAND

Department of Political Science,

Ball State University, Muncie, Indiana, USA

On 15 June 1989, the British Greens amazed the pundits and themselves by winning 15 per cent of the national vote (compared with 0.6 per cent in 1984) in the European Parliament election. In six Euro-constituencies they finished as the second strongest party, winning as much as 25.4 per cent of the votes. In 77 out of 78 constituencies the Greens outpolled the Social and Liberal Democrats, and everywhere they outdistanced the Owenite Social Democratic Party (SDP). Their share of the votes soared to the highest of any green party in the European Community! Under proportional representation, the British Greens would have received twelve seats (instead of zero) in the European Parliament, which would have been four more than the internationally predominant West German Greens won.

The British Greens are hardly a 'flash' party. Their formation in February 1973 makes them Western Europe's oldest organized green party. However, for its first sixteen years, the party remained an obscure party, which political scientists ignored or lumped together with many fringe or 'nonserious' minor parties in Britain.[1] The British electoral system is notoriously unkind to national third parties, even well- established ones such as the Liberals. While small green parties were winning seats in nine West European national parliaments, British environmentalists chose for the most part to work through established interest group and party politics. After its disappointing 1987 general election campaign, the Green Party seemed little more than another British case of minor party futility.

But two years later in the aftermath of the Euro-election, national polls indicated that the Greens were Britain's third party in terms of popular support.[2] Why did the small Green Party emerge so suddenly from obscurity and what are its future prospects? To address these questions, we begin by reviewing the Green Party's meagre development during 1973–87. Then we will examine the changing political environment, 1988–9 election results, and subsequent developments. We will conclude by placing the emergence of the British Greens in a wider framework, including some North American observations.

The Development of the Green Party, 1973–87

In 1972 The Ecologist generated considerable debate by publishing a comprehensive plan for coping with Britain's environmental problems called 'The Blueprint for Survival'. However, its proposed unified politicized environmental movement did not materialize. But in 1973 a small group of activists around Coventry formed an environmentalist party named simply 'People' which adopted the 'Blueprint for Survival' as its manifesto. In 1974 they nominated five candidates in the February general election and four candidates in the October general election with meagre results. In 1975 the party changed its name to the Ecology Party. Programmatic disputes caused some of its early activists to resign, and party membership grew barely at all. During 1976-8, the obscure party ran candidates in scattered local council elections and won three seats. The party was on the verge of foundering when new leaders emerged in 1977.

In 1978 the Ecology Party, with only 500 members, no national office, and no paid staff, decided to 'go for broke' by nominating at least 50 parliamentary candidates in the next general election in order to qualify for free broadcast time. Party activists perceived themselves as a radical party which addressed the causes and not the symptoms of contemporary crises. The small party's electoral manifesto, 'The Real Alternative', which argued the case for a steady-state economy and against economic growth, received some national press attention. In the May 1979 general election the party won 0.13 per cent of the national vote (1.6 per cent where it ran candidates). In the June 1979 European Parliament election, the party struggled to contest three of Britain's 78 seats and won 3–4 per cent of the votes in these constituencies. As a result of its heightened visibility during these campaigns, party membership rose to over 5000 in 1980.

During 1981–3, the Ecology Party increased its number of local candidates and elected a few councillors, but its membership declined sharply. Despite a MORI May 1983 poll suggesting that 12 per cent of the electorate might vote for the Ecology Party, its 109 candidates won only 1 per cent of the votes where they contested seats in the general election, less than in 1979 (Parkin, 1989, pp. 223–4). In the June 1984 European Parliament election, the Ecology Party's seventeen candidates also averaged a smaller share of the votes contested than in 1979.

At its September 1985 conference, the party voted to rename itself 'The Green Party' in order to make the linkage with more successful West European green parties and to prevent other British parties from 'poaching' the identity. During 1985-7, the party's performance in local elections improved slightly, and party membership grew to 8000. In the 1987 general election the British Greens' 113 candidates won 0.3 per cent of the national votes. They averaged 1.4 per cent in their constituencies, better than in 1983 but less than in 1979. During 1973-87, the Greens had little appeal for protest voters in parliamentary by-elections. If one judges party 'success' by the number of elected representatives, the People/Ecology/Green Party's success after fifteen years had been slight - about 100 local councillors, mostly at the parish level.

A number of external factors have worked against the emergence of the Green Party as an electoral force. First, there have been legal/institutional barriers. Britain's first-past-the-post electoral system is a most formidable obstacle for any small party which lacks geographical strongholds. Furthermore, British electoral law deters 'trivial' candidacies by requiring constituency deposits, which the Conservative government in the mid- 1980s raised to £500 in general elections and £1000 in European elections (while lowering the threshold for saving one's deposit from 12.5 per cent to 5 per cent of the votes). In contrast to West Germany, there is no legal provision in Britain whereby parties obtaining a certain percentage of the votes qualify for public funding. Also, the federal system of West Germany provides opportunities for a new party to build up its credibility by winning state parliamentary seats. In the British unitary system, success in winning local council seats normally brings little in terms of resources, experience, or visibility transferable to national politics. Though small British parties may be able to qualify for a campaign allotment of free broadcast time, it is infinitesimal compared with the daily coverage which the London-centred mass media continuously devote to those parties represented in Parliament.

Second, the nature of party competition has been a complicating factor. The Labour and Conservative Parties can draw upon not only considerable organizational resources but also the long socialization of partisanship among the citizenry, which new parties can not. However, the protest vote for nationalist and Liberal candidates in the 1970s indicated growing discontent with the performance of both major parties. Survey data revealed the loosening of the traditional nexus between class and party. The left-right polarization of Labour and Conservative programmes after 1979 provided an historic opportunity for party system change. Benefiting from generous media coverage, professional leadership, and about 180 000 grassroots members, the SDP/Liberal Alliance sought to seize the centre of the British political spectrum. Thus, the small Ecology Party (Green Party after 1985) confronted a formidable competitor, which the West German Greens did not confront, in presenting itself as the 'real alternative'.

Third, the British Greens' unfavourable political environment has involved the pattern of interest articulation. The West German Greens sprang from a widespread base of nonpartisan citizen action groups focused on environmental and social problems neglected by the major parties. With rare exceptions, British conservation groups have wanted nothing to do with a 'radical' ecology party. British environmentalists have sought reforms through 'respectable' channels, such as the established parties, public enquiries, and advisory committees, whereas many West German environmentalists have had little faith in system responsiveness. In the early 1980s the West German Greens' political opportunity structure was such that they could broaden their appeal to become 'the' eco-peace party. Although the Ecology Party took similar stands regarding nuclear disarmament, it was totally overshadowed by the anti-militarist left wing of the Labour Party and by the revived Campaign for Nuclear Disarmament (CND). Furthermore, in West Germany, feminists and other human rights activists joined forces with the Greens; in Britain these activists largely ignored the Ecology Party.

Fourth, the level of public concern about environmental problems and the (real or perceived) responsiveness of the established parties to these problems obviously shapes the electoral opportunities of a green party. During the 1970s, the environmental awareness of the British general public lagged behind that found in West Germany, which one could attribute in part to the two countries' diverging economic circumstances. Within each of the major British parties, pro-environmental 'ginger' groups reflective of the concerns of segments of the attentive public appeared. Despite such intraparty groups, the major party leaderships were preoccupied with economic development. The Liberals had the largest 'green' streak among their membership; in 1979 the Liberal Assembly, to its party leadership's dismay, passed a motion challenging conventional assumptions about economic growth. During the 1980s as public opinion polls indicated growing concern about environmental problems, ecological themes became increasingly evident in parliamentary debates, at national conferences, and in election manifestos. Most of this party rhetoric can be described as 'technocentric' environmentalism (Owens 1986, pp. 195-201). The Conservative, Labour, and Alliance leaderships subsequently added environmental provisions to their programmes, which were dominated by other priorities. According to the Green Party's *General Election Manifesto* (1987, p. 1), being 'green' means much more than reformist environmentalism which tinkers with the status quo:

> Green politics is about building a new way of life, one that is based on our respect for our planet and humility about our role in it. We need to stop building on the quicksand of materialism, patriarchy, competition, and aggression. We are sinking faster than most people think.

Nevertheless, the environment did not become a major campaign issue during the 1987 general election.

Fifth, there are internal factors which help to explain the nonemergence of the Green Party as an electoral force in British politics. Because the Greens rely almost exclusively on members' dues and donations, their budgets have been meagre. In 1988 the total income of the national office was £48 000; it employed only two full-time and two part-time staffers. While these limiting characteristics are involuntary, there are others which the Green Party voluntarily adopted. The Greens deliberately organized themselves as a 'weak' party organization. However, the same 'anti-party' characteristics which may attract activists at the outset may repel voters in the long run. This possibility has not bothered the 'anarchist' minority tendency within the party, which has emphasized direct actions rather than elections to get the party's message across (Rüdig and Lowe 1986). The 'anarchists' have vigorously resisted changes proposed by the 'electoralists' which might strengthen the party's central organization.

The Green Party strives to implement grassroots democracy within its organization. The Annual Conference, with its overloaded agenda, is the supreme policy-making body. The Party Council has functioned as an unwieldly administrative body of 25 members meeting quarterly. Attempts to institute a smaller executive board, which would frequently meet, have been turned back by grassroots opposition. Like the West German Greens, the British Greens since the early 1980s have embraced collective leadership and imposed restrictions on tenure: three co-chairs are selected annually by the Party Council and are limited to three consecutive years. Proposals which would allow for the selection of one or two national spokespersons, who could provide a focus for media coverage and voter identification, have failed. Despite the national leadership's lack of power resources, hostility against 'the faceless bunch of centralist bureaucracies called the Party Council and Conference' (Econews, August 1986, pp. 2–3) has not been rare. Noteworthy are the continual national office pleas for basic information from the local parties, which are not only more autonomous than their counterparts in the major parties but also more diverse in organization and orientation (McCulloch 1983).

In short, there are external and internal factors which 'explain' the Green Party's lack of impact in British politics during 1973-87. The external factors seem the powerful ones since the more successful green parties in Western Europe share many organizational characteristics with the less successful British Green Party. In view of its hostile setting, in the words of one Belgian Green, 'It is a matter of astonishment that a Green party exists in Britain at all' (Parkin 1989, p. 215).

E. GENE FRANKLAND

The Green Movement, 1988-89

During 1988–9, the highly institutionalized framework of British electoral politics did not change, nor did the Green Party transform its structure, programme, or strategy. Therefore, this section concerns itself with how changes in the nature of party competition, interest articulation, and public opinion have contributed to the sudden emergence of the Greens as an electoral force. According to Berrington (1985, p. 449), the chances of a breakthrough by a new party are greatest when there is expansion of the electorate, growth of a new clientele (attitudinal or social), reactivation of existing groups by major events, and decline of loyalties to established parties. Despite signs of potential system change, the SDP/Liberal Alliance waned as it was 'waiting for something to turn up'. The Alliance's credibility as a vehicle for new forces was handicapped by 'a vague, centrist ideology, and indistinct issue positions' (Clark and Zirk 1989, p. 218), which critics characterized as promising a 'better yesterday'. During 1988–9, the successor Social and Liberal Democrats suffered through not only a 'fratricidal' rivalry with the rump SDP but also an identity crisis, which was symbolized by public disagreements over the merged party's proper short name. While the Green Party lacked the organization, the finances and the visibility of the former Alliance parties, its identity was unambiguously and radically 'green' at a time when the environmental movement was surging as never before in Britain. And many journalists, environmentalists, and politicians had increasingly taken to using the new label.

During 1988–9 environmental crises became regular front-page stories in Britain's mass media. Global problems, such as ozone layer depletion and the greenhouse effect, rivalled regional problems, such as North Sea seal deaths and acid rain, and local problems, such as unsafe drinking water and green belt encroachment, for attention. Green consumerism had shifted from the fringes into the mainstream of the economy. For example MORI polls indicated that 19 per cent of British adults had chosen one product over another because of its environmental-friendliness in 1988; the figure had risen to 42 per cent in 1989 (The Times, 30 June 1989). Other polls showed increasing public concern with the seriousness of a growing list of environmental problems and the professed willingness of many to pay for environmental improvements. Between December 1988 and July 1989, the environment as an important issue moved from being mentioned by 5 per cent of the public to 35 per cent, putting it ahead of all other pubic concerns, such as the health service and unemployment (The Times, 3 July 1989 and 31 July 1989).

According to press reports in the spring of 1989, 20,000 Britons per month were joining environmental groups. The full spectrum of groups from the most respectable to the most radical were benefiting from this surge of public concern (Today, 7 April 1989). Friends of the Earth and Greenpeace are two groups which took up the 'green' identity before it came in vogue and have been more 'political' than large, long-standing conservation groups, such as the Royal Society for the Protection of Birds. During 1988-9, Friends of the Earth saw its paid-up membership climb from 31 000 to 125 000 while Greenpeace supporters jumped from 150 000 to 281 000.[3] The overwhelming majority of even active environmentalists are 'reformists', but the minority who are system-challenging seems likely to grow given the backlog of environmental problems that threaten to overwhelm the capacities of government. Organized interest groups to maintain their nonpartisanship continued to distance themselves from the Green Party. But given the undeniable commonality of their environmental concerns, the latter profited from the rapid growth of the former. The Green Party saw its membership increase from 8000 to 10 000 between September 1988 and May 1989.[4]

'Politicians change colour', The Economist declared in its cover story of 15 October 1988. Because of the Thatcher government's insensitivity to such problems as acid rain and nuclear wastes, Britain had become known during the 1980s in environmentalist circles as 'the dirty man of Europe'. But in her September 1988 speech to the Royal Society, Mrs Thatcher abruptly put herself on the side of 'sustainable economic growth' and against atmospheric pollution. Later pronouncements made it clear that, in contrast to the Greens, she saw no incompatibility between expansive economic growth and better environmental protection. At the Conservative party conference (which had seventy-four green motions on its agenda) in October 1988, Thatcher reclaimed conservation as a traditional Tory concern. In the spring of 1989 she hosted an international conference on ozone depletion and staged a Cabinet seminar on global warming. On the other hand, her government remained committed to the expansion of nuclear power and to the privatization of water authorities despite widespread public misgivings about environmental consequences. Growing threats by developmental projects to the English countryside mobilized local citizens whose objections were vocalised by Conservative backbenchers. The Thatcher government announced that a 'Green bill' to give substance to its rhetoric would be forthcoming.

At their first conference, the Social and Liberal Democrats (SLD) in September 1988 stood at 8 per cent in the Harris Poll (far below the typical 20 per cent plus performance of the former Alliance). The Democrats claimed to have a party membership of 85 000 (about half the combined total for the Liberals and SDP before their contested merger). At the same time, the Owenite SDP rump claimed 30 000 members and had 5 per cent in the Harris Poll. The Democrats' new leader, Paddy Ashdown, proclaimed that 'the green approach' must be at the core of the SLD's politics and deplored the Thatcher government's dismal environmental record (*The Independent*, 30 September 1988). The Democrats voted for the phase-out of civilian nuclear power but without a specific timetable. At its September 1988 conference, the SDP voted for the new nuclear power plants and SDP leader David Owen's speech omitted 'ecology' from his party's core issues: security, democracy, and prosperity (*The Times*, 20 September 1988).

Within the SLD, the Green Democrats were launched as the successor group of the (more numerous) Liberal Ecology Group and the (less numerous) SDP Greens. The Green Democrats, who claimed hundreds of supporters, have sought to promote green values within the SLD, to inform the party's elected representatives, and to develop links with the wider green movement. In 'Towards a Green Democracy' (February 1989) they maintained:

> The Green Party does not have a sufficiently pragmatic approach to be a real party of Government, although their existence as a party is essential as a reminder of Green fundamentalism.

The Green Democrats encouraged doubts about the practicality of support for the Green Party because of its small size, inexperience, and lack of expertise. Former Liberal MP Michael Meadowcroft (1989) was more sharply critical because of the authoritarian and illiberal implications of the writings of the Greens. The Green Democrats viewed the prospects for 'greening' the Labour Party about as unpromising as those for the Conservative Party.

In the aftermath of Labour's third consecutive general election defeat, its National Executive Committee set up seven policy review groups to attempt to make the party more electable. Jeff Cooper of Socialist Environment and Resources Association (SERA) reported, ' The Physical and Social Environment was included in the list ... at the very last minute, only at the insistence of a NEC member of SERA' (1988, p. 5). Though SERA numbers over 1000 members and includes 32 MPs, it has been candid about the uphill struggle involved in placing environmental policies at the core of Labour's programme because of the trade unions' resistance. At the Oct-ober 1988 Labour Party Conference, the delegates passed a motion 'calling for the next Labour government's economic programme to take full account of the urgent need to protect the environment' (*The Guardian*, 8 Oct-ober 1988). Kinnock's conference speech, which was preoccupied with other themes, did challenge Mrs Thatcher to prove the sincerity of her environmental conversion with actions to control pesticides, prevent ocean dumping, and reduce atmospheric pollution. The final report of the Policy Review Group on the Physical and Social Environment released in May 1989 provided an extensive list of institutional and policy reforms 'to put Britain back in the forefront of ideas and actions to improve our environment' (p. 67). Its authors saw proposals, such as a Ministry of

Environmental Protection, as providing a long-term, coherent approach to environmental problems. But critics found a lack of integration with Labour's other policy reviews, which support the 'same old expansionist policies' (Irvine 1989, p. 9).

Thus, during 1988–9, the major parties responded to the surging green movement by making themselves look more pro-environment. The extent and credibility of their adaptations to green issues were conditioned by their leaders' simultaneous attention to established intraparty interests. Despite Ashdown's enthusiasm, even the distance the SLD could move towards being Britain's real (electable) green party was limited, as indicated by defections of disgruntled pro-environment Liberal councillors.

In 1988 the Green Party began to show up for the first time in the national opinion polls. The Harris Poll in October indicated only 1 per cent of respondents would vote for the Green Party. However, it provided encouragement by finding that 50 per cent of the public believed that the environment as an issue over the next five years would be 'very important', and 11 per cent of the public thought that the Green Party would best protect the environment, which put it ahead of the percentage for the Democrats (The Observer, 23 October 1988).

Recent Election Results

Historically, British parliamentary by-elections have provided the opportunity for protest votes against the governing party. Parties take them seriously, since despite lower turnouts they are seen as weathervanes of changing public moods. In those five occurring between July 1988 and May 1989, the Greens continued to lose their deposits but were clearly outpolling the fringe candidates (see Table 1). They scored a minor breakthrough in the two by-elections which occurred on 15 June 1989, with the Euro-election. Though losing its deposit in Glasgow Central, the Green Party finished ahead of both the Democrats and the SDP. And in Vauxhall the Greens won 6.1 per cent of the votes and thus saved their first deposit ever in a Westminster election. In each of the four constituencies also contested by the Green Party in the 1987 general election, their votes edged upward in 1988 (or 1989) while the combined electoral shares of the SLD and SDP were lower than the Alliance's 1987 share in five of seven constituencies.

In the May 1989 country elections, the two centre parties also saw their votes declining while overall there was a swing to Labour. The Greens only won one county council seat while the SLD held on to some 400 seats and the SDP, fourteen seats. But the Greens' percentage of the votes (where contested) rose sharply compared with that in the last county elections in 1985 (see Table 2). Eighty per cent of their candidates won more than 5

Table 1 Parliamentary by-election results: percentages

Kensington (14 July 1988)		Glasgow Govan (10 November 1988)	
Conservatives	41.6	SNP	48.7
Labour	38.1	Labour	36.9
SLD	10.8	Conservatives	7.3
SDP	5.0	SLD	4.1
Green Party	2.4	Green Party	1.1
Others (10)	2.0	Others (3)	1.7
	99.9[a]		99.8[a]

		Richmond [Yorks] (23 February 1989)	
Epping Forest (15 December 1988)		Conservatives	37.2
Conservatives	39.4	SDP	32.2
SLD	26.0	SLD	22.0
Labour	18.7	Labour	4.9
SDP	12.2	Green Party	2.8
Green Party	2.0	Others (4)	0.9
Others (4)	1.7		100.0
	100.0	Glasgow Central (15 June 1989)	
		Labour	54.6
Vale of Glamorgan (4 May 1988)		SNP	30.2
Labour	48.9	Conservatives	7.6
Conservatives	36.2	Green Party	3.8
SLD	4.2	SLD	1.6
Plaid Cymru	3.5	SDP	1.0
SDP	2.3	Others (3)	1.2
Green Party	2.0		100.0
Others (5)	2.9		
	100.0		

Vauxhall (15 June 1989)	
Labour	52.8
Conservatives	18.9
SLD	17.5
Green Party	6.1
SDP	—
Others (10)	4.8
	100.1[a]

[a] Because of rounding, figures do not add up to 100.0

Table 2 Local election results of the green party since 1985

Year and type of election	No. of seats contested	No. of votes received	Average percentage of the votes in seats contested[a]
1985 English/Welsh Counties	249	33 372	3.41
1986 English/Welsh District; Scot Regional; London B.C.s	428	62 287[b]	3.43
1987 English/Welsh	427	67 863[b]	3.62
1988 English/Welsh /Scot. District	396	58 470	4.14
[1988/89 District and County by-elections]	[46]	—	[6.90]
1989 English/Welsh Counties	646	190 000[c]	8.64

[a] average in one seat contests where there were at least three candidates besides the Greens (which allows better comparison to general elections).
[b] Total vote inflated by preferential voting in multi-seat contests where there was only one Green candidate.
[c] Twenty-six local results still unreported.
Source: Chris Rose, Green Party election coordinator

per cent of the votes in four-or-more cornered contests while 31 per cent exceeded 10 per cent in such contests. The Greens managed to defeat the SLD in 26 per cent of their confrontations, the SDP in 50 per cent, and Labour in 11 per cent (Matthissen and Rose 1989, pp. 1–2). By winning overall about 190 000 county votes the Greens moved for the first time ahead of the SDP as Britain's fourth party.

In its Euro-strategy document, the Green Party set five objectives for its European campaign: to field a full slate of candidates; to achieve the fourth largest number of votes; to win an aggregate total of at least 500000 votes; to save its deposit in target seats (fourteen were listed); and to show the importance of Green representation in the European Parliament (Green Party 1988, pp. 2–5). Though the Greens came no closer than 45679 votes (in the Cotswolds) to electing a Member of the European Parliament (MEP), all their other objectives were more than satisfied. They fielded a full slate of 78 candidates in Britain (plus one in Northern Ireland); they ranked as the third party; they won 2 292 696 votes (see Table 3); and they saved all their deposits. In the 1984 European elections the Greens nomi-

Table 3 European elections 1984 and 1989

Party & rank	No. of candidates	Total votes	Percentage of votes cast	Seats won
1984 European Elections				
1. Conservative	78	5 426 761	40.76	45
2. Labour	78	4 865 220	36.55	32
3. Liberals	39	1 358 169	10.20	0
4. SDP	39	1 233 488	9.27	0
5. SNP	8	230 610	1.73 [17,8][a]	1
6. Plaid Cymru	4	103 031	0.77 [12,2][a]	0
7. Green Party	16[b]	74 176	0.56	0
8. Others	10	21 348	0.16	0
		13 312 803	100.00	78
1989 European Elections				
1. Labour	78	6 153 453	40.06	45
2. Conservative	78	5,331 097	34.71	32
3. Green Party	78[b]	2,292 696	14.93	0
4. SLD	78	944 769	6.15	0
4. SDP	16	75 856	0.49	0
5. SNP	8	406 686	2.65 [25,63][a]	1
6. Plaid Cymru	4	115 062	0.75 [12,89][a]	0
8. Others	25	41 403	0.27	0
		15 361 022	100.01[c]	78

[a] Percentages in brackets are those applying within Scotland or Wales only.
[b] In both elections, there was also one candidate nominated by the Greens in N. Ireland, whose results are not included in this table.
[c] Rounding error

nated sixteen candidates (plus one in Northern Ireland), won 0.56 per cent of the ballot with 74 176 votes, finished behind not only the four national parties but also Welsh and Scottish nationalists, and lost all their deposits. Besides the upsurge of the Greens, the 1989 Euro-results revealed a national swing from the Conservatives to Labour and the collapse of the centre parties since 1984.

The Greens finished ahead of both the SLD and the SDP everywhere, except in Cornwall and Plymouth where the SLD outpolled them. In six southern English constituencies, by winning over 20 per cent of votes, the Greens finished ahead of labour and replaced the SDP/Liberal Alliance as the second strongest vote-getter. The Greens outpolled the Plaid Cymru in three of four Welsh constituencies though the latter had more votes in

Table 4 Correlation of the Greens' percentage of votes with other parties' percentage of votes in Euro-constituencies (Pearson's r)

Party	England	Scotland	Wales
Labour	−0.79	−0.62	+0.85
Conservative	+0.67	+0.14	−0.75
SLD	+0.16	+0.41	−0.25
SNP	—	+0.54	—
Plaid Cymru	—	—	−0.95
Number of constituencies	66	8	4

Source: Chris Rose, Green Party election coordinator

Wales owing to its strong showing in North Wales. Scotland was the Greens' weakest region (7.25 per cent); where they ranked fourth behind Labour, the SNP, and the Conservatives.

The Greens did the best in English constituencies dominated by the Conservatives (Rose 1989, p. 29). In Wales the data suggest the opposite: Green votes were highest in Labour-dominated constituencies (see Table 4). There is a strong negative correlation between the Greens' percentage of the votes and Labour's in England and Scotland, which seems to indicate they were competing for the same floating votes, but in Wales the strong negative correlation is between Conservative votes and Green votes. Overall, there is a strong negative correlation (−0.71) between the percentage of Green votes and the percentage of working-class residents (based on the 1981 census) within the Euro-constituencies, which means that the Green Party, as expected, did better in middle-class constituencies.

Historical comparison is limited because the Greens contested only fourteen English constituencies in the 1984 Euro-elections. According to Chris Rose's analysis of the 1984-9 net movement of votes for the Conservatives versus the Greens and for the Alliance versus the Greens, 'there is a stronger negative correlation with the Conservatives (−0.70) than with the Alliance (−0.59)' in these constituencies (1989, p. 6). The correlation between the percentage changes of Labour and Green votes is only +0.05. Using poll data, one study reported that 29 per cent of Green voters in the 1989 Euro-elections had voted Conservative previously, 19 per cent Labour, 16 per cent SDP, and 11 per cent SLD (*New Statesman and Society*, 14 July 1989). Thus, the basic picture suggested is that the Greens largely drew votes away from disgruntled Conservatives and former centrist voters in a low-turnout election (averaging 36 per cent).

With no government at stake, the European Parliament elections exem-

Table 5 Regional growth of green votes: 1987 green percentages of electorate compared with 1989 green percentages of the electorate[a]

Region	1987 General %	1989 European %	Growth factor
South East	1.11	6.95	6.3
South West	1.38	7.87	5.7
London	1.04	5.76	5.5
Britain	1.00	5.39	5.4
Midlands	0.99	5.39	5.4
North East	0.81	4.30	5.3
Wales	0.89	4.58	5.2
North West	0.90	4.26	4.7
Scotland	0.77	2.99	3.9

[a] See note 5.
Source: Chris Rose, Green Party election coordinator

plify what Karlheinz Reif (1984) terms 'Second-Order Elections'. In these elections, many partisans who are moderately interested in politics don't bother to vote; some who are disappointed with 'their' party's perform- ance send a midterm message of protest, and otherwise tactical voters choose with their hearts and not their heads. Many pundits were inclined to view the Greens' vote as a spectacular, but transitory, protest phenom- enon. To deal with doubts about 'real growth', one can recalculate the Green votes as a percentage of the electorate and compare this figure with the results obtained by Green candidates in the 1987 general election (where they contested seats).[5] (See Table 5.) These 'deflated' results in- dicate significant growth of Green votes over the last two years, particularly in the South East. Scotland ranks as the lowest region not only for 'real' votes but also for 1987–9 growth, the upswing of the SNP being the complicating factor. Elsewhere the Greens' vote potential seems large enough to be relevant to the tactical considerations of the major parties.

Reactions and Outlooks

National polls indicated that the Greens' level of popular support jumped from 3–4 per cent before Euro-elections to 7–8 per cent afterwards, matching the combined totals for the SLD and the SDP. Furthermore, the

MORI poll (20-26 July 1989) found that the Greens enjoyed a large sympathy potential: 24 per cent of respondents said that the Greens understand problems, 20 per cent said that they have sensible policies and that they are representative of all social classes (The Times, 31 July 1989). The late summer controversy about Britain's import of PCBs (toxic wastes) from Canada is but one example of why 'genuine' Greens are unlikely to fade soon from public view.

After 15 June 1989, the governing Conservative Party found itself occupied with countering the appeal of a small party, which ironically Environment Secretary Nicholas Ridley, as recently as his radio interview of 30 November 1988, did not even know existed (Econews, Feb/March 1989). In the opinion of some Tory backbenchers, the Thatcher government's espousal of environmentalism since September 1988 had backfired, raising the credibility of the Greens. The Conservative Research Department rushed out a pamphlet portraying the Greens' policies as extremely left-wing and hinting at something sinister in the Green Party's nonhierarchical structure. Ridley attacked the Greens' Euro-platform as 'unscientific rubbish, based on myths, prejudices and ignorance' (The Times, 11 July 1989). On the positive side, Mrs Thatcher utilized the Group of Seven summit in July 1989 to give 'high profile' exposure to her government's environmental concerns. Also, in her midsummer cabinet shake-up, Thatcher replaced Ridley with Chris Patten, who had the reputation of being more technically competent and more politically attuned to the voters' environmental sensitivities.

While enjoying a revival of electoral support and a midterm lead in the polls, Labour in a general election campaign needs the support of those disgruntled Conservatives and Democrats who voted for the Greens on 15 June. Kinnock blamed his party's lack of environmental credibility on the national press. The central argument of Labour was simply that it is the only party strong enough to defeat the Conservatives and to bring new priorities into government. As Labour MPs Armstrong and Mowlem succinctly concluded, 'Green politics MUST not become an issue of protest. For all our sakes, it must become an issue of power' (New Statesman and Society, 30 June 1989).

Paddy Ashdown's SLD saw itself nationally overshadowed by a 'real' green party, though the Democrats[6] retained local bases of support as indicated by their 18 per cent of the votes in the May 1989 county elections. The new leader's strategy of eliminating the rump SDP and replacing the Labour Party as the alternative to the Conservatives no longer had much credibility. Ashdown maintained that the Greens are not destined to become established as the third force of British politics because voters will become disillusioned as they learn more about the Greens' stands on controversial issues, such as unilateral nuclear disarmament.[7] On the other hand, the SLD's claim to be the 'Green Party of Government' seemed 'hollow' and unlikely to appeal either to voters who follow the Greens' logic of protest or to voters who follow Labour's logic of power.

From the Greens' point of view, their Euro-election breakthrough was more than a 'flash-in-the-pan' because there had also been positive trends in local elections and encouraging parliamentary by-elections. After 15 June 1989, the party enjoyed a higher media profile than at any time in its history. And predictably, its membership rapidly grew from 10 000 before the Euro-election to 15 000 four months later. For a party which has relied almost totally on membership dues for its budget, this meant badly needed finances for staff development. Attention turned to translating the party's momentum into fuller slates of candidates in the May 1990 local elections.[8] Green optimists maintained that, under the right circumstances, the Greens could soon elect their first MP in a parliamentary by-election (Andrewes 1989, p. 5). Even without by-election miracles, one can expect considerably more than 113 Green candidates in the next general election though a full slate of candidates would require four times the sum of the Euro-election deposits. Observers noticed in the 1989 county elections that the other parties' candidates paid much more attention to environmental issues where Green candidates were also on the ballot (Spring and Green 1989); such could also be anticipated as the consequence of a greatly expanded number of Green parliamentary candidates in the next general election.

Along with the new electoral opportunities come some formidable organizational challenges for the Green Party. Because the Greens have been deemed a relevant party by the mass media and the major parties, they can expect fuller but also more critical attention. The party needs to develop the media skills to maximize positive publicity and to formulate short-range and medium-range policies which can stand up in comparisons with the other parties. Trends toward professionalism, however, have provoked grassroots opposition even when the party was barely more than a cosy club. Those who see the Green Party as a prototype of the alternative society (rather than as a 'tool' for getting there) have immense difficulties relating to the necessity of party leadership with organizational resources to coordinate local efforts (Irvine and Ponton 1989, pp. 145–6). The perennial dispute over optimal decentralization is likely to be reinvigorated as the party leadership tries to advance the Greens' national image. For example, during spring 1989, there were outcries about how the European election manifesto was written without sufficient grassroots input.

The British Greens have evolved in a more gradualist, less conflictful manner than have the West German Greens. To be sure, there are political culture differences, but also the British Greens during their development have not been anywhere near the levers of power, compared with the West German Greens, whose *Fundis* and *Realos* have engaged in bitter in-fighting over party strategy. Because of the marginality of the British Greens in their party system, factionalism has not threatened to splinter the party. However, major differences of opinion do exist regarding the party's strategy, which one would expect to become more evident if its role in British politics grows. For example, former co-chair Penny Kemp, a self-described 'fundi', denounced the compromising of green principles in order to appeal to more voters and, furthermore, declared, 'As I see it, our role in participating in institutions is to make them ungovernable' (1989, p. i). A colleague (Clayton 1989, p. ii) provided the counterview:

> Do we want to be a minority party with unrealistic policies, agitating on the fringe after individual power, or do we want to be a mainstream party that cares about people, with policies based on reality, well organized ... and worth voting for?

Porritt and Winner maintained that the Greens could benefit from some 'genuine political debates' about the role of the party given its 'harsh electoral setting' (1988, p. 77).

A question (which the West German Greens have continuously debated) is how the party should relate to other parties. Should there be joint candidacies with green-minded members of other parties? Should there be informal stand-down agreements or formal electoral pacts with other parties? Should the Greens participate as a party in some future anti-Thatcherite 'rainbow' movement or even currently as individuals in the socialist Chesterfield conference? Should Liberal councillors who defect to the Greens be required to resign their seats and run again as Green Party candidates? A more relevant Green Party can not avoid such questions in the future.

At the September 1989 Green Party Conference, an emergency motion which advocated collaboration with Labour and the SLD, so that there would be one candidate standing solely on the issue of proportional representation in each parliamentary constituency, failed for lack of a two-thirds majority. Neither Labour nor the SLD would have accepted such an offer under existing circumstances. Labour's clear lead in the polls gave it no reason to strike early deals with small parties. And with his policy review process successfully completed, Kinnock saw Labour well-positioned to win back moderate voters from the Conservatives in the next general election. At the September 1989 SLD conference, Ashdown opposed electoral pacts with other parties, especially with the 'narrow-minded, authoritarian, anti-internationalist' Green Party (*The Times*, 12 September 1989).

Given distinct signs of the reviving two-party tendency of British national politics, the Greens are likely to find their Euro-election share tightly squeezed in the next general election. It would take a dramatic series of ecological disasters during the run-up to the election to demonstrate to the voters the inadequacies of the major parties' reformist environmentalism. Otherwise, the conventional issues of economics, social services, defence and leadership can be expected to reassert themselves in the campaign at the Greens' expense. Even to hold their current popular support against the powerful 'wasted vote' argument when government is actually at stake will require greater professionalism from a party organization which has made a virtue out of its amateurism in the past. But this cannot be ruled out since the doubling of the Greens' membership since 1988 is likely to have brought more 'electoralists' into the party.

The most likely scenario for the near future is for the party to elect significantly more local councillors during the early 1990s. The Greens stand to benefit from the lower turnout of voters and the lower constraint of partisanship in local elections. Their electoral successes should give impetus to national pragmatists who favour structural reforms which moderate the Greens' 'anti-party' features and who favour political strategies which embrace interparty cooperation. Barring the British equivalent of Chernobyl, Green MPs are unlikely to be elected in the absence of deals with other parties in the 1991 (or 1992) General Election. Because of the heightened environmental sensitivities of the public, the Green Party should be able to increase its share of the national votes a couple percentage points compared with 1987. However, it is hard to conceive of a major breakthrough by the Greens in such a 'First-Order Election' without electoral reform, which would be possible only after the election of a 'hung' parliament. The Greens themselves see theirs as a long-term struggle and look to the late 1990s for their Westminster breakthrough.

Conclusion

After years of frustration in a hostile party-political environment, the small Green Party suddenly emerged as an electoral force in 1989. The British electoral system had not changed and the likelihood of any reform seems to be less now than in the mid 1980s. However, the waning of the centre parties as a credible third force provided an opening for the Greens as a vehicle for midterm protest voters. The green vote in the Euro-elections can be seen as a complex phenomenon because one could protest against the Thatcher government, against Labour, against the Democrats, and against the party system itself (Marquand 1989).

Environmental issues were moving toward the top of the public agenda, which Mrs Thatcher's conversion experience graphically confirmed in 1988. The Democrats claimed to be a green party but their image was fuzzy. Even SERA's activists were a bit dubious about the depth of Labour's environmental convictions in the late 1980s. Most voters probably knew (and cared) little about the small Green Party's specific policies, but they knew that its candidates stood unequivocally on the side of environmental protection. In addition, the Greens' anti-materialistic stance may have appealed to those voters morally concerned after ten years of Thatcherism with the manifestations of societal greed (Benton 1989, pp. 10-11). Environmental pressure groups, preserving their mainstream nonpartisanship, maintained their distance from the 'radical' Green Party during the local and European campaigns. The environmental lobby, however, quickly rallied to the defence of the Greens in midsummer 1989 when Ridley attacked their pollution data as misinformation. It is also possible that Kinnock's revision of Labour's nuclear disarmament policy will allow the Greens to gain support within the ranks of the Campaign for Nuclear Disarmament (CND). In short, there are some signs of a changing political opportunity structure.

Does Green politics have a future in Britain? In the sense of 'light green' environmentalism, the answer is obviously 'yes'. The total membership of the most prominent fifteen environmental groups grew from 1.8 million in 1980 to 3.8 million in 1989 while the trade unions' membership fell from 12.1 million to 8.7 million (Lohrer 1989). In recent years, all the major parties (and the Welsh and Scottish nationalists) have been incorporating more environmental themes into their rhetoric and programmes. And all have intraparty groups which pressure their leaderships to go even further in their reform proposals. But does the small Green Party, which sees itself as 'dark green' and advocates fundamental changes of the system, have a future as more than an additional pressure upon the major parties? Before 1989, despite the theories of value change in post-industrial societies, political scientists agreed that the answer was 'no' because of Britain's plurality electoral law and two-party pattern. The early successes of green parties on the Continent were generally facilitated by their political systems' proportional electoral laws and multi-party patterns. The emergence of the British Greens can be seen as evidence that formidable and deeply rooted legal/institutional barriers have begun bending under the pressure of societal forces, at least in 'Second-Order Elections'.

Are there trans-Atlantic implications from the emergence of the Green Party in British politics? The American political system also has a plurality election law and a traditional two-party pattern. And 1988-9 saw surging memberships in environmental groups, heightened public concerns about environmental quality in the polls, an ecological disaster from the Exxon *Valdez* oil spill, and public posturing by President Bush as 'the environment President'. The pro-environment Citizens Party, which in the 1980 Presidential election did about as poorly as the Ecology Party did in the 1983 general election, quickly disintegrated as a national party while the Ecology Party persevered to become the Green Party. The second national gathering of US Greens in June 1989 shied away from establishing a national party in favour of developing as a grassroots political movement, which may selectively contest local elections.

Third parties confront even more formidable institutional/legal obstacles in the US than in the UK. For example, ballot access laws are complex, diverse, and deliberately 'rigged' against third parties by major party legislators. Owing to the vastness of the country (and of many states), campaigns require substantial organizational and financial resources. Because new parties tend to lack these resources, the mass media tend to ignore them. The national Democratic and Republican parties are loose coalitions of state and local parties, groups, and leaders which tend to absorb the more popular issues of those rare third parties which are able to pose an electoral threat. During the twentieth century, the more successful national third parties in the US have been focused on charismatic personalities while, during the nineteenth century, they were rooted in regional economic protest. US Greens neither have nor want 'superstars' as leaders. And, with their doubts about economic growth, they are unlikely to appeal to economically disadvantaged regions of the country. Citizen discontent about local environmental problems is typically expressed by nonpartisan activities (lobbying, contacting, and litigating). Given the continental diversities of American politics, the (rare) electoral successes of local Greens to date have had no contagious effect.

The emergence of the British Greens may have somewhat more relevance for Canadian Greens than American Greens. Canada shares geographical vastness with the US, but its government follows the British parliamentary model. And its electoral politics are more party (and less candidate) focused than America's. Historically, third parties have been more successful in Canada than in the US. Though sharing the plurality electoral system, Canadian ballot access is less restrictive than American. And Canadian law provides for partial reimbursement of campaign expenses for parliamentary candidates receiving 15 per cent or more of the votes. The mass media in Canada have been more generous in their coverage of small parties than in the US.

The Canadian Greens, who began as a federal party in 1983, have failed to score any breakthroughs in provincial or federal elections. They have remained a highly decentralized party movement whose membership is smaller than the British Greens. Green activism seems largely concentrated in pockets within British Columbia and a couple of other provinces. Environmental problems, such as acid rain and toxic chemicals, have contributed to a growing Canadian sensitivity to green issues, to which the major parties have begun to respond in recent years. The Greens considered their 2 per cent of the votes in the 1989 Quebec provincial elections as a 'great' success. The British Greens' upsurge in the Euro-election was heartening for Canadian Green activists, who also see themselves as 'a long-term alternative to the mainstream parties' (*Green Party News* [British Columbia], Autumn 1989).

During the 1980s, the small but real successes of European Greens, especially of the West Germans, have had a powerful 'demonstration effect' on nascent green parties throughout the world. The emergence of British and French Greens in June 1989 makes the future of the European Green movement somewhat less dependent on the fortunes of the West German Greens, who often seem determined to tear themselves apart. The French Greens also won a larger share of their country's Euro-votes than the West German Greens; they elected nine MEPs (one more than the latter). Though denied its twelve MEPs by British electoral law, the Green Party is represented in Strasbourg. Its sister parties have granted it votes within the Green Euro-parliamentary Group, a position on the Group's executive board, and a vantage point from which to press for uniformity of national voting systems in Euro-elections. Of course, success is unlikely in the near future. But the point is that no one knows what the political ramifications of Project 1992 will be in a decade. Green parties are a growing force in European politics, environmental problems and solutions transcend national boundaries, and Britain is increasingly becoming a part of Europe.

NOTES

1 The exception was the in-depth study by Rüdig and Lowe (1986) which sought to explain the 'stillborn' character of Green party politics in Britain.

2 The Green Party ended 1989 as the fourth strongest party (4 per cent) in the MORI poll, trailing the (renamed) Liberal Democrats (6 per cent) but leading the Owenite SDP (3 per cent) (*The Sunday Times*, 31 December 1989).

3 Data provided by the national offices of Friends of the Earth, UK and Greenpeace, UK respectively in August 1989.

4 Data provided by Chris Rose, Green Party national election coordinator, August 1989.

5 In the 1987 general elections, the Green Party contested about a fifth of the parliamentary seats, so regional results are projections from the actual constituencies results and are thus only roughly comparable. Assuming local parties do not nominate candidates in totally dismal circumstances, the 'projected' results probably overstate regional support levels in 1987.

6 As a result of the October 1989 postal ballot of SLD members, the party's official short name was changed from the Democrats to the Liberal Democrats in order to appease its MPs (*Manchester Weekly Guardian*, 22 October 1989).

7 See *The Sunday Times*, 18 June 1989. However, many Green constituency campaigns highlighted the party's anti-NATO, unilateralist, and anti-economic growth policies (Andrewes 1989, p. 4).

8 In the 1989 county elections, the Greens contested only 20 per cent of total council seats.

REFERENCES

Andrewes, T. (1989). '14.9%', Green Line, No. 74 (July-August), p. 4.

Benton, S. (1989). 'Turning Green', New Statesman and Society (23 June), pp. 10-11.

Berrington, H. (1985). 'New parties in Britain: Why some live and most die', International Political Science Review, Vol. 6, pp. 441-61.

Clark, H. D. and Zirk, G. (1989). "The dynamics of third-party support: The British Liberals, 1951-79', American Journal of Political Science, Vol. 33, pp. 197-221.

Clayton, S. (1989). 'Letter to editor', Econews, No. 46 (August-September), p. ii.

Cooper, J. (1988). 'Behind closed doors, Labour listens', New Ground: Journal of Green Socialism, No. 18 (Summer), p. 5.

Green Democrats (1989). 'Towards a Green Democracy', discussion document (February).

Green Party (1987). General Election Manifesto. London: Heretic Books.

Green Party (1988). 'A strategy for the European elections', party document (October).

Irvine, S. (1989). 'Hard Labour', Econews, No. 46 (August-September), p. 9.

Irvine, S. and Ponton, A. (1989). A Green Manifesto. London: Optima.

Kemp, P. (1989). 'No compromise on Green values', Econews, No. 45 (June-July), p. i.

Labour Party (1989). 'Meet the challenge, make the change: A new agenda for Britain', policy review document.

Lohrer, H. (1989). 'Nach dem Wachstum - neue Herausforderungen', Kommune (October).

Marquand, D. (1989), 'Labour's fantasy', New Statesman and Society (7 July), p. 19.

Matthissen, J. and Rose, C. (1989). 'Green Party 1989 county council election performance: A preliminary report',unpublished Green Party document.

Meadowcraft, M. (1989). 'Green identity - party or movement?' Challenge: Newsletter of the Green Democrats, No. 7 (Spring), pp. 5-7.

McCulloch, A. (1983). 'The Ecology Party and constituency politics: the anatomy of a grassroots party', paper presented at UK Political Studies Association annual conference, Newcastle.

Owens, S. (1986). 'Environmental politics in Britain: new paradigm or placebo', Area, Vol. 18, pp. 195-201.

Parkin, S. (1989). Green Parties: An International Guide. London: Heretic Books.

Porritt, J. and Winner, D. (1988). The Coming of the Greens. London: Fontana.

Reif, K. (1984). 'National electoral cycles and European elections 1979 and 1984', Electoral Studies, Vol. 3, pp. 244-55.

Rose, C. (1989). 'The Euro-election June 1989: Green Party performance', unpublished report.

Rüdig, W. and Lowe, P. D. (1986). 'The withered "greening" of British politics', Political Studies, Vol. 34, pp. 262-84.

Spring, J. and Green A. (1989). 'The Green Party's great leap forward?', Green Line, No. 73 (June), p. 3.

2. Party Activists versus Voters: Are the German Greens Losing Touch with the Electorate?

THOMAS POGUNTKE

Research Unit for Societal Developments
University of Mannheim, Federal Republic of Germany

The Loss of Political Relevance

More than a decade ago, the German Greens participated in a nationwide election for the first time. After some initial successes of green and alternative lists in local and *Land* elections (cf. Müller-Rommel and Poguntke 1990), the first direct elections to the European Parliament in June 1979 were used as the first serious test of the national electoral potential of a green party that was yet to be founded: still uncertain whether it would be wise to become involved in party politics, green activists used a special provision of the electoral law for the European election and ran as 'Other Political Organization – The Greens' (*Sonstige Politische Vereinigung - Die Grünen*). Although the 5 per cent hurdle of the German electoral law prevented the Greens from winning seats in the European Parliament, the result of 3.2 per cent gave them the confidence to go ahead with the foundation of a national party in January 1980. It came as a reassurance when the Green List of Bremen won the first green seats in a *Land* parliament in October 1979.

Although a regionally based Swiss group and the Belgian Greens managed to win seats in a national paraliament before the German Greens were represented in the Bundestag (Müller-Rommel and Poguntke 1989, p. 13), the German party has undoubtedly attracted superior national and international attention because they were, from the outset, potential holders of the balance of power in the Bundestag: ever since the formation of the Christian Democratic-Liberal government in 1982, the most promising Social Democratic strategy for a return to power was a red-green coalition. Furthermore, the German Greens were the first to enter a government and attain ministerial responsibility when they formed a coalition with the SPD in the *Land* of Hesse in the autumn of 1985.

Because of this strategic position in the German party system, the Greens had a very pronounced impact on the political agenda in the Federal Republic (Poguntke and Schmitt 1990). Furnished with their international reputation and ample financial resources as a result of generous state subsidies for election campaigns, the German Greens were able to influence several emerging green parties in Western Europe.

In a way, the West German Green Party is the 'prototype' of middle-class-based New Politics parties in West European democracies (Müller-Rommel 1982a, b; Rüdig, 1985; Kitschelt 1988; Poguntke 1987a, 1989a). Common to all green parties that mobilize on the new politics conflict is an open, participatory party organization that encourages rank-and-file participation on all levels of party politics. Also, New Politics party activists tend to prefer unconventional, direct, and elite-challenging forms of political participation (Barnes and Kaase et.al. 1979; Poguntke, 1987b). Inevitably – and intentionally – this leads to a conflictual style of internal party politics where all relevant positions and factions are given time and space to argue their points.

Even from this perspective, the German Greens appear to be particularly conflict-ridden. On the other hand, electoral fortunes of the party have been relatively stable thus far. The vast majority of Green supporters, however, do not seem to share the ideological preoccupations of Green Party activists. Diverse social profiles could contribute to the explanation of this phenomenon. Alternatively, a built-in organizational bias might work in favour of ideologically highly motivated party activists. This chapter seeks to provide tentative answers to these questions by analysing the social background of party voters and activists as well as the respective mechanisms of the Green Party organization.

The image of the German Green Party is marked by an almost masochist obsession with internal political conflict. Particularly since the collapse of the first red-green *Land* government in Hesse in February 1987, internal strife has paralysed the party almost completely. Nevertheless, the electoral performance of the Greens remained relatively stable. The only serious setback was the Hamburg *Land* election of May 1987 where the fundamentalist Green-Alternative List lost 3.4 per cent. However, having entered the campaign with a comfortable 10.4 per cent from the preceding election, this defeat was not taken very seriously by the green public. By and large, it was regarded as a reduction of the Green Party to its 'normal' size. Yet, this complacency may not be justified: membership figures have stagnated around 40,000 for several years and the German Greens were, together with the Dutch red-green alliance, the only 'green' party that could not improve its performance significantly in the 1989 European elections (Niedermayer 1989, p. 478).

More problematic, however, has been the loss of the party's ability to have an impact on the political agenda of the Federal Republic. Despite the fact that a series of genuinely green issues have captured public attention in the late 1980s, the Green Party has lost its prominent position in the public debate. When it became evident in December 1987, for example, that pivotal sections of the West German nuclear industry were involved in illegal activities (the so-called *Transnuklear*-scandal), political energies of the Greens were fully absorbed with factional strife and emergency meetings in Bonn.[1]

Similarly there was hardly any political reponse to the ratification of the INF-treaty which meant the fulfilment of a political demand that had been constitutive for the emergence and electoral success of the party. Even when all other political parties debated the seal disease at the North Sea coast in the summer of 1988, any remarkable green initiative was absent. Another striking example was the inability of the Green Party to react conceptually to the developments in Germany after the opening of the border between East and West Germany.

In view of the bitterness of internal faction fighting, the conspicuous lack of substantive points of contention is somewhat puzzling. There is little real programmatic debate inside the party that would aim at a partial revision of green programmatic positions. As far as long-term goals such as the utopia of an ecologically restructured economy or the realization of a nuclear-free world are concerned, there are hardly any open disputes. The subsequent brief analysis of the internal green 'landscape' will demonstrate that strategic disagreements between 'Realists' and 'Fundamentalists'[2] represent the heart of the matter.

Another Debate on Revisionism?

Undoubtedly, the choice of strategy is related to different concepts of the state and the role of parliamentary politics. Many green activists adhere to various shades of Marxist-inspired analyses of the state as an agent of the capitalist system which they in turn hold responsible for the outlook of environment and society. From this perspective, the real power resides with those who run the industrial system and politics is primarily seen as a phenomenon of the superstructure.

This interpretation suggests that there is little to be gained from the attempt to attain political control over the state machinery. Alternatively, the system should be challenged frontally, through mass movements. This concept of societal 'counter power' (*Gegenmacht*) rests on the convinction that it is possible to effectively limit the power of state and industry through mass mobilization. Furthermore, it implies that the parliamentary arena is not considered to be the place where important decisions are made. Instead, it is primarily regarded as a useful arena to voice political opinions and mobilize people for extra-parliamentary action.

The Realists, on the other hand, are influenced by the traditional Liberal concept of the state that regards it as a relatively neutral and powerful instrument of those who have gained political control over it. Unlike classical Liberals, however, green or alternative moderates are considerably more sceptical about the real power of parliamentary politics. They do not deny the power of the industrial system, but nevertheless believe in the capacity of the state to influence the course of events.

Consistent with their preference for extra-parliamentary politics, Fundamentalists usually seek to forge broad alliances. Whereas the Realists keep a close eye on their (parliamentary) respectability, radical New Politics proponents are less willing to denounce new social movement activists who get involved in violent confrontations with the police. However, this is primarily a strategic, not a substantive, disagreement. Both tendencies are opposed to violent action, but the Fundamentalists argue that it is necessary not to isolate extremist activists who share their goals.

Green Factions

In principle, the internal battle line runs between Realists and Fundamentalists. However, the picture is complicated by 'subfactions' that nevertheless tend to align with either Fundamentalists or the moderate Realists. By and large, the 'Eco-Libertarians' tend to side with the Realists in the debates, whereas 'Eco-Socialists' and 'Radical Ecologists' build the fundamentalist camp (cf. Murphy and Roth 1987, pp. 309-12). Although the minority faction of radical feminists, who tend to approach virtually all political problems from a feminist perspective, frequently support fundamentalist positions, they represent a current in its own right. Since feminist positions are almost conventional wisdom in the Green Party, they are not very influential as a separate political force. Rather, feminism has penetrated all green factions to a greater or lesser extent.

As a result of the exacerbting factional strife since 1987, a centrist faction (the so-called 'Grüner Aufbruch'), which attempts to forge a 'centre-right' alliance, has gained influence. The centrist strategy had an overwhelming success at the Duisburg party conference of February 1989, where no outright proponent of funamentalist positions was elected to the federal executive. Before the moderate breakthrough, fundamentalist politicians had dominated the federal party organization for several years. In fact, the federal party has been one of the last fundamentalist strongholds, whereas most of the Land parties have always been more pragmatic.

Obviously, a thorough analysis of the competing strands of Green factions would be an endeavour of its own. Inevitably, such a study would need to analyse the political biographies and traditions of these factions and relate them to the major currents of – sometimes specifically German – political thought as well as to the political history of the Federal

Republic.[3] Therefore, only a few prominent aspects of Green factionalism will be mentioned in this context.

Basically, there are three essentials that tend to arouse internal Green conflict; the position towards the use of violence; the debate over possible coalitions; and the question whether the state monopoly of legitimate use of force should be accepted.

State Monopoly of Force

The already mentioned three pivots of the factional debate have strong ideological connotations. As is often the case with highly ideological issues, they have little immediate relevance for practical politics. However, because of their symbolic value, they play an important role in the contemporary German debate.

All three aspects are intimately related to the 'biography' of the Green Party as an offspring of various protest movements. Green identity has developed through the ongoing resistance against policies which were implemented by parties of the dominant consensus in the Federal Republic. Such resistance sometimes involves the violation of existing legislation: in the struggle against the deployment of intermediate-range nuclear missiles or the construction of nuclear plants a higher-order legitimacy is set against the principles of the legal system. The continued involvement in such conflicts makes it very hard for some Greens to recognize the state monopoly of the legitimate use of force as an abstract principle which may nevertheless be violated in order to induce political reform (cf. Neumann 1988). The dialectics are not easily accepted by all green activists: the legitimacy of state action in the pursuit of certain policies must be acknowledged although the legitimacy of the policies themselves is questioned![4] This problem has frequently fuelled heated debates between Fundamentalists, who are reluctant to accept this principle of reformist politics, and Realists who struggle for its unambiguous approval in order to enhance the political respectability of the party.

The debate is confused further by the ambivalent meaning of the German word for 'force' which can also mean 'violence'. Green politicians defending the state monopoly of force have been accused frequently by their own ranks of justifying violent state action such as police violence.

Violence

There is absolutely no dissent among Greens so far as violence against persons is concerned. Non-violence is one of the four basic principles of the party which are codified in the preamble of the federal party programme. The Greens pride themselves of being the only pacifist party in Germany.

Things become more complicated, however, when violence against objects comes on the agenda. Again, this is related to the biography of the party. The 'destruction of destructive devices' has a long traditon in the history of civil disobedience, particularly in the pacifist movement. The second, more prominent, aspect refers to the recurring debate over violence after incidents in which peaceful demonstrations have turned violent. Knowing from experience that violent clashes are not always sparked off by protesters, many Greens have often refused to denounce civil protesters' violence indiscriminately.[5] Prominent Green politicians have argued that peaceful activists sometimes have found themselves in situations where the use of violence was a comprehensible reaction of self-defence. In sum, the Greens are reluctant to denounce people who - against their own intentions – have been compelled by police actions to react violently.[6] However, this reluctance is far stronger in the fundamentalist camp, whereas leading Realists have repeatedly called for the unambiguous denunciation of violence against people.

In the public debate, such a differentiating position lends itself to misunderstandings. Many SPD politicians have used this issue in conjunction with the debate on the state monopoly of force in order to rule out any cooperation with the Greens: a position which facilitated papering over cracks opened through the strategic debate inside the Social Democratic Party. It would be misleading, however, to qualify the Social Democratic position as merely tactical: a constitutive trauma of the SPD is the party's fear of being identified with anti-national, anti-statist elements. It dates back to the nineteenth-century anti-Socialist legislation of Bismarck and has been re-vitalized by the division of the German state after 1945 and the establishment of a Communist East German state under the ideological flag of 'real existing Socialism' (cf. Smith 1982, pp. 214-5).

Coalitions

Obviously, the positions towards violence and the state monopoly of force are intimately related to the choice of political strategy. Activists who have no confidence in piecemeal reform tend to prefer radical extra-parliamentary action - which makes it hard to accept explicitly the state monopoly of force and to exclude violent-prone protest groups from protest activities. Consistently, Radical Ecologists and Eco-Socialists tend to be extremely critical of possible coalitions with the SPD and prefer extra-parliamentary mobilization over governmental responsibility. Realists and the small group of Eco-Libertarians are to be found on the moderate, reformist side of internal Green battle lines. Not surprisingly, the heated internal debate over the merits and shortcomings of the 'rotation model' (Poguntke 1987b) polarized the party along the same dividing line: Reformists who aim at coalitions necessarily favour more personal continuity, which is clearly a systemic requirement of modern parliamentary politics (Poguntke 1989b). Those, however, who regard parliament primarily as a platform for extra-parliamentary mobilization have no inherent interest in adapting to the organizational norms of parliament.

Is the Party in Tune with the Electorate?

The preceding discussion has shown that possible coalitions with the SPD represent the core of the conflict. It is therefore legitimate to use this issue as a parameter for the identification of the relative weights of realist and fundamentalist positions among the green electorate.

The results from electoral research are staggering: Asked whether they would favour a red-green coalition if the election outcome facilitated such an arrangement, 94 per cent of the green supporters opted in 1983 for a coalition (Forschungsgruppe Wahlen 1983, p. 28). Despite exacerbating internal conflicts in the following years, almost the same proportion adhered to the realist position before the 1987 election (85 per cent) (Forschungsgruppe Wahlen 1987, p. 60). Despite this overwhelming realist majority among the Green electorate, federal Green Party conferences have not endorsed unambiguous coalition strategies before the elections of 1983 and 1987.

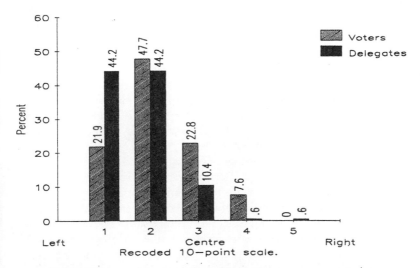

Figure 1 Ideological profile: Green voters and delegates (*Source*: Eurobarometer 25, 1986; conference survey 1985)

The debate over reformism is obviously related to the conventional left-right continuum. Consistently, the ideological profile of the green electorate is – compared with the party delegates – less pronounced. Figure 1, which is based on a recoded 10-point scale, shows that the delegates have a clear lead over potential green voters in the most left-wing category. Taken together, 88.6 per cent of the delegates, but just 66.6 per cent of the electorate are left of the centre.[7]

Social Characteristics of Green Party Elites

One possible explanation for the remarkably different degrees of radical-ism could be a different social profile of green activists and green voters. Although a direct inference from social position to political orientations is not possible, empirical findings that would show that economically marginalized groups dominate Green Party politics could provide impor-tant clues for further research and analysis.

In fact, it has been suggested, for the German case, that the Green Party should primarily be understood in terms of a party of economically deprived counter-elites who see their legitimate career prospects frustrated by the saturation of the West German labour market as regards social sciences, teachers, etc. (Alber 1985, p. 220; Bürklin 1984, pp. 45-7, 202-2; 1985a, b).

Empirical evidence for this argument is not very convincing. A study that has collected relevant data on 235 Green parliamentary deputies[8] and members of the federal leadership (BUVO) between 1979 and September 1985 (Fogt 1986) comes to the following results: like green voters and party delegates, most members of the party elite belong to the generations of the extra-parliamentary opposition or the subsequent new social movements (54 per cent). On all levels, the Green Party is the prime representative of the two youngest generations.

This representation, however, is imperfect: teachers, for example, were heavily overrepresented among mandate holders in the early years of the Green Party [9]. Meanwhile, the figures have approached the Bundestag average - which is, of course, also characterized by a disproportionate presence of teachers (Fogt 1986, p. 20; Emminger 1985, p. 369). However, this occupational category can hardly serve as a good example of the 'counter-elite' argument: German teachers are comparatively well-paid civil servants with secure life-time employment and ample holidays.

On the other hand, these economically secure green activists share their political preoccupations with a sizeable group that is characterized by an insecure occupational status: Fogt includes in this category all those who are unemployed, have frequently changed jobs, or work in the 'alternative economy' (26 per cent) (Fogt 1986, p. 21). However, the adequacy of this definition is questionable. After all, the autonomy to change jobs freely or the option for occupation in the alternative sector may conform exactly with the aspirations of Green politicians who attempt to realize their political visions at least partially in their private lives. In social terms, the Greens are clearly both the party of the economically secure and the insecure. Both categories, however, share one important characteristic: they are distant from the sphere of economic production!

The foregoing description of social characteristics of Green Party elites is only of illustrative character. Specific conditions of the West German parliamentary system render a systematic comparison between MPs and voters largely meaningless. There is a built-in bias in the legislation regulating job security of MPs that privileges members of the civil service. Particularly, people in non-career positions, such as teachers, are attracted by a political career [10]. Nevertheless, there are no conspicuous findings that would explain the contrast between party and voters.

In order to analyse the relationship between green activists and voters, results from a survey of Green Party delegates are compared with data from the Allbus social science survey.

The survey of delegates was carried out at the Offenburg Conference in December 1985, 25 per cent analysable responses were received. The Allbus 1984 survey elicited data on 246 green voters.[11]

The Social Background of the Green Party: Identity of Voters and Activists?

Occupation

Members of the various shades of the new middle classes are clearly the most numerous group among Green Party delegates, closely followed by students and young men serving the military or civil duties (Table 1). The dominance of middle-class values inside the Green Party is highlighted even more if we take a closer look at the category of self-employed. Only four out of twenty-five are business owners who are – as a social category – likely to be relatively distant from the ideas of the New Politics: their immediate dependence on the performance of the economy is not conducive to the development of New Politics-inspired political preferences. The others are self-employed members of the liberal professions who may not be all that different in their social and attitudinal moulding from members of the new middle class.

Although there was no specific category for civil servants, the identity of civil servants proved to be stronger than the categorizing force of survey questions and a substantial number of civil servants mentioned their specific status on the questionnaire[12]. Some even noted their vocation as teachers. Taken together, these two groups represent 10.1 per cent of the total, which is a result worth reporting given the fact that this figure may underestimate the true number of civil servants for the reasons just mentioned.

Unemployed are only slightly overrepresented among Green Party delegates and voters. Hence, there is little indication of an economically deprived counter-elite.

In the light of the self-proclaimed Green ideal of grass-roots democracy,

Table 1 Social Composition of Green Party Delegates
and Voters[13]

	Percentage of Delegates	Percentage of Voters
Self- employed	13.1	2.9
New Middle-class [a]	35.0	32.9
Worker	7.9	7.3
Student, services [b]	24.1	26.9
Unemployed	12.6	10.1
Other [c]	7.3	19.9
Total	100.0	100.0

[a] Includes 'white collar workers' and 'executive director' (Angestellter and Leitender Angesteller). No specific category for civil servants (Beamte) was included.
[b] 'Services' includes men doing their military or social service.
[c] 'Other' includes farmers, fishermen, pensioners, housewives and house husbands.
Source: Allbus 1984; conference survey 1985.

close similarity of the social profiles of voters and party activists is certainly a value in its own right. Both noticeable deviations do not cause any severe theoretical problems: the relatively large portion of self-employed among Green Party delegates is due to many delegates in the liberal professions. And the considerably larger proportion of voters falling in the category 'other' is mainly caused by the almost complete absence of pensioners from the Green Party conference. Given the 'ambiente' of these conferences and the length of the usual marathon debates (cf. Poguntke 1987b), it is evident that it is much harder for the older generation to participate in the Green Party than to support it with the ballot paper.

Income

Unfortunately, the figures of Tables 2 and 3 are not directly comparable, because the surveys measured gross and net income. Nevertheless, the underlying pattern is quite similar: there is a strong over-representation of people on low-income categories which is likely to be primarily a corollary of the low average age of green activists and supporters. At the same time, however, there is considerable spread across all income categories which indicates a substantial economic saturation of parts of the samples. As always, survey data on income levels has to be read with particular suspicion, because people do not often distinguish correctly between gross and net incomes. Nevertheless, the data do not support arguments that we are essentially confronted with an economically deprived group.

A very high level of education of party delegates is common to all Bundestag parties: in 1979 the percentage of delegates of established parties with

Table 2 Income per capita (gross)[a] of Green Party delegates

German Marks	Percentage
Under 1000	47.3
Under 2000	28.7
Under 3000	13.2
Under 4000	7.2
Under 5000	3.0
Over 5000	0.6
Total	100.0

[a] Computed from household income and number of persons living in household.

Table 3 The income per capita of Green voters (monthly net income, Allbus 1984)

German Marks	Percentage
Under 1000	50.0
Under 2000	27.6
Under 3000	14.1
Over 3000	8.3
Total	100.0

Abitur ranged from 64 per cent (SPD) to 82 per cent (FDP) (Schmitt 1987, p. 132).

Although it is not entirely accurate to equate attendance of the highest-level eductional institution with passing the final exam at this school, it may be justifiable for comparative reasons. Furthermore, owing to the required minimum age[14] of Green Party delegates, most of those who are still in eduction will be either close to their Abitur or already enrolled at university. Therefore, we can collapse those 'still in eduction' and those with 'university eduction' into the category 'Abitur'. As is the case for all other parties, those active inside political parties tend to be higher educated than the respective groups of voters (see Figure 2).

So far no conspicuous social differences between voters and activists have been found. Similarly, the age profiles of green voters and delegates, are almost congruent (see Table 4). Two-thirds are 35 years of age or

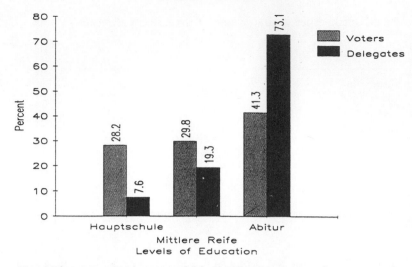

Figure 2 Education: green electorate and delegates. The West German education system has a comparatively rigid structure. The Hauptschule is the lowest secondary school. Mittlere Reife is an intermediate school leaving certificate, and the Abitur is the highest school qualification, entitling the successful candidates to a university education.

younger. Almost halt ot the Green delegates have been socialized politically during the heights of the extra-parliamentary movement of 1968, the so-called APO-generation.[15] Six years earlier, in 1979, virtually nobody from this so-called APO-generation was a delegate for one of the established parties.[16] Evidently, this substantial lack of political integration and representation of a whole political generation is an important part of the explanation for the emergence and the success of the Green Party. After all, 1979 was the year when the Greens dared to participate in the first national election (Euro-election).

One decade after the APO-activists had called for the 'long march through the institutions' a mere 2 per cent of the APO-generation had arrived at the Social Democratic Party congress! It is important to note, however, that we are not talking about the APO-activists themselves: they are hard to grasp because they were just a small minority of their own - 'affluent'-generation. But their vociferous political activity moulded the socializing environemnt of those who were mainly too young to participate actively in the student unrest: a 35 year old Green delegate at the Offenburg conference was just 18 in 1968.

The APO-activists are submerged amongst those who were between 36 and 55 in 1985. It seems reasonable to assume that at a Green Party conference the majority of this age group is comprised of former APO-combatants.[17] Frequently, they have been suspected to be the driving force behind the Green Party. However, a more detailed breakdown of the results

Table 4: Age profiles of Green Party delegates and voters

Age	Percentage of Delegates	Perentage of Voters
under 36	67.5	69.7
36 - 55	27.9	20.1
over 55	4.6	10.2
Total	100.0	100.0

from the conference survey shows that they hardly play a dominant role in the party: they are only the third-largest group, behind the APO-generation and youngest cohort that has been socialized in the period of the new social movements of the 1970s.

Political Selection and Green Party Politics

The analysis of social backgrounds of party activists and green voters hardly explains the substantial ideological gap between federal party activists and green voters. It can be argued, however, that political radicalism has as much to do with decisive political experiences as with political value orientations moulded through social class and period effects. From this perspective it is reasonable to expect those who lack experience with practical politics and piecemeal reform to be more radical and fundamentalist. Furthermore, those who are frequently involved in violent clashes with police forces are obviously less willing to become part of the governmental machine that is responsible for their bruises.

This leads us to the following set of hypotheses that seek an explanation in the specific organizational characteristics of the Green Party and the related structure of the political process in the Federal Republic. It is suggested that there are several effects of the Green Party's organizational structure which encourage those who are more radical to participate in federal politics. Clearly, there is a feedback effect of this selective mechanism: fundamentalists who remain outside parliamentary politics will lack the moderating effects of institutional socialization.

¶ *Green ideology emphasizes practical reform at the grass roots. Those who believe in reform are therefore likely (a) to be involved in local politics and (b) not to be primarily concerned with 'big politics' (cf. Kitschelt 1989a).*
¶ *People active in local council politics - and hence likely to be more pragmatic - will lack additional time to go to exhaustingly long federal party conferences.*

¶ It is therefore likely that many pragmatists are willing to leave conference 'slots' to activists who are not involved in local or regional politics (cf. Kitschelt 1989a, p. 163; 1989b, p. 406). Hence, federal party conferences will not be representative of the ideological composition of the party as a whole.

¶ The federal and administrative structure of the Federal Republic make for a large number of parliamentary mandates which are more attractive to Realists than to Fundamentalists. The former are obviously more likely to run for mandates because they believe in the possibility to bring about change through parliamentary work. This is particularly true for local and regional politics. In conjunction with low membership figures, the principle of strictly separating office and mandate has led to a situation where few - if any - prominent realists are available for positions in the party leadership. Obviously, the separation of office and mandate explains much of the gap between party leadership and the electorate. Unlike in established parties, moderate parliamentarians have no possibility of controlling party politics through institutionalized leadership.

It is consistent with this argument that it was for the first time at the Duisburg party conference of February 1989 that two Members of Parliament were willing to resign their parliamentary posts in order to be elected to the federal leadership. Before that, the Realists' wing of the party had always been short of convincing candidates for the federal leadership. It was the dominant expectation among realist circles that it would always be possible to rely on the structural overweight of parliamentary politics. Hence, activities of the federal party leadership were regarded as being comparatively unimportant (Poguntke 1987b). Only when it became apparent that the damaging effect of factional strife was endangering the survival of the party, political emphasis shifted back from parliament to the party organization.

¶ Whenever there is the real chance for alternative politics to gain a foothold in governmental power structures, there are strong pressures from the grass roots to deliver the goods. Particularly on local and regional levels, there are multi-fold possibilities for the alimentation of alterntive subcultures through political leverage of Green Party politicians. Clearly, this factor has thus far been absent in federal politics, allowing federal politicians to be more concerned with keeping their hands clean ideologically. The example of the Berlin red-green coalition formed after the elections of January 1989 shows, however, how strong these forces are even in a Land party that has always been prominent for its radicalism.

Clearly, all these suggestions are largely theoretically grounded and would need further systematic empirical investigation. Also, other factors would need to be considered in a comprehensive attempt to account for the phenomenon of a political gulf between party activists and supporters. However, even this restricted perspective indicates the importance of organizational and institutional factors for political action. In some cases, they may weigh heavier than social background or political value orientations. Furthermore, it has been shown that specific selection processes are at work within the Green Party organization which lead to the biased representation of party activists with different political motivations in corresponding political arenas.

The developments after the 'German Revolution' of November 1989 indicate that the Green Party has still not succeeded in coming to terms with organizational impediments to efficient political performance. It was only by the end of February 1990 that the parliamentary party of the Bundestag and the federal council (Bundeshauptausschuß) could agree on statements on the question of German unifiction. After a phase of increased political visibility in the wake of the formation of the Berlin red-green coalition and the looming likelihood of a so-called 'traffic light coalition' of Liberals, Social Democrats, and Greens in the case of a 'Republican' success in the 1990 Bundestag elections, the Greens have again been backstaged on the political scene. As a result, in January 1990 the party had fallen below 8 per cent in a monthly poll commissioned by the weekly magazine Der Spiegel for the first time since early 1989 (Der Spiegel, No.9, 1990).

These results illustrate how dependent the Greens are on getting continued political attention. Being a party that is neither blessed with a highly loyal electorate nor with a strong and committed membership base (Poguntke 1990), it is more dependent on political seasons than established parties. Empirical analyses have shown that Green supporters are far more loyal to issues than to the party as such (Poguntke 1990; Inglehart 1989, p. 385). Their continued survival in parliamentary politics is therefore highly dependent on their ability to maintain a firm place in the centre of the political debate – which always means, in the context of West German political culture, potential relevance for coalition formation. In order to secure this, the party needs to continue closing the gap between voters and activists, a task which has been tackled by the Centrists of Antje Vollmer and her political allies.

NOTES

1 On 12 December 1987, a common meeting of the parliamentary party, the party executive and members of all Land parties was convened in order to prevent a split of the party (cf. Die Grünen 1988a)

2 These are the conventional labels in the German debate.

3 Ample relevant material is contained in studies that focus on the early history of the German Greens and its organizational forerunners (cf. Klotzsch and Stöss 1984; Papadakis 1984; Langguth 1983; Brand 1985; Brand et.al. 1984; Hallensleben 1984; for documentary evidence see Die Grünen 1988a,b)

4 See the debate between the Green MPs Antje Vollmer and Otto Schily (who has recently left the Greens to join the SPD) in: Der Spiegel, No. 13, 1985, pp. 75-78; see also STZ (Stuttgarter Zeitung), 5 January 1987).

5 Even conservative newspapers have criticized excessive police violence,

and some police actions have been declared illegal by law courts. See the
FAZ (*Frankfurter Allgemeine Zeitung*) report on a demonstration at the nuclear
site of Brokdorf; FAZ 7 June 1976. Another example is the 'Hamburg en-
circlement', where several hundred citizens were surrounded by police
forces for more than 12 hours, STZ 13 June 1986; FAZ 14 June 1986; Der
Spiegel No.25, 1986; STZ 7 March 1987.

6 Press photographs from demonstrations against the nuclear reprocessing
plant near Wackersdorf show elderly people collecting and filling up beer
cans for streetfighters (*Der Spiegel*, No. 30, 1986)!

7 Figure 1 is based on the data from the Offenburg conference survey (see
note 11) and the Eurobarometer 25 (March 1986), which was commissioned shortly after the Offenburg conference. Although the small sample
size of the Eurobarometer makes the data less reliable than the Allbus
surveys, it is preferred here.

8 On the *Land* and federal levels.

9 The 'outlier' was the *Land* parliament of Lower Saxony with 73 per cent
teachers.

10 Apart from the head teacher, there is hardly any formal hierarchy among
the teachers of a given school. Promotions affect only the level of payment.
Civil servants are also promoted regularly while they are on leave for a
political position.

11 The survey of Green Party delegates was conducted by the author. All
conference delegates were asked to fill in a questionnaire; approximately
25 per cent responded. Allbus is a national social science survey organized by the centre for survey methods and analysis (ZUMA) of the University of Mannheim.

12 The very low number of missing cases (3.5 per cent) indicates that it was
no problem for all respondents to assign themselves to one of the given
categories in a meaningful way.

13 Percentages in all subsequent tables are based on the number of valid responses. This is the most straightforward way of standardizing across tables with varying numbers of missing cases.
The total number of usable responses was:

	Delegates	Voters
Table 1	191	246
Table 2/3	167	192
Table 4	197	244
Figure 1	163	53
Figure 2	197	245

The category 'don't know / no reply' was treated as missing. All tables
are significant on the 0.001 level (chi-square test).

14 According to the party statute, the minimum age is 18, but three respondents were only 17.

15 See Schmitt (1987, p. 133) for the grouping of age cohorts. APO = Ex-
tra-parliamenary Opposition.

16 Schmitt calls this generation 'Protest-Generation' (Schmitt 1987, p. 132).

17 See also Fogt (1986) on this problem.

REFERENCES

Alber, J. (1985). 'Modernisierung, neue Spannungslinien und die politischen
Chancen der Grünen', *Politische Vierteljahresschrift*, Vol. 26, pp. 211-26.
Barnes, S. H. Kaase, M. et.al. (1979). *Political Action*. Beverley Hills: Sage.
Brand, K.-W., Büsser, D., and Rucht, D. (1984), *Aufbruch in eine andere Gesellschaft:*

Neue soziale Bewegungen in der Bundesrepublik. Frankfurt/Main, New York: Campus.

Brand, K.- W. (ed.) (1985). Neue soziale Bewegungen in Westeuropa und den USA: Ein Internationaler Vergleich. Frankfurt: Campus.

Bürklin, W. P. (1984). Grüne Politik. Opladen: Westdeutscher Verlag.

Bürklin, W. P. (1985a). 'The German Greens: The post-industrial non-established and the party system', International Political Science Review, Vol. 6, pp. 463-81.

Bürklin, W. P. (1985b). 'The split between the established and the non-established left in Germany', European Journal of Political Research, Vol. 13, pp. 283-93.

Die Grünen (1988a). Die Krisen-Klausur im 'Pantheon', Protokoll der gemeinsamen Sitzung des Bundeshauptausschusses der GRÜNEN mit VertreterInnen der Landesvorstände und den Abgeordneten der GRÜNEN IM BUNDESTAG am 12. Dezember 1987 in Bonn.

Die Grünen (1988b). Grüne Perspektiven. Kongress vom 16-19. Juni 1988 in und um Haus Wittgenstein / Bornheim-Roisdorf.

Emminger, E. (1986). 'Die "grüne" Schule', Politische Studien, Vol. 36, pp. 368-79.

Fogt, H. (1986). 'Die Mandatsträger der Grünen: Zur sozialen und politischen Herkunft der alternativen Parteielite', Aus Politik und Zeitgeschichte, No. 11, pp. 16-33.

Forschungsgruppe Wahlen (1983). Bundestagswahl 1983. Mannheim: Forschungsgruppe Wahlen.

Forschungsgruppe Wahlen (1987) Bundestagswahl 1987. Mannheim: Forschungsgruppe Wahlen.

Hallensleben, A. (1984). Von der Grünen Liste zur Grünen Partei? Die Entwicklung der Grünen Liste Umweltschutz von ihrer Entstehung in Niedersachsen 1977 bis zur Gründung der Partei Die Grünen 1980. Göttingen: Muster-Schmidt Verlag.

Herzog, D. (1982). Politische Führungsgruppen: Probleme und Ergebnisse der modernen Elitenforschung. Darmstadt: Wissenschaftliche Buchgesellschaft.

Herzog, D. (1975), Politische Karrieren. Selektion und Professionalisierung politischer Führungsgruppen. Opladen: Westdeutscher Verlag.

Inglehart, R. (1989). Culture Shift in Advanced Industrial Society. Princeton N.J.: Princeton University Press.

Kitschelt, H. (1988). 'Left-Libertarian parties: Explaining innovation in competitive prty systems', World Politics, Vol. 40, pp. 194-234.

Kitschelt, H. (1989a). The Logics of Party Formation: Ecological Politics in Belgium and West Germany. Ithaca, NY: Cornell University Press.

Kitschelt, H. (1989b). 'The internal politics of parties: The law of curvilinear disparity revisited', Political Studies, Vol. 37, pp. 400-21.

Klotzsch, L. and Stöss, R., (1984). 'Die Grünen', in Stöss, R. (ed.), Parteien-Handbuch: die Parteien der Bundesrepublik Deutschland 1945-1980, Vol. 2, Opladen: Westdeutscher Verlag, pp. 1509-1598.

Kolinski, E. (1988). 'The West German Greens - A women's party?, Parliamentary Affairs, Vol. 42, pp. 129-49.

Langguth, G. (1983). Protestbewegung. Köln: Verlag Wissenschaft und Politik.

Müller-Rommel, F. (1982a). '"Parteien neuen Typs" in Westeuropa: Eine vergleichende Analyse', Zeitschrift für Parlamentsfragen, Vol. 13, pp. 369-90.

Müller-Rommel, F. (1982b). 'Ecology parties in Western Europe', West European Politics, Vol. 5, pp. 68-74.

Müller-Rommel, F. and Poguntke, T. (1989). 'The unharmonius family: Green parties in Western Europe' in Kolinski, E. (ed.), The Greens in West Germany: Organisation and Policy Making. Oxford: Berg, pp. 11-29.

Müller-Rommel, F. and Poguntke, T. (1990). 'Die Grünen' in: Mintzel, A. and

Oberreuter, H. (eds.), *Parteien in der Bundesrepublik Deutschland*. Bonn: Bundeszentrale für Politische Bildung.

Murphy, D. and Roth, R. (1987). 'In viele Richtungen zugleich. Die Grünen - ein Artefakt der Fünf-Prozent-Klausel', in Roth, R. and Rucht, R. (eds.), *Neue soziale Bewegungen in der Bundesrepublik Deutschland*. Bonn: Bundeszentrale für politische Bildung, pp. 303-24.

Neumann, E. (1988). 'Traumen - Kämpfen - Verwirklichen', *Grüne Blätter*, No. 5, pp. 4-5.

Niedermayer, O. (1989). 'Die Europawahlen 1989: Eine international vergleichende Analyse', *Zeitschrift für Parlamentsfragen*, Vol. 20, pp. 467-487.

Papadakis, E. (1984). *The Green Movement in West Germany*. London: Croom Helm.

Poguntke, T. (1987a). 'New politics and party systems: The emergence of a new type of party?', *West European Politics*, Vol. 10, pp. 76-88.

Poguntke, T. (1987b). 'The organization of a participatory party - the German Greens', *European Journal of Political Research*, Vol. 15, pp. 609-33.

Poguntke, T. (1989a). 'The new politics dimension in European green parties,' in: Müller-Rommel, F. (ed.), *New Politics in Western Europe*. Boulder, Co.: Westview, pp. 175-94.

Poguntke, T. (1989b). 'Basisdemokratie als grünes Gegenmodell?' *Der Bürger im Staat*, Vol. 39, No. 4, pp. 255-8.

Poguntke, T. (1990). 'Unconventional participation in party politics: The German experience', paper presented to the ESF/ESRC Conference on Political Participation, University of Manchester, January 1990.

Poguntke, T. and Schmitt, H. (1990). 'Die Grünen: Entstehungshintergrund, politisch-programmatische Entwicklung und Auswirkung auf andere Parteien', in: Schmid, J. and Tiemann, H. (eds.), *Die Zukunftsdiskussion in Parteien, Verbänden, und Kirchen*. Marburg: SP-Verlag.

Rudig, W. (1986). 'The Greens in Europe: Ecological parties and the European elections of 1984', *Parliamentary Affairs*, Vol. 38, pp. 65-72.

Schmitt, H. (1987). *Neue Politik in alten Parteien. Zum Verhältnis von Gesellschaft und Parteien in der Bundesrepublik*. Opladen: Westdeutscher Verlag.

Smith, G. (1982). *Democracy in Western Germany: Parties & Politics in the Federal Republic*. 2nd ed. London: Heinemann.

3. The Evolution of the Irish Ecology Movement[1]

SUSAN BAKER

Faculty of Business and Management

University of Ulster at Jordanstown, Newtonabbey, Northern Ireland, UK

Introduction

Ireland is sometimes called the Emerald Isle, famous for its magnificent scenery, its unspoiled coastline and its salmon and trout fishing. Unfortunately, the harsh reality of rapid industrialization since the 1960s in Ireland belies this rather idyllic and romantic picture. Like many peripheries which have experienced colonial rule and, since their independence, have experienced subsequent dependent industrial development, Ireland has also experienced environmental destruction. In fact, although a member of the European Community (EC) and sharing many of the political features common to West European democracies, the pattern of the island's environmental destruction suggests that it has more in common with Third World countries than with its more developed European neighbours.

But, like many of these underdeveloped states, Ireland is also experiencing the emergence of ecological consciousness and with it the development of an active environmental movement. This movement is shaped both by Ireland's cultural and political proximity to the European continent and its dependent industrialization. The movement therefore combines features of environmental movements found within the developed world as well as those emerging in the underdeveloped states.

This duality means that study of the movement in Ireland offers unique opportunities. On the one hand, it can provide insights into the nature of the European movement and, on the other, can bridge the gap between analysis of First World environmentalism and that of the Third World. Furthermore, there is increased realization that the cause of environmental degradation lies with western anthropocentric models of economic development. As a consequence those concerned with the re-establishment of an ecologically balanced approach to the world increasingly turn for help to communities which have maintained the traditional patterns of interaction with the natural world. Ireland, situated as it is between both the First and Third World, offers a unique stepping stone for those wishing to undertake this task.

This chapter examines the evolution of Irish ecologism and its political manifestations from the late 1960s until the present time. It is analysed within the context of wider national and international developments which occurred during this period. 'Ecologism' refers to the political analysis of ecological deterioration, which seeks a solution to environmental damage in political, social and economic action. Ecologism, especially in the late twentieth century, has influenced political ecology groups to work for a re-orientation of economic, social and political activity away from behaviour that has a negative impact upon the environment towards behaviour that acts in harmony with the natural world.

The emergence onto the political stage of political ecology groups, not least within parliamentary politics, has spurred a variety of theoretical explanations. Theories seek to explain the origin of these groups and to indicate their significance for political, social and economic life in both the short and long term. These theoretical accounts remain, however, predominantly unidisciplinary. Thus, in order to find ecologism's place within the history of ideas, philosophers, as the historian Bramwell has pointed out, critically assess the past dominance of Cartesian understanding of nature, where homo sapiens is seen as discontinuous, that is, as standing apart from and threatened by, non-human nature. They look instead to Heideggerian philosophy and the return to the pre-Socratic understanding of human beings existing in a continuous and harmonious relationship with the natural world (Bramwell 1989). Similarly, the approach by Christian theologians to the environment has recently been influenced by the move from Hellenistic philosophy to a more biblical approach. This emphasizes the holistic nature of the human person, who exercises stewardship in a material world that is fundamentally good because it was created by a loving God (Daly 1988). Social scientists, on the other hand, concern themselves with the study of ecologism as a social movement. However, they present different approaches to the understanding of social movements. One approach stems from American sociology. It analyses social movements in terms of 'resource mobilization', that is, in terms of the mechanisms through which movements recruit their members and the organizational forms through which mobilization of both human and social resources take place (Eyerman and Jamison 1988). These analysts may also focus upon the personal motivation that leads to participation in social movements and, influenced by Olsen's rational choice theory, examine the self-interest of environmental activists (Olsen 1971). While not wishing to over emphasize the differences between the American and the European approaches, European social scientists, on the other hand, can be seen as chiefly focusing attention on social movements as carriers of political projects, as historical actors. Initially strongly influenced by the works of Alan Touraine, this approach sees the new environmental and peace movements in Europe not as resource mobilizers but as agents of social transformation (Touraine *et al.* 1983). Within this approach sociologists may also seek to relate the development of ecological activists to upheavals in the social and life spaces of the younger generations of the late twentieth century. Drawing upon American analysis some theorists argue that this creates what is known as a 'political opportunity structure' for activism (Lowe and Rüdig 1986). Attempts have been made to achieve a synthesis between the American and European approaches within sociology (Cohen 1985).These approaches have, however, been criticised. Eyerman and Jamison (1988) for example point out that they fail to address the substantial methodological and contextual differences between the two approaches.

As the decade of the 1980s drew to a close, political scientists also began to examine the phenomena. This is chiefly a result of the influence that ecologism is having upon both party formation and the voting behaviour of the electorate. Focusing attention away from the study of social movements as such, they debate whether or not the class-based cleavages, traditionally understood as the prime force shaping the voting behaviour of the Western world, are changing. Attention is thus focused upon attitudes to the environment and whether what Inglehart terms 'post-materialist value changes' will result in the emergence of a fundamentally new type of politics (Inglehart 1977; Müller-Rommel 1982).

There are, however, obvious limitations associated with conducting analyses of ecologism within the confines of one discipline alone. Chief among these is the restriction this places upon the ability to grasp the various dimensions involved in the phenomenon of ecologism and to understand their interrelationship. This is especially important as political ecologists undertake both analysis and action in what they refer to as a 'holistic' manner: one that addresses in an interconnected manner the various dimensions of people's relationship to the natural world, be it through consumption, production or leisure activities, and that stresses the necessity of holistic solutions to the environmental crisis. In this sense an interdisciplinary framework that utilizes concepts, ideas and theories from a variety of approaches seems most appropriate.

Furthermore, many of these accounts suffer, as Lowe and Rüdig (1986) rightly point out, from an lack of reference to the actual concern of political ecology groups, namely 'ecological crisis'. Theoreticians thus pay little attention to either the local, national or global issues that spur ecologists into action and they thus fail to present a contextual understanding of ecologism. As a further consequence, analysis either shows a lack of attention to the empirical context within which specific groups operate or pays too much attention to the empirical mapping of specific groups of activists with no reference back to theoretical issues.

There has similarly been a tendency to address ecologism in a somewhat static manner. This often assumes that there exists a shared analysis among activists, a common understanding of what is needed to address the issues and an agreed method of organizing ecological groups in order to win a say in shaping policy towards the environment. However, ecologism, like all philosophies, is the outcome of a complex set of influences. Political ecology groups draw upon those influences in a variety of different ways and to meet a variety of different needs. There is need, therefore, to unpack the treatment of both ecologism philosophy and the activists groups that draw their inspiration from this philosophy. This needs to be done in a way that allows for a fuller understanding of the complexity of the issues involved as well as the manner in which these issues are addressed by political ecology groups.

In what follows an attempts is made to address the complexity of influences, ideas, policies and organizational forms of ecologism as is manifest in one country, Ireland. Attempt is also made to do so in an interdisciplinary manner: the political, ideological, social and economic factors that influence ecological consciousness and action in Ireland are examined. Ireland offers distinct advantages for such a study, as it not only has a variety of political ecology groups but also as a dependently developed periphery offers us a new and different framework for analysis not present in discussions of ecologism in advanced industrial countries. We begin the examination of the ecological movement in Ireland with an analysis of the nature of the Irish state and its economy.

The Political Economy of the Irish state

Before 1922 Ireland, both politically and economically, could be said to have been a 'classically' dependent country. Ruled directly from Westminster in London the economic base of the country was locked into an agricultural and trading relationship with the centre that left it both economically underdeveloped and politically marginal. It had more in common with the Third World economies analysed by the *dependencia* school than with the capitalist economies of its European neighbours (Baker 1987a).

Despite the partial political independence of 1922 the Southern part of Ireland continued to experience a relationship of economic dependence with Britain. Up until the 1950s the economy was primarily based upon subsistence farming and the export of raw material and labour (Meenan 1970). This relationship was maintained despite the fact that for the bulk of the period from 1922 to 1958 a policy of economic self-sufficiency, 'economic nationalism' had been implemented by the dominant Irish political party, Fianna Fáil. One of the chief reasons for the continued economic difficulties of the post-independence period was that, with the partitioning of the island, the majority of the industrial bourgeoisie remained with the United Kingdom, that is, in the North of Ireland. This left the Southern Irish industrial bourgeoisie both weak and ineffective and thus unable to bring about the economic development sought by the policy of economic nationalism.

The policy of economic nationalism was one expression of the dominant ideology in Irish political culture: that of Republican-Nationalism. This ideology is the single most important influence upon political life in the South of Ireland. Republican-Nationalist ideology and what is known as 'the national question' influences Southern Irish policy making at both the national and the international levels. For example, the decision to join the European Community (EC) in 1972 was taken in the hope that membership would make the border between the North and the South of decreasing economic relevance and thus increase the chances of national unification. Similarly, the decision not to join NATO, despite EC membership, was an expression of the belief that the participation of the Republic in international military affairs would be a source of political embarrassment and that political neutrality should continue as long as Ireland remains partitioned (Raymond 1984).

The policy of economic nationalism, however, was abandoned by the Fianna Fáil Government in 1958. The immediate reasons lay in the failure of the policy to bring about economic development, resulting in a series of crises in the 1950s. This change was also influenced by post-war reconstruction in Europe, an important feature of which was the change in the structure and nature of the multinational company. The multinational company moved from being predominantly a trading company to being involved in foreign direct investment in several sites simultaneously (Barnet and Müller 1975). The new phase of the multinational company was seen in Ireland as capable of bringing the economic development that the island so urgently sought. Thus in the late 1950s institutions, such as the Industrial Development Authority, were re-oriented towards the task of attracting foreign direct investment into Ireland (Baker 1987a). A policy of export-oriented economic expansion achieved through reliance upon foreign direct investment has subsequently remained the major plank of Government economic policy in Ireland.

By the late 1960s the economic structure in Ireland had undergone radical change. The island now has an urbanized industrial economy. Close examination of the modernization and industrialization of the Irish economy reveals, however, a surprising continuity with the past. The structures of dependency, present during and immediately after the period of 'colonial' rule, have remained. Its more visible features, however, have changed. The economic, fiscal and trading relations that once existed between the rural, underdeveloped and peripheral economy and the centre in London have been replaced by a developed industrial economy reliant for its economic development on the continued presence of the multinational companies engaged in export-oriented foreign direct investment. This investment has been shown to have little upstream or downstream linkages with the Irish economy, which can be described as a 'platform' production process (O'Farrell and O'Loughlin 1980). In short, the Irish economy has, in the last twenty years, changed from being a dependent underdeveloped economy to being a dependently developed one (Crotty 1986). That dependent industrialization has not resulted in the expansion of the home industrial base, and the industrial bourgeoisie remain economically weak (Bew and Patterson 1978).

The Emergence of Social Movements in Ireland

The changes that took place in the Irish economy in the 1960s and 1970s must not be seen in isolation. Rather, they were related to wider social changes occurring on the island at the time. These changes included: demographic changes, with a growth in the population experienced for the first time since the 1840s, much of it occurring in the Dublin region; secondly, a general rise in the standard of living; thirdly, an introduction of non-fee-paying secondary level education and increased access to third level education; fourthly, the arrival of television in 1962 and a decrease in the rigorous nature of Irish censorship (Baker 1987a); and finally, a decline in the importance of the Roman Catholic Church in state and political affairs, bringing with it the arrival of hitherto taboo topics as legitimate areas for discussion on the political stage (Garvin 1981). This 'modernization' of Irish society widened outlooks, increased employment prospects, facilitated travel and cultural exchange and raised expectations among the Irish population. The rapid economic and social changes of the period disrupted what had hitherto been a closed and relatively stable society. In particular, the scramble to 'catch-up' with the development of its European neighbours through industrialization and modernization had disruptive effects upon the accepted political and social processes and relationships that had existed throughout the island. Furthermore, entry into the modern industrial age was also to bring ecological disruption and with it an increased concern about the negative impact of the drive towards industrialization and modernization.

It was against this background of rapid industrialization and cultural and social modernization that 'new' social movements began to appear in Irish society. For example, the 1970s saw the birth of the 'new' women's movement, including single issue groups campaigning for access to contraceptives (for example the Contraceptive Action Programme) and divorce (the Divorce Action Group) as well as groups concerned with consciousness raising and gay rights. Many of these groups were established by the student population in university towns, as access, albeit limited, to third level education opened up to the wider population.

The Irish anti-nuclear movement is one such example. This was the first movement in Ireland to address itself to issues of an ecological nature. Before that there had been some concern about nuclear issues but these were addressed exclusively in terms of Irish neutrality. There had also been a resource protection group concerned with the appropriation of Irish mineral wealth by multinational companies, but this expressed itself in traditional Marxist terms. If we wish therefore to understand the subsequent evolution of Irish ecologism we must begin with an analysis of the Irish anti-nuclear movement. Following analysis of the anti-nuclear movement, the subsequent anti-toxic industry movement, Irish mining controversies and then the current 'green' movement are examined.

The Anti-nuclear Movement

The Irish anti-nuclear movement arose within the context of the state's decision in the 1970s to generate electricity in Ireland by building at least one nuclear power station. Much of the impulse for this decision came from Fianna Fáil, the dominant Irish political party. They actively encouraged the state-run Electricity Supply Board to push ahead with its nuclear plans. Fianna Fáil's support for nuclear power was a reflection of their belief in sustained industrial growth, a belief that had formed the basis of the Party's economic policy since the 1958 industrial initiative of the then party leader, Seán Lemass. There may also have been a nationalistic motive behind the enthusiasm with which the Party greeted this technology: the desire that Ireland should, like its advanced industrial neighbours, display its arrival into the modern industrial age by participating in new technological developments like that of nuclear power (Baker 1988). Fianna Fáil were supported in their pro-nuclear stance by all the main political parties, including the Worker's Party and Fine Gael, the later albeit cautiously. The Labour Party also gave support to the nuclear plans during their period of participation in the 1973-7 Coalition Government. However, many of the Party's major supporters were against nuclear power, including some of the larger trade unions.

Development of the Movement

At first, the news that a nuclear power station might be located at Carnsore, County Wexford, was met with a positive response at the local level. It was not until 1973-4 that doubts began to arise concerning the proposal. After an initial series of informal meetings local individuals organized into the Nuclear Safety Association. Similarly Friends of the Earth (FoE) was established in Dublin in 1974. Later a branch of FoE was also established in Cork and was to prove to be among the strongest and most active of the FoE groups in Ireland (Dalby, 1984-5). By 1978 there was a strengthening of existing groups and the formation of several new groups so that the major coalition representing the Irish anti-nuclear movement developed. These new groups included Nuclear Opposition Wexford, formed in 1978, a year which also saw the formation of anti-nuclear groups in Cork, Limerick and Galway. The development of this coalition, however, was not always smooth.

On the one hand there were groups such as FoE who wished to conduct its campaign against nuclear energy through the use of the legal and administrative processes available within the state. While they wished to see changes, often of a radical nature, they intended to achieve these through working within the system in a non-violent way. They adopted traditional organizational structures, with executives, a chairperson, etc., and formal membership, and were a branch of 'FoE Worldwide'

On the other hand, there were groups including the anarchist Belfast Just Books Collective and the extreme-left Revolutionary Struggle, who accepted the policy that Ireland should remain nuclear free 'by any means possible', violent if necessary. These groups wished to see a national movement develop along what was referred to as 'autonomous' lines. Autonomous in this sense meant that groups were free to develop their own policy and strategies and were not to be held accountable at any regional or national level to any other groups or organizational structure. For them, small, local and autonomous groups, without formal membership and interwoven through a network of informal contact, and more appropriate and truly democratic. These groups wished to see a mass movement develop outside traditional parliamentary politics. Many were on the far left, had been in existence before the nuclear controversy developed or were active in issues other than the nuclear one, and saw nuclear power as but one example of capitalist technology requiring mass opposition. Furthermore, unlike FoE, they did not wish to become involved in campaigning for, or conducting research into, alternative energy sources, such as solar or wind power. They saw this as a means cf providing capitalism with a way out of its energy crisis. These groups wished to change the system but from the outside, that is, they did not wish to restrict their activities to the established political, administrative and legal structures nor did they wish to restrict themselves to non-vlolent means.

With the development of these tensions the movement split in 1978. After this split the movement developed along two lines: groups who wished to work within the system, and those who wished to work from outside it. The split is significant in that it was to act as a major influence upon the formation of the cleavage lines subsequently found throughout not only the anti-nuclear movement but the ecology movement as a whole.

Interactions Within the Movement

Despite the divisions within the movement a surprising amount of joint activity was to be found and the contact between groups was most noticeable at the national level. The bulk of the anti-nuclear campaign, however, was conducted within the context of loosely woven, informal and locally based campaign groups. These numbered at one point approximately 102 separate groups and operated throughout Ireland, both in the North and the South. A series of newspapers, the most important of which were *Rebel*, *Dawn* and later *Red Herring* played an important role in information dissemination [2]

The Issues for the Movement

The anti-nuclear movement, while initially focused around opposition to the Carnsore nuclear power station, became almost immediately involved in other nuclear-related issues. The proximity of the British Windscale/ Sellafield nuclear re-processing plant to the Irish east coast and its contamination of the Irish Sea became an immediate target for opposition. A similar concern was the dumping of radioactive waste off the south-west coast of Ireland, especially by Britain. Furthermore, nuclear weapons, the use of nuclear medicine in Irish hospitals and of radioactive isotopes in factories, the training for a nuclear future through the use of the small-scale nuclear installation in University College Cork, all became specific focuses of concern. In many cases ad-hoc single-issue groups were established to conduct campaigns around these concerns. The Dublin Clean Seas Campaign, for example, was formed to oppose the Windscale/Sellafield plant while The Lough Anti-Nuclear Group was formed in 1980 in Cork around the campaign to halt the nuclear training programme at the city's university. Similarly, Help Organise Peaceful Energy (HOPE) was formed to conduct a campaign against the dumping off the south-west coast, a group that was formally launched in May 1980. In April 1986, this group organized into the national group 'Earthwatch'. Other 'outside' groups also become involved. For example, The Irish Transport and General Workers Union, the largest Irish trade union, adopted an anti-nuclear stand and a Trade Union Campaign Against Nuclear Power was launched. John Carroll, the Union President, had consistently opposed nuclear power and was, for example, involved in editing a book on the dangers of nuclear technology with Petra Kelly of the German Green Party (Carroll and Kelly 1980).

A major overall concern of the movement was that the presence of a nuclear electricity generating plant would threaten Irish neutrality by impelling its participation in the arms race. Both plutonium and enriched uranium are associated with civil nuclear energy and they can be used in the making of nuclear weapons. Many in the movement felt that Irish neutrality would be compromised by involvement in the proliferation of nuclear weapons. Furthermore, as it was more likely that the Irish nuclear power station would use reprocessing plants abroad, the movements remained unconvinced by Fianna Fáil's assurance that the use to which the by-product of the Irish nuclear programme would be put would be carefully monitored. Many in the movement saw nuclear technology as a closed cycle, which began with uranium mining, moved through the production of electricity and ended with the production of nuclear weapons. Thus participation in any part of the process was seen as involvement in the wider nuclear cycle.

Two major campaigns formed the national focus of the anti-nuclear movement's activities. The most important of these was the campaign against the proposed nuclear reactor at Carnsore Point. Before this came to a climax, vigorous campaigns were mounted against the mining of uranium in Leinster and, most noticeably, in Donegal, organized by the Leinster Anti-Uranium Group and the Donegal Uranium Committee respectively (Baker 1988).

The success of the Donegal campaign in particular added both determination and strength to the anti-nuclear campaign simultaneously being conducted around the Carnsore proposal. However, it is this latter campaign which was to prove the major focus of group discussion and activity within the Irish anti-nuclear movement. This was facilitated by the decision in 1978 by anti-nuclear groups to occupy the site of the proposed station and to conduct a festival there. This was to be the first of five national festivals, known as 'The Carnsore Festivals'.

The Carnsore festivals were important events for the anti-nuclear move-ment. For the movement they encouraged, strengthened and consolidated their anti-nuclear stance, yet paradoxically they were also to widen the internal divisions. After the first festival many international contacts were made and the four other annual festivals were subsequently attended by many from abroad. Contacts from the USA, France and Italy, especially among those who were participating in the Italian 'Il Movimento', including Lotta Continua per il Communismo, a Italian political left-wing group, were of particular importance. At this point members of the Irish movement began, in turn, to attend international events and this exposed them to new ideas from abroad. The campaign in the USA after the accident at the Three Mile Island plant at Harrisburg, and the campaign against the nuclear plant at Plogoff in France attracted particular Irish support. This influence and the group's own increasing involvement in the anti-nuclear campaign in Ireland widened the area of concern of these groups and made the divisions within the movement all the more marked.

Thus, the more radical groups, many of whom, it will be remembered, had always seen the nuclear issue as but one example of production to which they were opposed, became increasingly concerned with other aspects of domestic and international policy. These included a rejection of industrial policies such as that proposed by Fianna Fáil, which required major energy inputs; and from the opposition to multinational companies who wished to engage in uranium mining there followed a questioning of the whole role of multinationals not only in the Irish economy but internationally; a similar progression from concern about the nuclear arms race to the involvement of Northern Ireland in NATO to the 'national question', that is, the partition of Ireland; and a linking of concern with the European Community energy policy to a wider critique of the European Community itself and also the USA through critique of its 'Atoms for Peace Programme'. The groups working outside the system increasingly began to see nuclear power as but one example of a capitalist and toxic production process designed to increase the profitability of international capital at the expense of local and indigenous people. These groups were, in short, presenting a neo-Marxist critique of political economy, one that was increasingly expressed in nationalist terms.

Other groups, especially those working within the system, were on the other hand moving towards life-style issues, alternative energy sources and what may be called 'green politics'. Many of the individuals involved were to become involved in Comhaontas Glas (known originally in English as the Green Alliance, later as the Green Party). They began to share features in common with the international green movement. They were, in short, forming into a European style political 'green' movement (see below).

Following from the momentum of the Carnsore festivals, the political parties began to take note. The combination of opposition activities resulted in Fianna Fáil conceding a public inquiry on the issue of the Carnsore proposal. This decision, however, did not defuse the opposition as Fianna Fáil had hoped. If anything it had the opposite effect as it opened up participation in the debate to those who either would not or could not participate in the group activity typical of the anti-nuclear movement. After the Government's announcement, opposition to nuclear power widened and deepened. In response to this Fianna Fáil were forced to concede further and establish an Interdepartmental Committee to examine the nuclear issue in 1979. Despite pressure from the groups the Interdepartmental Committee's report was not made public and it is unclear whether it was ever completed. However, what is clear is that the promised public inquiry never got off the ground. In effect the idea was dropped, probably because holding the public inquiry would have made the government's energy policy all the more subject to public scrutiny. Furthermore, the task of dealing with the controversy was made all the more difficult by the decision of Fine Gael to reconsider its position of nuclear energy. Thus unanamity of agreement between the major parties began to break up.

In addition to internal political opposition a number of external factors also acted against the Government and played into the hands of the anti-nuclear movement during the later phase of the campaign. The nuclear accident at Three Mile Island in the USA, the down turn in economic activity and the failure of energy demand to accelerate as much as was predicted all acted to decrease the urgency and certainty with which the policy was being pursued. Despite these outside influences, however, there can be little doubt that the movements' ability to utilize these developments to expose the weakness of the Party's position was a major factor in shaping the final outcome of Ireland's nuclear energy policy. As a consequence in 1980 Colley, who had replaced O'Malley as Minister of Energy, was forced to announce the postponement of the Carnsore plans. Fine Gael likewise acted and published its *Aspects of Energy Policy* in which it stated, albeit cautiously, that it was no longer committed to nuclear power (Fine Gael 1980).

The Toxic Industry Movement

It will be recalled that as the anti-nuclear campaign progressed a number of activists began to become interested in other related areas. As a result many became increasingly aware of other production processes already in existence in Ireland that posed threats to the environment similar to those posed by nuclear power. This was particularly true for the far left group Revolutionary Struggle which, as time progressed, began to devote more of its activities to this area.

Concern about the potential environmental and health damage that industry could bring was most noticeable in the Cork area, located at the mouth of one of the world's great natural deep-water harbours. The Industrial Development Authority (IDA), the body chiefly responsible for industrial development strategy in Ireland, had in the 1970s decided that the resource of Cork harbour could be utilized to attract further foreign direct investment into Ireland. The IDA therefore adopted a strategic development plan of zoning Cork Harbour for chemical and pharmaceutical plants. As a result Cork has a high concentration of foreign-owned chemical and pharmaceutical plants and these factories became the chief target of environmental activists.

Throughout Irish industrialization there have been many incidents of local objections to the location of particular plants. Most noticeable among them were objections to Pfizers in the early 1970, Alcan in 1974, Schering Plough in 1974 and Beechams 1977. However, it was not until a group called the Cork Noxious Industry Action Group was established around 1980 that the first signs of objections to the policy of attraction of foreign direct investment into Ireland, as well as concern with the environmental impact of this policy began to receive national prominence. This group was initially formed by members of the Cork Anti-Nuclear Group. Its chief concern was subsidiaries of multinational companies whose production process involved the use or the production of toxic substances. The Cork group devoted its attention to campaigning, information gathering and educational activities. One of the most significant campaigns it became involved in was that against a subsidiary of an American company, Raybestos Manhattan, which had a plant in Ovens, County Cork. Initiated by local *ad hoc* groups, including the local residents' associations in the Ovens and Ringaskiddy areas, this campaign was to grow to encompass eighteen groups and last from 1976 to 1980. The campaign resulted in the closure of the plant (Baker 1987b).

There were two immediate consequences of the success of the Raybestos Manhattan campaign. First, it encouraged other community groups to undertake similar campaigns. Second, it focused attention on another related issue, the disposal of the toxic by-products produced by factories already in operation in Ireland.

Community Opposition to Toxic Industry

Other groups followed from the example of the Raybestos Manhattan campaign. In 1978 Cork FoE, for example, though still active on the nuclear question, began to devote attention to plans by Eli Lilly/ Elanco to open a branch factory in Dunderrow, on the western side of the Harbour. This led to the formation of the Bandon Valley Protection Association. Opposition, however, soon extended to areas outside Cork, for example, the state-owned NET factory in Arklow and the Japanese Ashi plant in Mayo. The most important case to develop was that of the opposition to the chemical plant Merck, Sharp and Dohme in Tipperary.

The Merck, Sharp and Dohme plant opened in 1976 and two years later the first complaints about damage to health resulting from the plant were made by a local farming family, the Hanrahans. The following two years saw an number of similar complaints from the dairy and farming families in the area, especially relating to ill-health among farm animals, although chiefly made by the Hanrahan family (Keohane 1989). Following these complaints and the increasingly vocal concerns of the local community a report on pollution and the dangers of emissions from the factory was commissioned by the Tipperary County Council. This action failed to halt the first death of a farm animal in 1981 that was attributed by the family to pollution from the factory. Within a year the family were claiming that the deaths of sixty-seven of their cattle were directly attributable to the emissions from the plant. A High Court writ was served by them in 1982 against the company. During the next three years while the court case dragged on, the Hanrahan family, Merck, Sharp and Dhome, the National Farmers' Association, the County Council, the Minister for Agriculture and the Creameries as well as the Institute for Industrial Research and Standards (subsequently to be restructured and renamed Eolas) became embroiled in a bitter controversy. Conflicting evidence about pollution levels and their potential effects on humans and animals was presented by different parties and debates about the degree of culpability of the company began (The Irish Times, August, October 1982; August 1985; July 1988; The New Scientist, October 1985).

Given the number of different interests involved, the dispute began to take on national importance, with the result that the Government set up an Interdepartmental Committee to monitor the situation in 1982. In 1985 the High Court decided against the family and they were ordered to pay £1 million costs. This resulted in the public auction of the Hanrahan farm animals and equipment, an emotional event that brought wide coverage by the national media. However, following appeal in 1988, the Supreme Court decided in favour of the Hanrahan family, a decision that came too late to save the livelihood of the family.

The case was very important at the local level. It raised issues of allegiances both to political parties within the County Council as well as to the National Farmers' Association. It also had a direct impact upon relationships within the community: the divisive issue being that support for the family on the one hand and, on the other, concern that too much publicity could adversely affect the marketing of all of the local farmers' produce, especially milk to the local creamery. However, the real significance of the case lies in its impact at the national level. This impact was manifest at a variety of different levels and should not be underestimated.

First, the Hanrahan's were a traditional family, rooted for generations in the locality. Their actions were not therefore easily dismissed, as had been all to easy in other cases where objectors were often newly arrived rural dwellers, seeing the rural countryside as a place to live out alternative lifestyle choices that often have little in common economically or socially with the traditional community of the region. Secondly, and more importantly, the family were engaged in dairy farming and the factory was located in the heart of rich pasture land. As a consequence, the case forced policy makers to confront two conflicting interests: those of agriculture and industry. This was a conflict of interest that is especially important in a newly industrialized country where agriculture is still an important component of the gross national product (GNP). Third, the case brought a new set of interests into the environmental arena, in particular, the farming community, and this, as we shall see below, was to prove very influential at a later date. Fourth, the controversy brought Irish industrial policy on to the agenda for discussion in a new way. In particular, the issue of continuous and appropriate monitoring of the emissions from existing factories was raised. Furthermore, the long drawn out legal proceedings pointed both to the lack of evidence and, when available, the conflicting nature of the evidence on the degree of and dangers associated with the emissions from the Merck, Sharp and Dohme plant. This in particular highlighted the lack of knowledge by the policy makers and planning agencies who were charged with the industrialization of the Irish economy. This in turn led to the linking of concern with environmental protection to a critique of industrialization policy based upon the attraction of foreign industry investment, and forced a more general debate on environmental protection and the type of industry being attracted into Ireland by the IDA. Fifth, the controversy also focused attention upon the IDA itself and added to the continuing questioning of the lack of accountability mechanisms, which prevent the IDA's attraction strategy being subject to public scrutiny and to public influence. Sixth, the case opened up a new set of strategies, the legal route, to the antitoxic industry movement. Merck, Sharp and Dohme is considered to have made an important legal precedent within Irish law. Previously the difficulty facing people had been to prove a direct link between the ill effects of pollution and the putative case. The Supreme Court decision considerably lightened the burden on the plaintiff to show that a particular factory is the source of the problem (Keohane 1989). Furthermore, the opening up of the legal route widened the net of potential activists willing to become involved in opposition to toxic industry. Before that case activism had often been confined to those willing to engage in behaviour more typical of 'new' social movements, such as protest, leafleting and demonstrations. Finally, the determination and ultimate vindication of an individual family in the face of the resources of a large multinational company, legal and bureaucratic delays, huge financial costs – a determination that required very real sacrifices – fired the imagination of the country in an extra-ordinary way. This was to give strength and inspiration to other local communities faced with development plans to which they were opposed.

An important example of this influence is to be found in a recent case of community opposition to the IDAs proposal to allow a USA pharmaceutical company, Merrell Dow, to locate in Killeagh in East Cork. This proposal had led to the establishment of a Womanagh Valley Protection Association. This group opposed the siting of the plant arguing that the Killeagh area was prime agricultural land and that pollution from the plant could potentially threaten this (The Irish Times, December 1988, September 1989; The Sunday Tribune, 10 September 1989). Initially their campaigning was limited to the effort to have the factory relocated at a more appropriate site in the Cork harbour area. The group, drawing its strength from the successful Hanrahan case, strongly believed in the adoption of legal proceedings arguing that natural justice was on their side and that this would be vindicated through the courts. However, as the campaign developed and other groups became involved, including the Concerned

Citizens of East Cork and West Waterford and the Concerned Citizens against Merrell Dow, the emphasis shifted from the desire to relocate the plant at a more suitable site to principled opposition to the plant. This was based upon the belief that the presence of the plant posed unacceptable environmental hazards to the local people and the ecosystem.[4]

These local groups formed as a result of a far wider alliance of interests than previously experienced when such actions were undertaken in the early 1980s. However, this did result in polarization of the community, as seen for example by the establishment of a Killeagh Pro-Industry Group in the area (*The Imokilly People*, 8 June 1989). The campaign lasted until 1989 and succeeded in forcing a much publicized appeal to an Bord Pleánala, the body responsible for planning permission appeals and, as in the Hanrahan case, finally resulted in a High Court action. In 1989, as a consequence of the delays brought about by this opposition, Merrell Dow withdrew its proposal to build a plant in Ireland, although the company denied that this was the reason (*The Irish Times*, 5 September 1989).

This action came as a serious blow to the IDA, who had consistently argued that the success of their plans to further develop Cork harbour rested to a large measure on their ability to attract Merrell Dow into the area (*The Irish Times*, 2 June 1989). Failure to do so weakened their image abroad while at the same time forcing on to the public agenda even more issues concerning the environment, especially the IDA's monitoring of the environmental record of companies it seeks to attract to Ireland.

Another important case that is currently attracting national attention is that emerging against the IDA's proposals to attract Sandoz to Ringaskiddy, also in Cork harbour.[5] Sandoz is the Swiss pharmaceutical company which was involved in the Rhine pollution in 1986. This campaign is being conducted by numerous groups, including the newly formed Responsible Industry for Cork Harbour Group, a somewhat conservative group chiefly composed of local residents on the western side of the Harbour (*The Irish Times*, October-November 1989; 14-15 December 1989). However, a total of 200 objections against the plant were lodged by national and local groups with Cork County Council. The outcome of this has yet to be decided, but it is becoming critical to the IDA as mounting environmental opposition not only undermines its development plans for Cork harbour but threatens its national development strategy. A recent Irish Times/MRBI opinion poll confirms this growing opposition. The poll showed that a majority (51 per cent) of Southern Irish people do not think that the IDA should attract chemical or pharmaceutical companies into Ireland (*The Irish Times* and Marketing Research Bureau of Ireland Ltd, November 1989).

Despite the national attention received by many of these campaigns the community opposition groups remain local in nature. These community groups are often, because of the IDA's preference for green field sites, rural in nature or develop within small towns.[6] There have been some attempts to unify this action and, for example, in 1981 many of the local groups opposed to toxic industry united under the umbrella of the Alliance for Safety and Health. The Alliance, like many of the more radical anti-nuclear groups previously in existence, framed their analysis in term of nationalist ideology. They argued that the presence of such a high degree of pene-tration of foreign direct investment into the Irish economy was a result of its colonial legacy. Furthermore, they argued that the solution to Ireland's toxic and nuclear problems lay not in regulation and monitoring but in the resolution of the national question, that is, the unification of Ireland and the re-appropriation of its natural resources by the Irish people. The Alliance remained in existence from 1981 to 1983. During this time it conducted a series of conferences and seminars and produced the first comprehensive report on toxic industry in Ireland, called 'Toxic Ireland: A Discussion Document' (n.d.). However, the Merrell Dow campaign led to another attempt to co-ordinate action and to share information among groups. In February 1989 Action for Safety and Health was established, a group who act as an information resource for the fragmented opposition to both the toxic waste dump issue and toxic industry as well as mining controversies. They also bring together activists from the community level at regular intervals to learn from each other and disseminate information.[7] To date the group has organized a number of national environmental conferences throughout Ireland.

Despite significant victories and the spontaneous opposition that currently arises to toxic industry, it is important not to overstate the significance of the anti-toxic movement. Many of the cases have been unsuccessful; activists have to a large measure failed to win the support of the trade unions and organized labour; the campaigns often take place within polarized communities; and, furthermore, within both individual groups and the movement as a whole, there can be different and sometimes conflicting interests. For example, some community groups are concerned to shift the location of particular plants while others present a more radical and principled objection to multinational companies locating in Ireland. Similarly, the development of the toxic industry movement has not been smooth, with the movement as a whole experiencing a lull in their activities in the mid 1980s and a re-birth as the 1980s drew to a close. This movement, lacking a steady development, remains somewhat nebulous. Its existence to a large measure is dependent upon the ability of local *ad hoc* groups to successfully launch campaigns of opposition to industrial development strategies for their area. Lacking a national organisational dimension, longer-term and planned goals, being reactive rather than primarily pro-active in nature, they are in a weak position in terms of their ability to influence the direction of a national industrial development policy so rooted in the ideology of all the main political parties since the 1950s. They should, therefore, be seen as indicative of the beginning of a questioning process within Irish society about economic and environmental policy not as the end product of that process.

This questioning, nevertheless, is having important consequences for national policy. In particular it has forced the present Fianna Fáil Government to consider more seriously the implementation of EC environmental policy, on which to date the Irish have had a poor performance record. Indeed the current Taoiseach (Prime Minister) Charles Haughey is determined that, during the Irish Presidency of the European Council in 1990, ecological issues will be very much highlighted (Geoghegan-Quinn 1989). Furthermore, the questioning had consequences for the formulation of new and tightening up of existing legislation on environmental protection, including the decision in 1990 to establish an Environmental Protection Agency in Ireland.

Community Campaigns Against Toxic Dumps

The emergence of campaigns against particular factories was, it will be recalled, only one of the developments that was influenced by the Ray-bestos Manhattan campaign. The second consequence was a broadening of awareness to encompass not only concern for the production process but also for the by-products of that process, including toxic waste as well as the transportation of toxic chemicals through both urban and rural settlements.

FoE Cork was the chief group which expressed concerned about the transportation of toxic products. In the early 1980s they campaigned for the introduction of national legislation to regulate this transportation. It is, however, the issue of toxic waste disposal that has been a focal point of concern for the Irish ecology movement, especially since 1981. It has also been a chief concern of the IDA.

The lack of toxic waste disposal facilities remains a source of considerable embarrassment to the IDA. As far as the IDA is concerned, its development plans not only for the Cork harbour area but for the country as a whole are threatened by the lack of toxic waste disposal facilities. First, they believe that it reflects badly upon their credibility, especially upon what they see as the national commitment to industrialisation through foreign direct investment. Secondly, the provision of a toxic dump was seen as increasingly important in the light of international concern about the exportation of toxic waste and the increased reluctance of not only Western European but also of developing countries to accept the importation of toxic waste from other countries. This is particularly important for Ireland as in 1982, following a series of accidents and the wrecking of the *Craigantlet*, a ship bringing a cargo of toxic waste from Ireland, the British Government restricted the importation of toxic waste for disposal from

Ireland (Keohane 1989). Third, the IDA argues that the continuous failure to resolve the problem gives increasing scope to what it refers to as 'the volatile environmental lobby', especially in the Cork region (The Irish Times, 21 November 1980 and 12 May 1980). It argues that the longer the problem remains unsolved the harder it will be to find a solution. Finally, the IDA argues, if there are to be toxic by-products of industrialization then it is better that they be disposed of in a monitored and secure manner making control, accountability and responsibility easier to maintain.

This last argument has caused divisions within the Irish environmental movement. On the one hand, there are those groups who argue that, given the presence of toxic industries in Ireland, it is better in the short-term to monitor their waste disposal and that this is achievable only by the establishment of a state toxic dump. This strategy would then be complemented by a longer-term goal: to achieve source-reduction so that the amount of toxic waste could be radically reduced or even eliminated. Groups holding this position included FoE and Bandon Valley Protection Association as well as more recent groups such as Earthwatch, formerly HOPE, and Greenpeace (see below). On the other hand, there are those who argue that any toxic waste disposal facilities, either at the national or local level would further legitimise toxic production, encourage the IDA to attract more industry of this nature into Ireland, and stifle the debate about alternative forms of production through the implementation of a short-term solution. Groups holding this position included the Cork Noxious Industry Action Group, Revolutionary Struggle, Green Action Now Group, The Alliance for Safety and Health, and Action for Safety and Health.

This division in the movement goes back to 1978, when the IDA announced that it had commissioned a report on standards and procedures for toxic waste disposal in Ireland. Much of the impetus for this came from the need to find a waste disposal site for the asbestos by-products of the Raybestos Manhattan plant. Various suggested sites in the County Cork area resulted in the emergence of local opposition, the most noticeable being the campaign backed by the the Irish Farmers' Association in Nohoval which lasted from 1978 to 1980 (Baker 1987b). Following such intensive campaigns, Cork County council informed the Government in 1980 that it would not provide the national tip head for toxic waste. Attention was thus shifted to Dublin and within months Dublin County Council voted to provide a site for toxic waste for industry at Dunsink, near Finglas.

Once the intention to proceed with the acquisition of a site for a national land-based toxic dump facility in Finglas was established, the Finglas Toxic Action Group was set up (The Irish Times, October 1980, January 1981, May 1981, August 1981, March 1982; The Cork Examiner, November 1978 and April 1979).[8] This group eventually became opposed to any type of toxic waste facilities. It launched a very active and vocal campaign and was subsequently joined by the Clondalkin and Baldonnel Toxic Action Groups, groups formed in the areas chosen as alternative sites. They succeeded in forcing the abandonment of these areas and, furthermore, to delay the plans for a state toxic dump.

All three of the initial areas chosen were in Dublin and the groups were heavily supported by the Dublin anti-nuclear movement. However, at the time, a number of new activists began to get involved, mostly arising out of community-based groups, such as residents' associations. This mobilization of support from what had hitherto been 'a-political' groupings was an important step for the ecology movement and many of these 'citizen initiatives' were subsequently to form part of the Comhaontas Glas, the Irish Green Party.

Residents' associations, it will be remembered, played an important role in the Raybestos Manhattan campaign and were to prove a fertile source of support for the environmental cause in Ireland. Traditionally, such groups are active at the local level, are single issue groups and composed of a fairly homogeneous membership. They are a modern phenomenon formed in the numerous urban housing developments that have occurred in Ireland since the development of the 1960s. Traditionally, their concerns are with the acquisition of facilities for the residents of a particular housing estate, for example, street lighting and sheltered bus stops. Their politicization on the toxic dump issue is not only a direct response to the state plans for areas such as Finglas and Baldonnel but also a consequence of the very active support that the Irish anti-nuclear and toxic industry movement gave to these groupings when they were fledgling concerns. In particular, attention should be drawn to the role of the Dublin Anti-Radiation and Toxic Action Group, a group formed by radical anti-nuclear activists in Dublin and as well to groups such as the Research Action Group who published the anarchist magazine *Red Herring*. Residents' associations brought a good deal of organizational skills as well as political acumen to the movement, the latter arising as a result of their experience with the manipulation of the clientelistic political culture in existence in Ireland. Despite the role played by urban groups, it is nevertheless important to note the centrality of rural community groups in shaping the Irish ecological movement.

Although the issue of toxic waste disposal has remained unresolved since the early 1980s, it took on a new urgency in 1989. Recent revelations about the 'disappearance' of toxic waste in Ireland and the high levels of contamination of areas where toxic waste is currently dumped have led both Earthwatch and Greenpeace to renew their calls for a solution. Furthermore, increased international pressure, combined with that from domestic sources, including the IDA, led the Fianna Fáil government to state in March 1989 that it intended to resolve the issue once and for all by the establishment of a land-based dumping facility and incinerator as quickly as possible (*The Irish Times*, 15 March 1989). It can be expected that the siting of both the national incinerator and the land based toxic dump will continue to give rise to community-based opposition. With Earthwatch launching a national campaign on this issue one can also expect that this protest will begin to take on even more of a national dimension.[9]

As we have seen, much of the activity around toxic waste dumping and toxic production process took place between 1980 and 1984. However, during the middle part of the decade groups such as the Research Action Group and Dublin Anti-Radiation and Toxic Action Group, and the Cork groups, Cork Noxious Industry Action Group, Bandon Valley Protection Association, as well as the national Alliance for Safety and Health ceased to exist. Cork FoE also effectively ceased to function, its members having become involved in such concerns as the Campaign for Nuclear Disarmament and Third World issues. By their nature these groups are usually ephemeral. Often formed by only a handful of activists, many of these groups lack formal membership or structures and operate with very limited resources. They are prone to internal disputes and continuous resource problems. Furthermore, those that become involved in direct action live an existence clouded in secrecy and thus are unable publicly to call upon support when needed. The Alliance for Safety and Health presents a typical example of such problems. Formed as an umbrella group it became heavily influenced, especially at the national level, by Revolutionary Struggle. This group was an extreme left-wing group adopting a very militant position on the national question and, in the mid-1980s, dissolved due to internal disputes. The Alliance for Safety and Health fell apart at the national level partially as a result of this.

Campaigns against Mining

Recently undertaken geological surveys have revealed that Ireland is richly endowed with mineral wealth. This has come as a surprise, for traditionally it was believed that Ireland was, except for a few small sites, almost devoid of mineral deposits. At present, prospecting licences for a number of these deposits have been issued to commercial companies with a view to issuing full mining licences at future dates. However, mining, like many of the other areas of recent economic development, has also resulted in vocal local opposition.

Opposition to mining first developed into national prominence in Ireland in the 1970s when a Dublin-based resource protection group began to campaign against the manner in which the state allowed multinational companies to operate Irish mines. However, this group was not environmental as such, confining its arguments to the issue of control over the profit resulting from mining and not to a principled opposition to mining as such.

The turning point in attitudes to mining came with the discovery of uranium deposits in the Glenties area of County Donegal. As uranium is a fuel for nuclear power stations, mining the uranium deposits was linked to the anti-nuclear campaign from the beginning. In particular, it was felt that not only would this particular mining impel Ireland into participation in the nuclear cycle, it was also feared that mining of a radioactive mineral such as uranium posed unacceptable health and safety risk to miners and to population of the locality. A well-organized opposition group, the Donegal Uranium Committee, which received widespread support from the Irish anti-nuclear movement, succeeded in halting the plans to mine the uranium. This campaign was active between the late 1970s and the early 1980s. Similar outcomes surrounded the discovery of uranium in Counties Kilkenny and Carlow (Baker 1988).

The importance of the uranium campaign lay in the fact that it was the first Irish campaign to address the health and environmental issues associated with mining, as opposed to concentrating attention on the distribution of the profits of mining operations. The anti-uranium groups involved in that campaign presented a principled objection to exploitation of a particular mineral. As was the case with Raybestos Manhattan, the successful outcome of this objection had a direct influence upon other communities facing mining operations. That influence included activists from the Donegal campaign giving information and organizational help to other groups, the most noticeable of which were the Lignite Action Group in County Tyrone and the groups opposed to gold mining in Connemara.

Opposition to lignite mining in Ardboe, County Tyrone, in the north of Ireland and to gold mining plans in Connemara, on the west coast of Ireland are the two most important anti-mining campaigns currently being conducted in Ireland. Furthermore, and especially in the case of the gold mining, they are also receiving widespread public attention.

The campaign against lignite mining is important because it directly linked environmental and economic issues to social issues and in so doing has extended the range of areas addressed by anti-mining groups. A brief history of the campaign reveals this importance.

Confirmation of the existence of commercially viable deposits of lignite along the western shores of Lough Neagh was given in the early 1980s. This caused immediate concern for wildlife groups such as the Royal Society for the Protection of Birds. The Lough, the largest fresh water lake in the British Isles, is an important sanctuary for over-wintering birds and its shore line is protected by the Ramsar Convention on the protection of wetlands (The Belfast Telegraph, 23 April 1986). Furthermore, the Lough is also a vital economic resource for the local community, with eel fishing acting as the most important source of income for the region. The loughshore community is tightly knit and many of its families have been settled in the area for over three hundred years. For them lignite mining was seen as posing unacceptable social, economic and environmental threats to both their community and the Lough.[10]

Lignite Action, the group formed to oppose the mining plans, drew its strength from the local community's strong Irish identity. However, unlike similar anti-mining groups, Lignite Action developed a positive action programme which sought to ensure the economic survival of the community through sustainable patterns of resource use. It saw itself therefore, not primarily as an opposition group but as a group of local ecologically aware people who wished to have a say in shaping their own development, to have that development reflect the traditions of the local community and to do so in a manner that can sustain community survival in the area.[11]

Lignite Action have been in existence since 1985 and throughout this period has engaged in discussion and debate with both the mining companies and with the Department of Economic Development Northern Ireland (DEDNI). The Department's main interest in the lignite deposits was in their utilization for the generation of electricity, a policy designed both to decrease dependence upon oil imports and to reduce the unit price of electricity production (DEDNI 1983). To date Lignite Action in its dealings with DEDNI has won important concessions, including access to the consultative process and the right to a public inquiry if full mining licences are to be issued (Baker 1989). However, the final outcome for the community remains to be seen.

Unlike Lignite Action, the anti-mining groups in the west of Ireland have not succeeded in gaining similar access to the decision making process. Thus, despite intensive campaigning, the groups opposed to gold mining, including the Mayo Environmental Group, continue to fight for the right to access to the policy process and to have Government see as legitimate the desire of a local community to have a say in shaping its own economic future. Other groups are also involved in the controversy, including Mining Awareness and Gold Environmental Impact Assessment (Gold EIA). Mining Awareness was established following concern with the general lack of information available on the environmental impact of gold mining and sees itself as a neutral information-giving and fact-finding group.[12] Gold EIA, on the other hand, are more critical of the mining process and wish to see a proper EIA, conforming to EC directives, conducted before any mining licences are issued for the area.[13]

As in the case of the lignite mining, local opposition to the mining of gold stems from both environmental as well as economic concerns. Modern gold mining processes utilize the toxic chemical cyanide and local people fear that its use could contaminate the local water table. As well as the long-term damage this could do to the local eco-system, the fear is that it could also have disastrous consequences for the fishing industry. Fishing, small-scale farming and tourism are the mainstays of the local economy. The area is also one of great natural beauty, and tourist interests fear that the despoiling of the rugged mountains of the district will effectively destroy the amenities of the area.[14] However, as is the case in the Lough Neagh area, the community is also divided in its response to mining. For some, especially for the small farmer existing on marginal land, leasing of land holdings to mining companies offers hitherto undreamt of possibilities of financial gain (The Connaught Tribune, 26 April 1989 and 27 April 1989; Alpha, 14 September 1989).

The gold mining controversy, however, is significantly different from other controversies in that it has a strong religious dimension. One of the chief sites of gold discovery is Croagh Patrick, a mountain that occupies an important place in Irish religious folklore and is regarded as Ireland's holy mountain. It is the site of an annual religious pilgrimage which attracts tens of thousands of pilgrims. The prospect of mining on this mountain has led the Archbishop of Tuam, Dr Joseph Cassidy, to condemn strongly all attempts to mine gold on Croagh Patrick (The Sunday Press, 30 April 1989). Given the importance of the Roman Catholic Church in Southern Irish society the Government can ill afford a controversy of this nature.

However, as mining controversies develop, not just in the west of Ireland but throughout mineral-rich regions, wider issues are coming to the fore. First, the need to begin to formulate a national policy on mining is becoming increasingly evident. In particular, dialogue between the various interests involved is required and policy needs to be formulated that takes account not just of multinational mining interests but also of local interests. Second, consideration has to be given to the balance between local economic activity, including tourism and fisheries, and the often short-term interests of multinational companies engaged in mineral exploitation in Ireland. Furthermore, as in other controversies, the issue of access to the decision making process by local interest groups as well as criticism of the planning apparatus is also coming to the fore. Historically, Government policy towards mining has been ad hoc and largely biased in favour of the interest of the multinational companies, but this approach is showing itself increasingly inadequate both in the context of new discoveries about Ireland's mineral wealth and in the face of widespread, local and highly organised environmental opposition groups.

The Emergence of European Style Green Politics in Ireland

Concern about nuclear power, toxic industry and mining operations are but three of the areas of concern of the Irish ecology movement. Other areas also exist, each in turn bringing activist groups engaged in campaigns on these issues to the fore. Such groups include, to name but a few: Dandelion Puppets in County Clare, a group using entertainment to carry the environmental message; Saor Collte Sheantruibh in Santry, a group wishing to save Santry wood from housing developers; Skerries Marine Mammal Watch and Killarney Nature Conservation Group as well as the Belfast-based Black Mountain Support Group and the Save the Cavehill Campaign, the latter two involved in protest against quarrying and mining. Other concerns include the possible health effects of waves from radio masts used for commercial radio as well as by the British Army in the border regions; the use and disposal of asbestos; the excessive turf cutting and drainage of Irish bogs; the rapid development of fish farming; and marine pollution, especially in the Irish sea.[15]

Although some of the above-mentioned groups have reached national prominence, many of them involved at the local level have not, receiving neither wide coverage in national newspapers and the media nor calling forth Government response at the national level. They are, none the less, important, especially in shaping the culture of ecologism in Ireland at the local level. However, this chapter is not seeking to give an exhaustive outline of all the groups involved in ecological issues nor of all the issues that political ecology groups address within Ireland. Rather it seeks to outline the main areas of concern and activities that are collectively shaping Irish ecological consciousness. There remains, however, one final group of actors not yet addressed by this chapter and these are among the most recent arrivals on the political stage in Ireland: what may loosely be called Irish 'green groups'.

Like the toxic industry opposition, the roots of green consciousness lie in the anti-nuclear movement, but the groups formed around this consciousness have undergone major transformation since the days of the Carnsore campaigns. Today there exist three main national green groups in Ireland: Earthwatch, Comhaontas Glas/The Green Party and Greenpeace. What characterizes these groups is that they address a wider range of issues than typically found among the other groups we have examined, groups that tend to be concerned with mining, industrialization or with nuclear power. The green groups, on the other hand, address issues across a broad spectrum of ecologism. This includes the above concerns but also incorporates national issues such as sea dumping, marine pollution, renewable energy and agricultural pollution. Furthermore, they address international issues such as rainforest destruction and ozone depletion and, in the case of the Comhaontas Glas, wider issues such as trade with the Third World, education policy, and the position of women in society. These groups see themselves as ecological in the widest sense of the term, that is, as not just concerned with creating a balanced interaction between human beings and the physical ecosystem at all levels but also with a new determination of social, political and economic lifespaces within the human world itself.

The first use of the name 'ecology' by an Irish group was by the Ecology Party of Ireland formed in 1981 by Christopher Fettes. Fettes was active in animal rights campaigning, a somewhat tangential concern to the mainstream groups at the time. He was also active in the vegetarian society and in the Esperanto movement. The Party attracted support from the less radical wing of the anti-nuclear movement, most noticeably those who favoured a centralized structure as opposed to the loose network that the movement had evolved. The Ecology Party was formed specifically as a political party and, thus, its main concern was and is with parliamentary politics. This was a formation which stood in sharp contrast to the other groups' activities at the time.

The Party contested the 1982 election but received only 0.22 per cent of the votes. Following this the Party joined with other groups in the period 1883–4 to form Comhaontas Glas, then known as the Green Alliance. Comhaontas Glas was an alliance of approximately ten groups that lasted from 1983 to 1986. It is seen by many as Ireland's 'Green Party', following along the lines of the German Greens. However, from the out-set, Comhaontas Glas had major problems. Essentially, these arose because it represented an alliance of groups which came from two very opposing traditions. On the one hand were those from within the anti-nuclear movement who were prepared to work inside the system, including groups such as the Tralee Anti-Nuclear Group. These groups were interested in parliamentary political activity, the formation of a centralized and highly organized group with formal membership and the development of a clear set of policies and manifestos with which people could be asked to identify. On the other hand, Comhaontas Glas was also composed of radical groups, including the Green Action Now Group and the Cork Green Movement who had another vision of what constituted green politics.

Green Action Now Group was a group formed directly from the Dublin Clean Seas Committee, a group whose chief concern was the closure of the Sellafield/Windscale reprocessing plant. Dublin Clear Seas Committee was in turn formed by the Research Action Group, who also organized the Leinster Anti-Uranium Group.[16] This group, like many of the Cork groups, was opposed to centralized structures and did not wish to devote its energies to parliamentary politics. Some of its members had strong anarchist tendencies. As the 1980s progressed, this group was joined by the Cork

Green Movement, formed by activists from the greater Cork area who had been involved in the anti-nuclear movement, the toxic industry movement as well as lifestyle issues such as spirituality and holistic medicine. They shared similar concerns to those of the Green Action New Group.

Despite the different outlooks of the groups, Comhaontas Glas was formed because activists believed that united action offered the best platform for success. However, both sides had different expectations of this alliance and this was to prove fatal. The more radical groups believed that the alliance could be tolerant of its varying traditions and that different and even conflicting positions could be held by its component parts. They believed, essentially, that the groups which composed Comhaontas Glas could retain a good deal of individual autonomy and that as an alliance it did not have to address itself primarily to parliamentary politics. The less radical wing, however, believed that common policies would have to be thrashed out and the more anarchist traditions brought to toe a party political line.

Following a good deal of tension Comhaontas Glas purged itself of Green Action Now Group in 1986, to be followed soon after by the resignation of the Cork Green Movement. In 1987 Comhaontas Glas formally changed its English name to the more appropriate Green Party. The purged groupings, on the other hand, formed themselves into 'The Alternative Green Network'. The Alternative Green Network was chiefly composed of Green Action Now Group and the Cork Green Movement and produced a newsletter called *Campaign Web*. However, by 1988 this network had effectively ceased to operate. One of the reasons for this was that its members had become increasingly interested in other areas of activity including solidarity work with both Latin America and the Third World.[17]

No longer burdened by internal disputes, Comhaontas Glas set about reorganising and re-working its policies. As a consequence of this Comhaontas Glas won a major victory with the election of a Teachtaí Dála (Member of Parliament) to the Irish Dáil in the June elections of 1989 (*The Irish Times*, 21 June 1989). Roger Garland, the first Irish Comhaontas Glas TD, was elected with a high number of first preference votes but without reaching the quota to represent a middle class suburb of Dublin[18] (*The Irish Times*, 23 June 1989). Since the election Comhaontas Glas has seen unprecedented growth in party membership. Membership stood at approximately 300–400 at the beginning of 1989. By February 1990 it had risen above the 1000 member mark. If the green societies in third level institutions are included, societies that are affiliated to Comhaontas Glas, then membership is increased to around 1500. Green societies exist in University Colleges Dublin and Cork, Trinity College Dublin, The College of Art and Design, and Kevin Street Technology College. Furthermore, new Comhaontas Glas groups have been established chiefly within greater Dublin, including

North Dublin, Wicklow and the Dun Laoghaire areas. Attempts to establish and restructure groups outside the Dublin area have also been successful, resulting in the re-establishment of a group in Cork (*Nuacht Glas*, May/June 1989 and Autumn 1989; *Alpha*, 22 June 1989). Comhaontas Glas now has affiliated groups throughout Ireland with noticeable weakness, however, in the western part of the country.

Such growth has not been without its problems for the Party. Resources are stretched to the limit and many of the new members lack political experience and expertise. The necessity to educate many of the new members further stretches the Party's resources at a time when it is under increasing pressure, especially from the media, to have ready policies on a wide variety of issues. Of particular difficulty for the Party is the formulation of policy on the 'national question', that is, on Irish unification, a policy which is at present undergoing review by the Party. Sudden growth can normally be expected to present such problems. However, these are all the more acute for a party that was formed from an alliance of very different interests. Furthermore, a radical commitment to decentralization is also needed in a party dominated by groups from the greater Dublin region.

Another of the national level groups is Earthwatch, formed by a group of activists in the Bantry area to protest against the dumping of radioactive waste off the south-west coast of Ireland. These activists had previously been involved in the Carnsore campaign. Earthwatch subsequently became heavily involved in the campaign against acid rain from the Money Point electricity generating station in County Clare. The group produces Ireland's only ecology magazine *Earthwatch*. It is committed to non-violence and is highly centralized. Earthwatch is a member of Friends of the Earth International. It has a number of groups operating at the regional and local levels, including in Dublin. It works in close connection with Greenpeace Ireland, which opened up a full campaign office in Dublin in 1988.

All of these groups raise a variety of issues that have come to be expected of green groups, including concern about agricultural pollution, ozone thinning and global warming, deforestation, land use, waste dumping, economic policy, trade with the Third World, education policy, resource use, recycling and also women's issues. It is interesting to note the international influence acting on these groups, including the fact that two of them are members of international organizations (Earthwatch being a member of FoE International, and Greenpeace of the international group of the same name). Comhaontas Glas is also strongly influenced by the European Green movement and is a member of the Eurogreens, who are in turn affiliated to the International Greens. Despite their international outlook they also address issues that arise within an Irish context, including the growth of fish farming, the establishment of an Irish Environmental

Protection Agency, Irish adherence to EC environmental protection legislation, mining and industrial development strategy. However, it is predominantly the local groups who are involved in the actual campaigning on these issues.

One of the major types of activity of the national groups is the conducting of campaigns of joint action. The most important is that aimed at the closure of the Sellafield/Windscale reprocessing plant in Cumbria. Sellafield/Windscale is seen by them as responsible for the high level of contamination of the Irish sea, which is now the most radioactive sea in the world. This has resulted in serious damage to fish and mammal life. The closure of this plant and the protection of the Irish sea is now the subject of a joint action programme by Greenpeace, Earthwatch and the Campaign for Nuclear Disarmament (CND) as well as Greenpeace UK.[19] A second main and related concern is the establishment of Ireland and its territorial waters as a nuclear free zone. The Irish ecology movement has worked in close contact with the peace movement on this issue, including such groups as North Atlantic Network and Portwatch, as well as the Dawn Collective. The peace movement is involved because the presence of nuclear-powered submarines and ships in Irish waters is seen as a direct affront to Irish neutrality. This involvement has a long history and the most noticeable overlap in activity between the peace movement and the ecology movement occurred in the 1970s and 1980s with the establishment of a 'peacecamp' at Bishopscourt, in the North of Ireland.[20]

All of the Irish political parties, including the present Fianna Fáil Government, have called for the closure of Sellafield/Windscale. The Irish County Councils and other local Government bodies have also been active in campaigning, demonstrations and protests against the plant, and they receive wideranging national support. One of the main reasons for this level of support is that national self-determination and national sovereignty are seen as threatened by the UK's continuous policy on Sellafield/Windscale. Neutrality is likewise tied to the national question. Neutrality, like nationalism, remain important political ideologies in Irish political culture, and groups such as Earthwatch, CND and Greenpeace are able to exploit this ideology not only in their Sellafield/Windscale campaign but also in the nuclear-free zone campaign.

Conclusion

This chapter has presented an overview of the evolution of the Irish ecology movement. This has been undertaken by dividing the movement's development into phases: beginning with concerns about nuclear power, examining the development of opposition to toxic industry, the anti-mining campaigns, and subsequently examining what may be termed Irish green politics. This has proved useful in a number of ways. In particular it has allowed us to situate the large number of groups that have been in existence throughout the last twenty years of the ecology movement in such a way that the distinctive concerns of the groups at different periods could be highlighted. This historical approach also enables us to see the movement as a dynamic one. However, it is important not to place too much emphasis upon the discrete nature of each phase. In the first place, the different phases overlapped, for example, the concern about toxic industry arose while the anti-nuclear movement was at the height of its activities. Similarly, individual groups and group members overlapped in their concern and actions across these different phases.

Another important distinction was between groups prepared to work within the system and those wishing to operate outside it. This distinction should not be exaggerated. Some groups, such as FoE, evolved from being 'insider' groups to become more radical on the question of styles of activism. Furthermore, an individual group may contain elements of both approaches or may choose to decide on tactics according to the nature of the issue under consideration. Thus, there are no hard and fast divisions between different types of groups nor does any one group fit completely and comfortably into any one category. In short, it is important that groups are seen as occupying positions along a continuum, positions that change depending upon the issue at stake, and that develop across time.

In terms of our understanding of current developments within Ireland, this analysis has pointed to a number of issues. First, it has shown that, in the face of the new critique of Irish industrialisation, the planning process has become stretched to the limit of its resources and also of its credibility. Thus, the issue of accountability by planners to the general public has been raised and the policy process seems incapable in its present form of addressing that issue. Furthermore, this critique also raises fundamental questions about access to the decision making process by ordinary people, access which at present is both restricted and, in so far as it is available, requires large resources and financial inputs. Second, it is clear that the movement is proving a fertile ground for the development of locally rooted and well-organised community action groups, especially in rural areas. This development may have a profound impact upon the future development of local politics in Ireland, a political dimension that has hitherto been dominated by political activists who have used local politics primarily as a stepping stone to national politics. Third, there is the emergence of a tension between development and the maintenance of traditional economic activity, especially agriculture. This tension does not simply mirror the usual rural/urban split but challenges directly the very foundation of Irish industrial policy: development through the attraction of foreign direct investment into Ireland. A recurring theme throughout has been the direct linkage between the policy of industrialization and the emergence of both anti-nuclear protest as well as protest against toxic industry.

The development of this opposition forms an important part of the dynamics of a healthy society: it is part of the renewal process of society whereby traditional methods, policies and institutional arrangements, including the planning process, are thrown open to question. Examination of this process can reveal much about the nature of the society within which they occur. However, from the point of view of the study of ecologism, what is interesting is whether or not this critique contains a transformational potential, that is, whether we are seeing the birth of a radical change in social, economic and political life as a whole. To answer this we need to turn to the ideologies of political ecology groups in Ireland.

Throughout this chapter the variety of different influences which shape ecological consciousness has been noted. Of particular importance is the fact that ecologists draw from traditional political ideologies, especially Irish nationalism. The linking of the national question to the environmental question was, as we have seen, increasingly evident as the Carnsore campaigns developed. Subsequently it was also expressed in the toxic industry movement and in 'green' politics. The centrality of the national question in Irish politics has shaped the Irish ecology movement in two ways. First, it has shaped the type of environmental problems occurring in Ireland; second, it has had a direct influence upon the analysis, strength and size of the support base of the movement. This is especially evident within the North of Ireland where traditional conservation groups predominate but where ecology groups remain weak and marginalized, despite the recent establishment of a branch of FoE. A new development, however, is also worth noting and that is the establishment of the Green Party of Northern Ireland. This new party was formally launched in February 1990 and hopes to be associated with both Comhaontas Glas as well as with the UK Green Party. We shall have to wait to see how its development will influence the emergence of ecological consciousness within the North of Ireland.

Thus, in the Irish case, it is premature to argue that ecologism is part of the creation of a new type of political culture: political culture in Ireland has always been based upon the national question and this continues to be reflected in the ecology movement's concerns and development. Thus, as far as the development of the politics of ecology is concerned, this analysis would caution those arguing that the modernization of Irish society is bringing with it the development of a more European like political system (Garvin 1981).

The variety of other influences that are acting upon political ecologists must also be noted. For example, traditional economic interest groups, especially the agricultural lobby, are strongly influenced by a belief in democratic participation in decision making and place their faith in the legal apparatuses of the state. Their critique is not presenting a fundamental challenge to the production system as such, rather they wish instead to have an equal right to participate in it. Yet these groups also present an ecological critique of production practices, even if this is limited to industrial as opposed to agricultural production methods

Similarly , the important role played by international influences is to be noted. This was seen in the early days of the anti-nuclear movement and later in shaping both the organizational form as well as the affiliation of present-day green groups. In the case of the more radical elements of the toxic industry movement, it has also influenced the emergence of a neo-Marxist critique of industrialization. In the case of other groups, especially Earthwatch, it has resulted in a concern for alternative and renewable energy sources as well as for a more 'holistic' approach to the earth.

In short the ecologist movement in Ireland has been shaped by a variety of different influences, some rooted in traditional Irish political culture, others stemming from international developments, especially in Europe. These range from the desire to relocate a factory away from a group's immediate area to a 'more suitable' site to a requirement that we reappraise the very way in which we approach the utilization of nature. Given this diversity, analysts looking from the examples of ecologism in Europe to the Irish case may wonder if all or indeed any of the groups we have outlined are really 'green' at all, questioning whether or not they conform to the type of political ecologism that is emerging on the European stage. Indeed, this chapter began with a definition of ecologism, framed in terms of a holistic approach to ecological deterioration, that may even exclude the majority of the groups which that analysis has revealed. However, this problematic may prove to be a good thing: in the context of the sudden growth of the phenomenon of ecologism no one group or style of politics has as yet a monopoly on the use of the title, least of all those found within advanced industrial nations.

NOTES

1 This chapter is based upon papers presented at the European Consortium for Political Research, Joint Session of Workshops, Paris, 10-14 April 1989, and at the UK Political Studies Association annual conference, University of Warwick, 4-6 April 1989.

2 *Dawn: An Irish Journal of Non-Violence*, Dublin: The Dawn Collective; *Rebel*, Dublin: Newspaper of Revolutionary Struggle; *Red Herring*, Dublin: Newspaper of the Research Action Group.

3 Alliance for Safety and Health, 'Making its Merck on Ireland', 'Hanrahan, Merch, Sharp and Dohme: A Chronology'.

4 Womanagh Valley Protection Association, paper to Action for Safety and Health Conference, University College Cork, June 1989.

5 Responsible Industry for Cork Harbour, paper to Action for Safety and Health Conference, University College Cork, June 1989.

6 A point made by a Member of Action for Safety and Health during discussion with the author, October 1989.

7 Author's discussion with member of Action for Safety and Health, October 1989.

8 Alliance for Safety and Health, 'Desperately Seeking a Toxic Dump', n.d. and Earthwatch, Number 11, Autumn 1989.

9 Earthwatch, Number 11, Autumn 1989.

10 Lignite Action, Lignite on the Loughshore Ardboe, Lignite Action, n.d.

11 Interview with Niall Fitzduff, Lignite Action, 22 October 1988.

12 Mining Awareness, Mining Awareness, n. d.

13 Gold Environment Impact Assessment, Gold EIA, n.d.

14 Interview with Peter Shanley, Mayo Environmental Group, Westport, 21 May 1989.

15 Traditional style conservation groups operating at the national level, including An Taisce and The Irish Society for the Protection of Birds, have not been examined. This is chiefly because they do not present a political analysis of ecological problems or of conservation issues. Nevertheless, they did play a role in the anti-nuclear movement. The Irish Conservation Society, for example, produced an information booklet on nuclear power: Blackith n.d.

16 Interview with a member of the Research Action Group, Dublin, March 1989.

17 Interview with member of Alternative Green Network, Cork, February 1989.

18 The voting system in use in the South of Ireland in the single transferable vote system. Large multi-member constituencies are used. Voters mark their ballot papers 1, 2, 3, 4... etc. against the candidates, according to their preferences. Once the votes have been cast the electoral officer establishes a quota. This is the minimum number of votes required to establish election as a candidate. Initially, if the candidate gains the quota on first preference votes he/she is elected. Votes over this number are superfluous and the surplus votes are distributed in accordance with the second preference on the ballot paper. Votes are transferred until the required number of candidates achieve the quota. If the required number is not reached the candidate with the highest number of votes is deemed elected without reaching the quota. For a fuller explanation see Sallis 1982.

19 Greenpeace, 'Clean Irish Sea: Information', Dublin: Greenpeace, n.d.; Interview with Greenpeace organizer, Dublin 1989; Earthwatch, magazine of Earthwatch, especially 1989.

20 The influence of the Irish peace movement on green politics in Ireland remains an area that is as yet unexplored. It is beyond the scope of this paper to attempt such a task. However, an interesting starting point would be to identify the reasons for the separate yet parallel development of the ecology and peace movements and to see if the present day developments in green politics is causing the two movements to intersect more frequently.

REFERENCES

Baker, S. (1987a).*Dependency, ideology and the industrial policy of Fianna Fail in Ireland,* 1958-1972, Florence: European University Institute, Unpublished Ph.D. thesis.

Baker, S. (1987b). 'Dependent industrialisation and political protest:Raybestos Manhattan in Ireland', *Government and Opposition,* Vol. 22, pp. 352-8.

Baker, S. (1988). 'The nuclear power issue in Ireland, The role of the Irish anti-nuclear movement', *Irish Political Studies,* Vol. 3, pp. 3-17.

Baker, S. (1989). 'Community survival and lignite mining in Ireland',*The Ecologist,* Vol. 19, No. 2, pp. 43-67.

Barnet, A. J. and Muller, R. E. (1975). *Global Reach: The Power of the Multinational Corporations.* London: Cape.

Bew, P. and Patterson, H. (1978). *Sean Lemass and the Making of Modern Ireland.* London: Gilland Macmillan.

Blackith, R. (n.d.) *Questions and Answers on Nuclear Power* Dublin: The Irish Conservation Society.

Bramwell, A. (1989). *Ecology in the Twentieth Century: A History.* New Haven CT: Yale University Press.

Caroll, J. and Kelly, P. K. (eds.) (1980). *A Nuclear Ireland?* Dublin: Irish Transport and General Workers Union.

Cohen, J. (1985). 'Strategy or identity: New theoretical paradigms and contemporary social movements', *Social Research,* Vol. 52, pp.663-716.

Crotty, R. (1986). *Ireland in a Crisis: A Study in Capitalist Colonial Underdevelopment.* Dingle: Brandon Press.

Derby, S. (1984-5). 'The nuclear syndrome: Victory for the Irish anti-nuclear movement', *Dawn,* No. 3,Winter pp. 7-24.

Daly, G. (1988). *Creation and Redemption.* Dublin: Gill and Macmillan.

Department of Economic Development Northern Ireland (1983). 'Northern Ireland Energy Issues: A Discussion Paper'.

Eyerman, R. and Jamison, A. (1988). 'Social Movements: Contemporary Debates', Lund: Department of Sociology, University of Lund.

Fine Gael (1980). *Aspects of Energy Policy.* Dublin: Fine Gael.

Garvin, T. (1981). 'Societal change and party adaptation in the Republic of Ireland 1960-1981', *European Journal of Political Research,* Vol. 9, pp. 269-85.

Geoghegan-Quinn, M., T. D. (1989). Address in Dublin Castle, 14 December 1989, by the Minister of State for European Affairs, on 'Ireland and the European Community' in opening the conference of the Irish Association for European Studies/Trans European Policy Studies Association on 'The Priorities of the Irish Presidency 1990', pp. 19-20.

Inglehart, R. (1977). *The Silent Revolution: Changing Values and Political Styles among Western Publics.* Princeton N.J.: Princeton University Press.

Keohane, K. (1989). 'Toxic trade-off: the price Ireland pays for industrial development', *The Ecologist,* Vol. 19, No. 4, pp. 144-146.

Lowe, P. and Rudig, W. 'Review article: Political ecology and the social sciences - the state of the art', *British Journal of Political Science,* Vol. 16, pp. 513-550.

Meenan, J. (1970). *The Irish Economy Since 1922.* Liverpool: Liverpool University Press.

Muller-Rommel, F. (1982). 'Ecology parties in Western Europe', *West European Politics,* Vol. 5, pp. 88-74.

Olsen, M. (1971). *The Logic of Collective Action: Public Goods and the Theory of Groups.* New York: Schocken.

O'Farrell, P. N. and O'Loughlin, B. (1980). *An Analysis of New Industry Linkages in Ireland.* Dublin: Industrial Development Authority.

Raymond, R. J. (1983). 'Irish neutrality: Ideology or pragmatism?' *Journal of International Affairs*, No. 603, pp. 30-41.

Sallis, E. (1982). *The Machinery of Government*. London: Holt.

Touraine, A.(1979). 'Political ecology: a demand to live differently now', *New Society*, 8 November 1979. pp.307-309.

Touraine, A., Hegedus, Z., Dubet, F. and Wieriorka, M. (1983). *Anti-Nuclear Protest: The Opposition to Nuclear Energy in France*, Cambridge: Cambridge University Press.

4. The Medium is the Message: Democracy and Oligarchy in Belgian Ecology Parties

HERBERT KITSCHELT
Department of Political Science
Duke University, Durham, North Carolina, USA

European ecology parties have placed new issues on the political agenda and have forced incumbent parties and governments to respond to them. At the same time, however, ecology parties have pursued a further and possibly more ambitious objective. Green party activists believe that the very style and practices of political mobilization which they have chosen may serve as a catalyst for the creation of a new participatory political culture that transcends the established patterns of indirect democratic involvement of citizens in public policy-making through elections and bureaucratic mass parties. The organization of green parties itself should provide the model and laboratory to explore opportunities for transforming Western democracies. In this sense, *the medium of political organization becomes its own message.*

The problem of democratic party organization is hardly new, and neither are the solutions that green parties have explored in order to facilitate internal party democracy. Electoral or party offices are rotated among party members in order to prevent the emergence of a small staff of political 'professionals'. All party meetings are public and party conferences are scheduled frequently to enable a maximum of party members or delegates from the grassroots party sections to have a say over key issues. Important decisions, such as the nomination of candidates for electoral office or the choice of strategies and programmes, and important resources (financing) should remain, wherever feasible, under the control of regional or local party sections rather than the national party leadership. Moreover, party members are expected to have a say over important choices through intraparty referenda and other methods of intraparty consultation (membership journals, etc.).

Although the *problem* and the institutional *solutions* to party democracy are not new and were first tried by organizations in the emerging working class movements of the nineteenth century, it remains open whether ecology parties can come up with *new democratic accomplishments* that fly in the face of conventional wisdom generally sceptical of democratic enthusiasm. If we follow the classical discourse on party democracy, as enshrined in Robert Michels' (1911) study of the German social democrats and labour unions in the first decade of this century, party democracy is bound to fail and give way to an oligarchy of party leaders. Is this 'iron law' of oligarchy the fate that will or may already have befallen ecology parties too? Or do ecology parties stand a reasonable chance of maintaining the programmatic linkage between their organizational medium of mobilization and their participatory message?

Before we can even attempt to address these questions by empirical studies, let alone formulate tentative answers, we must disentangle the 'oligarchy muddle' (Payne 1968), a complex array of conceptual confusions about 'oligarchy' and ambiguities concerning appropriate research strategies for research on the the power structure of complex institutions. One problem pertains to the meaning of oligarchy. What are the structural patterns that qualify an organization as oligarchical? What did Michels and his successors mean when they talked about oligarchy? Another problem involves our access to the reality of power relations we may wish to identify as more democratic or oligarchical. Should we rely on the interpretations of participants in the setting we study? Or must we search for 'objective' indicators capturing the behaviour of individual actors and their capacity to shape power relations?

I will begin with this last question and then address different conceptions of oligarchy and oligarchy theory as they have been expressed by social scientists and political activists. Based on these clarifications, I will explore the power relations in the Belgian ecology parties Agalev (in Flanders) and Ecolo (in Wallonia) based in a questionnaire distributed at party conferences in 1985. First, I will discuss the party activists' own interpretation of the oligarchy problem in ecology party organization. It is important to note already here that my survey included not solely party leaders, but also simple rank-and-file members who participate only occasionally in the parties' national political affairs. Thus, my sources are relatively unbiased and reflect the perceptions of a wide range of party activists. Second, I have confronted the militants' interpretations with some other methods of gauging the parties' power structures that provide more 'objective' information on the control of resources and involvement of militants in the choice of party strategies. Third, I will interpret the convergence and divergence of 'objective' and 'subjective' insights into Agalev's and Ecolo's power structure. Finally, my analysis enables me to speculate about the likely future of ecology party organizations and their chances of avoiding the fate that Michels predicted for all political parties.

Party Oligarchy as Analytical Construct and Practical Interpretation

Theoretical propositions in the social sciences, particularly those that have triggered intense controversies, often have a Janus face. On the one side, they are analytical constructs suggesting an empirically accurate and insightful explanation of social behaviour and institutions. On the other, they constitute practical interpretations of the social world employed by social actors, and not primarily scholars, to interpret the meaning and purpose of their own actions and come to terms with social structures and institutions. Examples of Janus-faced theories are particularly common in the realm of social power and political institutions. Class and stratification theories of social inequality and political mobilization, for instance, profess to supply not only objective representations of society, but are also arguments in the distributive political struggle for life chances. In a similar vein, the debate about the validity of pluralist, elitist, or structural conceptions of power to describe modern society is immersed in a political discourse on social reform and normative visions of democracy.

Michels' theory of oligarchy in voluntary political organizations also lies at the intersection between academic and political debate. It provides an analytical set of statements about the empirical limitations of democratic choice in complex formally organized collectivities, but at the same time has served political actors as an argument and a guide for practical action in order to create, govern, attack and change political organizations.

Scholars who attempt to test the validity of a Janus-faced theory that has become part of the actors' self-reflection in everyday social life and political discourse may choose between two alternative research strategies. First, they can gather and analyse evidence about the actual behaviour of individuals and the outcomes of their interaction, as they are identified by observing scientists. The actors themselves are not asked to comment on scholarly interpretative frames, such as the one developed by Michels. As a rule, this approach claims to evaluate theories against objective 'facts', although these 'facts' are already constituted within the researcher's interpretative framework.[1]

A second research strategy begins with the argument that social science research provides only a secondary interpretation of a social reality that is already interpreted by the actors themselves. Scholars can never pretend to have direct access to 'behaviour' and 'meaning' in social action and to be capable of bracketing the interpretations actors develop to constitute their social world. For this reason, social theories, as it were, represent secondary recodings of actors' interpretations and must rely on the social actors' primary conceptions of the social world.

Earlier in this century, especially the influential Chicago school of symbolic interactionism emphasized this methodological premise of social research. As a consequence, it attributed great importance to the reconstruction of the actors' point of view and understanding of social reality, as is evidenced by the well-known Thomas theorem that what individuals define as social reality has real consequences. The social sciences therefore must begin with the actors' subjective sense of society to shed light on the workings of social and political institutions.[2] In more recent decades the insight that social science is a reinterpretation of already interpreted social reality has been radicalized by ethnomethodology[3] and critical hermeneutics[4] research which has focused on the relationship between the social actors' and the scientific observers' interpretations of reality, and subjected the common social science research techniques to a thorough critique. Pushed to their most radical conclusion, these perspectives subscribe to a highly subjectivist and idealist conception of the social world: society is only revealed through the actors' talk and knowledge about society.

Instead of taking this extreme position, I propose that both the actors' 'subjective' interpretations as well as the scholars' 'objective' observations must be combined in social analysis. In contrast to radical objectivism, the actors' interpretations do matter. But subjectivist idealism ignores the fact that actions have objective, material effects and impacts that transcend the consciousness of the individuals who are involved, and give meaning to a sequence of exchanges. Social and political processes bring about intended consequences that cannot be reconstructed from the actors' perspective alone, but require a structural and behavioural analysis.[5] For this reason, it may be advisable to use both subjective and objective methodologies in the social sciences. The extent to which findings reached by these methods agree or disagree are themselves a problem for sociological and political theory.[6]

Research on Michels' 'iron law of oligarchy' has not only been surprisingly limited, but confined primarily to an assessment of the theory's validity from the observer's point of view. It employs data on the behaviour of actors in voluntary organizations, the preferences of rank and file participants and leaders, and the organization's actual collective strategies and purposes to determine how power is distributed internally.[7] Yet, to my knowledge, no studies have been undertaken that would directly tap the actors' 'subjective' knowledge and assessment of Michels' theory, even though the 'iron law of oligarchy' is widely known and intensely debated among activists in many political organizations, particularly voluntary associations and parties of the political Left that strive for a democratization of modern society.

Oligarchy as a Theoretical Construct

In his celebrated and controversial work on the rise of oligarchy in modern mass parties, Michels (1911) provides not one, but three different interconnected theories about the nature and the origins of oligarchy. The relationship between these three theories is not always clear and some of them have given rise to more dispute than others.

Michels' work contains a weak and a strong conception of oligarchy. The weak notion is directed against the claim of unitary, direct democracy that all citizens or members of an organization can participate in collective decision making. Building on Mosca's and Pareto's elite theories, Michels emphasizes the advantages of small groups in controlling social institutions. Going beyond elite theory, however, he also develops an additional 'strong' notion of oligarchy, according to which elites and masses inevitably have fundamental conflicts of interest.[8] In political parties, the leadership is always oriented towards the status quo and represents a conservative position, whereas the rank-and-file often call for more radical change.

Michels traces back the origins of 'weak' and 'strong' oligarchy to at least three causal mechanisms.[9] The first explanation is particularly useful for our understanding of 'weak' oligarchy. Beyond a certain size, defined by the number of participants and the task differentiation in the collectivity, all social institutions develop division of labour and hierarchical modes of coordination to satisfy purely 'technical' imperatives of efficiency. Modern political science can flesh out this argument that Michels (1911, pp. 61-80) presents in the first sections of his book in the following way: parties are purposive associations whose objectives (activating constituencies, vote getting, policy making) must be reached with a limited amount of resources (time, money, activists). Hence, parties must economize on costly transactions inside the organization in order to devote a maximum of attention to their external struggle. Hierarchies happen to be more resource-conserving than participatory democracy. In the language of the institutional economics of organization, one may label this first explanation of oligarchy a theory of transaction costs (see Williamson 1975).

For Michels, the theory of transaction costs is only the first step of his enterprise. He then goes onto examine the party militants' psychological drives and dispositions, and, building on LeBon's mass psychology popular at the end of the nineteenth century, couches his second key argument into the terms of a theory of membership lethargy (Michels 1911, pp. 81-116). Rank-and-file members of voluntary associations usually do not possess the intellectual and emotional abilities and the resources (time, money, information) to participate effectively in complex organizations.

Therefore, demanding tasks are delegated to professionals who have the resources and are sufficiently devoted to the party to carry out difficult and time-consuming missions. Moreover, Michels believes the masses have an emotional longing to identify with charismatic politicians who have dedicated their lives to politics and who master the techniques of demagogy and symbolic, if not ritualistic, acts that are designed to enhance the legitimacy and authority of their leadership.

Michels, however, treats the imperatives of transaction costs and membership lethargy as preliminary stages of his enterprise which prove only the necessity of a 'weak' form of oligarchy. But Michels wishes to argue for a 'strong' notion of oligarchy according to which the evolving party leadership becomes internally cohesive and united by a particularist self-interest that sets it apart from the rank-and-file. For this reason, he develops a third theory I will label a *theory of elite control*. Leaders look back on a career of upwards social mobility which has placed them in positions that enjoy high social esteem, and supply strong selective incentives (income, publicity, reverence, etc.). Party leaders derive special gratifications from their elevated position, the adoration of the masses, their superior access to political information, their face-to-face relations with members of the political elite in parliaments and the state executive. Leaders, therefore, will do everything to maintain their position and stifle whatever efforts the rank-and-file could make to endanger that position. Their prerogative is most easily preserved if they muzzle interparty opponents who call for radical social change, support at most incremental reforms, and otherwise defend the status quo. To ensure that their parties pursue such strategies, leaders will emasculate the rank-and-file and run the parties according to their own whims.

In the conclusion of his book, Michels distinguishes the three theories of oligarchy clearly and ranks their importance:

> Leadership is a necessary phenomenon in every form of social life ... Now, if we leave out of consideration the tendency of the leaders to organize themselves and to consolidate their interests, and if we leave also out of consideration the gratitude of the led towards the leaders, and the general immobility and passivity of the masses, we are led to conclude that the principal cause of oligarchy in the democratic parties is to be found in the technical indispensability of leadership. (Michels 1911, p. 364)

Yet while Michels attributes greatest importance to the theory of transaction cost in this quotation, most of his book elaborates the theories of membership lethargy and elite control – and it is here where inconsistencies creep into Michels' reasoning and where his critics have raised their strongest objections.[10] Michels builds on a simple dichotomy between 'leaders' and 'followers' (Beetham 1977, p. 14) that forces him to characterize both groups in contradictory and empirically unrealistic terms.

Based on LeBon's mass psychology, Michels initially conceives of the party rank-and-file as docile, irrational and submissive individuals under the spell of charismatic leaders. Yet later in the book, when he attempts to demonstrate the elite's dominance and conservatism, the masses occasionally reappear as radical driving forces of political struggles such as mass strikes (Michels 1911, pp. 169 and 284). Here the political lethargy of the masses is presented, not as the cause, but as the consequence of elite control; frustrated by the conservatism of their leaders, the radicalized masses turn away from politics. In yet other passages Michels abandons the assumption of a homogeneous 'mass' with a single political disposition altogether and discovers that grassroots activists express a plurality of political views and demands. The extent of rank-and-file participation, for instance, depends on the members' social background and the atmosphere of urban or rural party sections, as well as on such contingencies as the political issues that are placed on the agenda for decision making (see, e.g., Michels 1911, p. 87). We must conclude that Michels does not provide a logically and theoretically convincing account of rank-and-file behaviour in parties. Moreover, subsequent empirical studies of participation and factualism in parties have confirmed that the membership of mass parties is heterogeneous and that numerous factors influence intraparty mobilization.[11]

Similarly, Michel's account of party elites has serious theoretical and empirical flaws. On the one hand, Michels treats party leaders as a homogeneous group that is shaped by intra-organizational socialization and shares a common greed for money, status, and power (cf. pp. 129-48 and 205-8). Even in working class parties, the leaders begin to constitute a new petty bourgeois stratum and, in fact, recruit themselves increasingly from bourgeois circles (pp. 256-66). But on the other hand, this simplistic materialist psychology is not sufficient to account for political differences party leaders often express among themselves (cf. Lipset 1962, pp. 35-6). Even Michels (1911, pp. 172-6) admits that there are divisions within party elites on political strategy and that competition cuts down on elite autonomy in formally democratic parties which, in turn, increases the leaders' accountability to the masses. Moreover, leaders come from diverse social backgrounds that may generate persistent political disagreements among them.[12]

Nevertheless, Michels expects that the leaders' common organizational socialization and discipline will eventually prevail over such divisions (pp. 177-83). This hypothesis, however, is hardly borne out by modern party research. In many instances, leaders' economic and political self-interest to be reelected may in fact intensify intraparty competition and factionalism.

In others, Michels overestimates the extent to which leaders and the parties' bureaucratic stratum that is serving them are motivated solely by material incentives. Even in Michel's prime empirical case, the German Social Democratic Party at the beginning of the twentieth century, salaried offices and other material incentives were much less widely available than his account suggests.[13] Further, Michels almost entirely ignores the purposive motivations and incentives (cf. Wilson 1973) that attract individuals to the competition for leadership positions.

Thus, Michels' oligarchy theory does not account for the heterogeneity and internal pluralism within party elites and among rank-and-file activists, although the empirical relevance of these phenomena can hardly be questioned. As a consequence, Michels understates the forces that bring about a convergence between leaders and masses and the advent of 'responsible leadership'.[14] More generally, his theory does not reflect the *variability* of the relationship between leaders and masses. Empirically, Michels points out that the French socialist leaders in the first decade of this century moved further to a reformist strategy than their German counterparts, because the former were operating in a parliamentary democracy while the latter were fighting against an authoritarian regime (Michels 1911, pp. 132-3). Such contextual factors as the political regime form had played a role in Michels' early theory of political organization as a determinant of party organization. Yet they had vanished from his explanatory account by the time he was writing *Political Parties* (Beetham 1977, pp. 7-8). Empirical studies, however, show that the social base of ideology of a party's constituencies, as well as political regime institutions, affect the structure and strategy of political parties considerably (cf. Harmel and Janda 1982; Janda and King 1985; Kitschelt 1989a).

Michel's theory of transaction cost in political parties is relatively uncontroversial in the social science literature. Yet my brief review of the scholarly critique directed against Michels' 'iron law of oligarchy' shows that the convergence of 'weak' and 'strong' oligarchy is questionable. Technical constraints on democratic participation are not necessarily linked to membership lethargy or elite control in political parties. There may be sufficient rank-and-file involvement and competition among militants aspiring to leadership positions to maintain a close correspondence between elites and masses. Further, one might suspect that the emergence of 'strong' oligarchy depends on institutional and cultural contingencies not considered in Michel's theory. For instance, two-party systems with plurality voting rules may generate the greatest pressure towards 'strong' oligarchy and disparity between leaders and followers, because control of government office hinges entirely on the ability of party leaders to accommodate to the preferences of the median voter whose support can make or break a party's electoral victory. At the same time, they usually need not fear defection of their more radical supporters for want of effective party alternatives.[15] In multi-party systems with proportional representation, however, it is much less likely that leader and followers will be at odds over party programme and strategy.

Michels' only systematic explanation of different degrees of party oligarchy is based on a *life-cycle model* of organizational development: as parties age and become larger, 'strong' oligarchy gains an indestructible hold on the organization. Alternatively, we may hypothesize that there are a number of structural and cultural conditions that influence party organization. First, the nature and the mobilization of the social cleavage that defines a party's constituency may promote or suppress oligarchical tendencies. Thus, socialist parties, relying on an ideology of solidarity are more capable of oligarchical centralization than others (see Janda and King 1985). Second, institutional rules and conditions of party systems (electoral laws, the number of effective parties) influence organizational structure. Third, parties may be more oligarchical where they are in a strong competitive position, i.e. where small electoral gains among marginal supporters may increase their power to control government and public policy dramatically.

Applied to green parties, this alternative interpretation of oligarchy would predict that (1) by virtue of their ideology and social following, green parties will always remain less oligarchical than competing mass parties in European multi-party systems and (2) that the extent of green party oligarchy is a function of variable institutional conditions and strategic configurations. Hence, oligarchy is not the inevitable result of a 'life-cycle' process of party formation.

Empirically, my study of the Belgian ecology parties Agalev and Ecolo cannot satisfactorily disentangle causes for the extent to which each party has developed or refrained from oligarchy. At least in one respect, however, I will be able to throw some light on the variability of interparty power structures. For historical reasons, the rise of social movements that ecology parties wish to represent was stronger in Flanders than in Wallonia (see Kitschelt and Hellemans 1990, pp. 36-41). For this reason, one might expect a less oligarchical structure in Agalev than in Ecolo.

Oligarchy as Practical Interpretation and Guide to Political Action

Beyond scholarly critiques based on empirical investigations that employ 'objective' indicators of party oligarchy selected by academic observers, Michels' theory has also generated considerable debates among political activists. Conservatives and radicals disagree on the relevance of Michels' 'weak' theory of oligarchy according to which the scarcity of resources and the extent of transaction costs prevent grassroots participation. While

conservatives endorse Michels' view and believe that widespread participation in politics is impossible, radicals subscribe to a more voluntaristic
perspective and argue that Michels underestimates the desire of average
citizens to be politically active and the availability of resource and technologies to lower the high transaction costs of democracy.

Yet both radical supporters of unitary grassroots democracy, as well as
conservative pluralists, committed to a conception of democracy as elite
competition for voter support, endorse Michels' 'strong' theory of
oligarchy. They concur that party leaders subject rank-and-file activists to
their political control. Both also subscribe to a materialist psychology of
leadership, considering the longings for status, income, power and office
as the prime driving forces of political ambition among party elites. Yet
in contrast to Michels' classic study, both see a definite trade-off between
mass lethargy and elite control: elite dominance is so important and visible
precisely because followers are not lethargic, but press party leaders to
pursue goals incompatible with their personal and institutional interests.
Radicals and conservatives also agree that party democracy and electoral
democracy conflict with each other. Rank-and-file activists are
unrepresentative of the electorate at large. Both groups, of course, derive
very different political messages from these analytical agreements.

For radicals, party democracy has priority over electoral accountability.
A party should lead and transform the electorate, not reproduce the median
voters' limited political consciousness. Because radicals believe in a
voluntaristic theory of elite control that is not based on the 'technical'
impediments to party democracy, they argue that oligarchy can be
overcome if rank-and-file activists defeat a recalcitrant, conservative party
leadership. Even Michels himself started out as a radical syndicalist socialist
with a voluntarist theory of oligarchy that still held out some hope for
efforts to reverse the bureaucratization and conservatism of socialist party
elites (see Beetham 1977, pp. 5-10).

One of the probably most lasting and widely read radical libertarian
critiques of party oligarchy has been provided by Rosa Luxemburg who
was opposed to both bureaucratization and centralization as methods of
elite control.[16] In a critique of Lenin's pamphlet *What Is To Be Done?*,
(Luxemburg 1974, Vol. 1, pp. 432-4) claims that a strong party leadership
slows down the revolutionary mobilization of the masses. She also
chastised the bureaucratization and integration of the German Social
Democracy into parliamentarism and the careerism of petty bourgeois
intellectuals who, she believes, impeded the self-activation of the workers
inside the party (Luxemburg 1974, Vol. 1, pp. 437-40). Later, in the
debate on the political use of strikes, (Luxemburg 1974, Vol. 2 pp.
154-63) identified the union leader-ship, not the masses, as the obstacle
to revolutionary strike activity. In similar ways, the New Left critique of

contemporary democracies since the 1960s has argued that self-interested political leaders, coopted into the institutions of representative democracy, have abandoned their radical following and ceased to be democratic representatives of the lower classes.[17]

For conservatives, the normative problem of oligarchy derives from what they perceive as a conflict between party and societal democracy.[18] Because militants are radical zealots, they tend to be unrepresentative of the party's electoral constituency at large and unwilling to agree to party policies accountable to the voters. Hence, societal democracy can survive only if party elites prevent rank-and-file militants from exercising control over party strategy and policy. Parties that implement internal democracy, on the other hand, will ignore the voters and suffer electoral defeats. For conservatives, for instance, the performance of the US Democratic Party under the presidential candidacy of McGovern (Kirkpatrick 1976) or of the British Labour Party since the late 1970s (McKenzie 1982) serve as warnings of what will happen if ideological party activists get their way. For the sake of electoral success and accountability, parties have to forego internal democracy.[19]

Michels' original theory, its scholarly empirical and theoretical critiques, and the radical and conservative discourse on power in political parties thus lead to different expectations of how transaction cost, membership lethargy, and elite control are related to each other (Table 1). For Michels, all three arguments were mutually supportive and contributed to the 'iron law' of oligarchy. Radicals and conservatives, however, while they disagree on the significance of technical resource constraints in party democracy, do see a clear trade-off between membership lethargy and elite control. An active radical membership is confronted with a dominant moderate elite. The scholarly literature, finally, sees merit in the transaction cost theory of constraints on party democracy, but comes to no general conclusion about membership lethargy and elite control; Michels' law is not as 'iron' as he suggested, at least for his 'strong' conception of oligarchy.

One way to test the adequacy of Michels' original theory or of its three competitors is to ask party militants themselves to evaluate each of the underlying three arguments I have identified. How relevant do party militants find theories of transaction costs, membership lethargy, and elite control as interpretations of their political involvement? Are these theories competing or complementary in the activists' view? Since I do not subscribe to a purely subjectivist research methodology and social theory, I will treat these interpretations as only one of several sources for evidence on a party's actual power structure. We must also examine the power distribution in political parties from the observer perspective. If the observer and the participant views on party power lead to different

Table 1 Four views on the problem of oligarchy in political associations

Impediments to organizational democracy	Michels' original theory	The conservative political discourse	The radical political discourse	Social science research findings
1 Transaction costs	Yes	Yes	No	Yes
2 Membership lethargy	Yes	No	No	(Variable)
3 Elite control	Yes	Yes	Yes	(Variable)
Linkage between different elements of oligarchy	Mutual supportive relationship between the impediments of democracy: 'iron law' of oligarchy	'Iron law' of the conflict between party activists and leaders		Contingent relationship between masses and elite: no 'iron law'

conclusions, we must find ways to reconcile these discrepancies. The militants' interpretations of power structures respond to two different, but inextricably interrelated, cues: a cognitive cue provided by the militants' own actual experiences and observations in the parties, and a normative cue provided by the militants' ideological predispositions. Both dimensions can be partially separated by examining the assessment of party oligarchy by subgroups of activists, divided by ideological leanings and involvement in party affairs. If normative cues rather than actual experiences of oligarchy emerge as a key determinant of the militants' interpretations, however, the 'objectivist' interpretation of power structures is not automatically the only trustworthy path to assessing the true power structure of a party, as I will explain in the last section of this chapter.

The Data

The following study is based on a survey among militants in the Belgian ecology parties Agalev in Flanders and Ecolo in Wallonia. The parties were founded in the late 1970s, but emerged from precursor organizations that go back to about 1972. In the 1980s, the parties established themselves as an electoral force to be reckoned with in Belgian politics by increasing their electorate in three consecutive elections and receiving 7.1 per cent of the national vote in the 1987 election.

Ecology parties are steeped in the tradition of radical democratic efforts to open political parties to broad participation and keep party leaders under the control of the rank-and-file. In Belgium, ecology parties strive for an egalitarian and libertarian transformation of society that couples economic redistribution and strict environmental restrictions on industry with a call for decentralized political institutions and a more open participatory democratic process. Quite naturally, the organization of the ecology parties themselves is a starting point for the party militants' to demonstrate the feasibility of a libertarian and democrative social reform. Both parties try to set themselves apart from what Belgians often call the 'particratie' of the established parties in which small groups of leaders in parliament, party executives, and affiliated interest associations are said to dominate the political decision making process (Ceulers 1977; de Winter 1981).

Agalev's and Ecolo's statutes single out internal party democracy as one of the four most important political goals. Inside the parties, debates on organizational democracy occur frequently and Michels' arguments are well known. The formal party structure therefore has taken considerable precautions against oligarchy. In both parties, the national party conferences are the highest organ which decides on the programme, strategy and executive leadership. All party members have the right to attend and vote at conferences. The candidates for parliament, however, are chosen within the individual electoral constituencies (*arrondissements*) by the regional party sections. Both party executives and members of parliament can serve a maximum of two consecutive terms. Their meetings are open to all party members. Thus, participatory openness, decisional decentralization, and the rotation of party leaders are meant to protect Agalev and Ecolo from oligarchical tendencies.

The survey among party militants was distributed to all participants at the Agalev and Ecolo national party conferences preceding the 1985 Belgian national elections. The 1985 meetings drew roughly 400 attendants, or about 20 per cent of Agalev's and Ecolo's combined membership. The questionnaires were handed out on the first day of the conference and 256 militants, or about 61 per cent of all conference participants, i.e. 13 per cent of all party members, returned the completed forms. Given that attendance at the conferences fluctuated hour to hour and presented considerable obstacles to the efficient distribution and collection of the questionnaires, this return is satisfactory and rules out gross sampling bias among the participants. Although a questionnaire of national party activists inevitably misses passive party members or militants who confine themselves to local party affairs, it reached a wide spectrum of activists. In fact, almost 50 per cent of the respondents indicated they were mostly involved in the local party sections. There is thus reason to be confident that the questionnaire is fairly representative of the parties at large.

The survey covers a wide area of topics, only a few of which will be analyzed here.[20.] I operationalized Michels' iron law of oligarchy by six statements to which militants could respond on a scale from 1 (completely disagree) to 5 (fully agree). Each theory of oligarchy is represented by two statements. These statements were listed in a random order. To check how 'subjective' evaluations of Michels' theories relate to 'objective' methods of studying party power, the survey provides a variety of data on the militants, political biographies, involvement in social movements and protest events, participation inside the party, and political views that can be related to their assessment of Michels' theory. Since the data are on two independent parties, one can assess the extent to which different perceptions of party oligarchy are due to individual practices and beliefs or to differences between the parties themselves.

Evaluating Michels' Oligarchy Theory

Agalev and Ecolo militants were asked to assess Michels' theory of trans-action costs by evaluating statements about the scarcity of time and re-sources for political consultation as obstacles to party democracy. Table 2 shows that three-quarters of all respondents see considerable merit in the transaction cost theory. Evaluations of membership lethargy, represented by statements concerning the militants' interest in and knowledge about national party affairs, elicit more guarded responses, but still a majority believes that membership lethargy is a problem for party democracy. Militants back Michels' theory of elite control significantly less than membership lethargy and transaction costs. Approximately one-third considers elite control to be an important impediment of democracy, while nearly one-half rejects this viewpoint (Table 2).

The structure of beliefs on party oligarchy comes into sharper relief in a second battery of questions which asked militants to rank the six different impediments of party democracy by singling out the first, the second, and the third most important impediments (Table 3). In this instance, mili-tants were compelled to weigh theories of oligarchy against each other. The two statements on transaction cost constraints on democracy beat membership lethargy by a margin of better than two to one as the most important impediments to democracy. Membership lethargy is considered to be of secondary and tertiary importance about as often as transaction costs. In all respects, elite control is perceived as the theory that is supported by the smallest number of party militants as a relevant obstacle to democ-racy.

Overall we can say there is considerable support for the theory of transaction costs, moderate support for the theory of membership leth-argy, and the least support for the theory of elite control. In ecology par-

Table 2 Impediments to democracy in ecology parties

Statements with which militants:	Agree[a]	Partially agree	Disagree[a]
[a]*Theory of transaction cost*			
1 Decisions must often be made too rapidly to consult members (N = 245)	57%	20%	23%
2 There is not enough personnel, time and means of communication to contact members (N = 242)	57%	19%	24%
Theory of membership lethargy			
3 Grassroots members have little interest in political problems at the national level (N = 241)	40%	25%	36%
4 The local members do not know enough about complicated national problems (N = 242)	33%	26%	41%
Theory of elite control			
5 People at the top make too little effort to include members (N = 238)	34%	24%	43%
6 The leadership does not want to risk its ideas (N = 229)	27%	25%	48%

[a] Categories collapse two values in the original questionnaire.

ties control are mutually reinforcing and combine to create a 'strong' oligarchy that subjects the rank-and-file to the leaders' self-interests. Yet, the traditional radical and conservative theories of party oligarchy are also not supported by our Agalev and Ecolo data. Contrary to both radical and conservative theory, elite control is seen as a less serious obstacle to party democracy than membership lethargy. Contrary to the radical theory, technical constraints are acknowledged as a limit on party democracy.

My findings also confirm the argument that 'weak' and 'strong' notions of oligarchy do not necessarily converge. Although democracy may be limited by technical imperatives and to some extent, by the modest engagement of the rank-and-file, these constraints do not necessarily translate into a systematic conflict between leaders and followers. Michels and Luxemburg, as well as conservative backers of 'strong' oligarchy such as McKenzie, did not sufficiently take the interaction between leader and followers into account. Radical militants who place themselves far from

Table 3 Rank ordering of impediments to democracy

	Most important	Second most important	Third most important	Not among most important
Theory of Transaction Cost				
1 Not enough means for consultation (N = 211)	32%	18%	18%	31%
2 Not enough time for consultation (N = 207)	28%	16%	21%	35%
Theory of Membership Lethargy				
3 Little knowledge of the rank-and-file (N = 209)	14%	23%	17%	45%
4 Little interest of members to national policy (N = 207)	11%	16%	21%	52%
Theory of Elite Control				
5 Little effort by the party leadership (N = 210)	12%	11%	11%	65%
6 Leaders will not risk own ideas (N = 210)	3%	12%	4%	82%

the party's dominant policy eventually leave the party. In turn, if membership attrition increases, party leaders will be forced to change their policy. Moreover, competition among party elites is likely to establish a fairly close link between leaders and followers.

The structure of beliefs underlying the militants' evaluations can be further clarified by a factor analysis of the statements on Michels' theory (Table 4). Factor 1 sets vigorous supporters of the lethargy theory who also endorse transaction cost theory against militants with greater scepticism concerning the technical and psychological limitations of organizational democracy. Factor 2 distinguishes supporters and opponents of elite control theory. The main divisions on the two factors are between a more voluntaristic view of party organization that denies transaction cost and membership lethargy or endorses elite control, on the one hand, and a more deterministic 'technocratic' view of party organization emphasizing the silent, unintended structural obstacles to democracy on the other.

The configuration of the factors provides at best highly indirect, weak evidence for a radical interpretation of party organization because those who emphasize the importance of elite control are less inclined to attribute relevance to the technical and motivational impediments of democracy. As

Table 4 Factor analysis of the militants' rating of oligarchy theories

	Factor 1: Resourcefulness of members and organization	Factor 2: Elite control
Theory of membership lethargy		
1 Little knowledge of the rank-and-file	+ 0.79	− 0.08
2. Little interest of members in national policy	+ 0.65	+ 0.14
Theory of transaction cost		
3 Not enough time for consultation	+ 0.63	− 0.25
4 Not enough means for consultation	+ 0.49	+ 0.17
Theory of elite control		
5 Little effort by the party leadership	− 0.01	+ 0.83
6 Leaders will not risk own ideas.	+ 0.07	+ 0.85

we will see in the next section, however, radical views of party oligarchy must be interpreted in the context of militants' broader political beliefs. The factor analysis lends most support to the argument in the social science literature that there is no tight link between 'weak' oligarchy (technical and psychological impediments to democracy) and 'strong' oligarchy (elite control).

The experience of ecology party activists thus does not fully support Michels' theory of oligarchy. At the very least, we must amend Michels' 'iron law' with an important qualification. While a weak theory of oligarchy is strongly confirmed, it does not necessarily translate into 'strong' oligarchy or elite control. There is a contingent relationship, not an iron law, that governs the linkage between 'weak' and 'strong' oligarchy. Moreover, it cannot be assumed that membership lethargy, as an aspect of 'weak' oligarchy, but also as a cause or consequence of 'strong' oligarchy or elite control, is an impediment of democracy in all voluntary associations.

Internal Interpretation and External Observation of Party Power: Comparing 'Objective' and 'Subjective' Assessments of Oligarchy

So far, my analysis has avoided two major complications in any study of party oligarchy. First, 'democracy' and 'oligarchy' cannot be measured as uni-dimensional, metric variables that would enable us to determine exactly how much democracy and oligarchy a particular party incorporates. At best, we can compare parties and identify which party is more or less democratic or oligarchic (Heidar 1984). The existing studies provide little support for reaching even this modest goal because a few comparative studies exist that employ sufficiently precise and similar measures of intraparty power relations.[21] In the Agalev and Ecolo study, there are at least two cases in which precisely the same measures of party oligarchy were employed. Since Agalev and Ecolo were founded independently of each other and have developed with little mutual interference in separate Belgian regions, we can compare them as independent cases.

The second difficulty in research on party oligarchy concerns the relationship between different methods of analysing party power. As the 1950s and 1960s debates on community power illustrate, research methods and research findings appear to be interdependent in studies of power relations. Empirical research employing positional and reputational concepts of power, for instance, are more likely to find elitist oligarchies than decisional approaches that identify actors and interests involved in particular decision making processes. Matters get even more complicated, when we confront these 'objectivist' approaches, relying on the researchers's secondary interpretation of social reality, with our 'subjectivist' approach in which social actors themselves assess the extent of oligarchy in a political party.

To cope with both problems of power analysis, I will first present a brief summary of findings on Agalev's and Ecolo's power structures that derive from a positional, decisional, and reputational power analysis I have reported elsewhere in considerable empirical detail.[22] Next, I will confront these findings with the militants' perception of oligarchy in Agalev and Ecolo separately. Finally, I will explore discrepancies between 'subjective' and 'objective' assessments of power in the two parties.

In 1985, Agalev and Ecolo had about 1000 members each. In Agalev, however, slightly less than 40 per cent of the members regularly participated in party affairs, in Ecolo the best estimates range from 20 to 25 per cent. Unlike Agalev, Ecolo tends to be dominated by a smaller group of activists, usually militants who were already involved in the foundling process of the party in the late 1970s. A *decisional* analysis confirms the differences between Agalev and Ecolo. Critical choices on party programmes, candidacies for electoral office, and the parties' strategy vis-a-vis potential coalition partners are more likely to be controlled by a small 'inner circle' of activists in Ecolo than in Agalev. In Agalev, regional party sections have complete autonomy over the choice of parliamentary candidates and important programmatic decisions have been made at conferences that diverged from the recommendations of the parties' official leadership. In Ecolo, no such instances have occurred.

Further, a *positional* analysis shows that Agalev has a greater turnover than Ecolo in the parties' executive and parliamentary offices. In Ecolo, the 'old guard' of the activists usually dominates the party executive. This executive closely supervises the permanent, salaried party employees, whereas in Agalev they enjoy greater political autonomy and influence.

Finally, a *reputational* analysis of power reveals that Agalev militants see a more pluralist distribution of power than Ecolo militants. In both parties, the executive committee is attributed the greatest power. But Agalev militants tend to see the parliamentarians, the national party conferences, and the secretaries as countervailing powers. In contrast, the power differential between the Ecolo party executive and any other party organ is perceived as much greater.

Based on decisional positional, and reputational evidence, then, I would predict that militants in Ecolo are more likely to endorse a 'strong' theory of oligarchy. To test this proposition with the subjective evaluations of Michels' theory, I have summed the rank orderings for each pair of questions operationalizing one of Michels' oligarchy theories. The statement that a militant believes to represent the most important impediment to party democracy receives three points, the second most important statement two points and the third one point. The remaining three statements are coded zero. Thus, the summed values for each pair of statements range from zero (low importance) to five (high importance).

Table 5 reports the summed rank orderings of impediments to democracy for Agalev and Ecolo separately. In both parties, the theory of transaction costs is still deemed to be the critical limitation on democracy, followed by the theory of membership lethargy and the theory of elite control. With respect to the latter two, however, significant differences between the two parties appear that disconfirm my prediction. Agalev militants consider the theory of elite control much more important than do their colleagues in Ecolo. Conversely, Ecolo activists subscribe to the theory of membership lethargy more willingly. If we follow these data, we must conclude that Agalev, rather than Ecolo, approximates the model of a 'strong' Michelsian oligarchy. How can we reconcile this discrepancy between the 'subjective' interpretation of power relations by the party militants and our 'objective' observations?

The discrepancy has two possible sources. On the one hand, it may be due to the fact that 'objective' investigations simply yield incorrect results and must be revised in the light of the militants' perceptions. On the other hand, it is possible that the militants perceptions are shaped by something

Table 5 Summed rank ordering of impediments to democracy in the eyes of Agalev and Ecolo militants

	Transaction costs		Membership lethargy		Elite control	
	Agalev	Ecolo	Agalev	Ecolo	Agalev	Ecolo
Least important (0-1)	21.6%	20.8%	50.8%	31.2%	58.8%	87.0%
Medium important (2-3)	43.1%	46.8%	38.6%	46.8%	31.3%	9.1%
Most important (4-5)	35.4%	32.5%	10.6%	21.1%	10.9%	3.9%
Average value	2.85	2.90	1.68	2.36	1.33	0.53
Pearson r	not significant		$+0.21^{**}$		-0.26^{***}	
	(N=130)	(N=77)	(N=132)	(N=77)	(N=131)	(N=77)

** $p \leq 0.01$ *** $p \leq 0.001$

other than their actual party experience. Militants may respond to evaluative cues which place their experience in a normative framework that shapes their view of Michels' theories. The 'framing' of Michels' theories may be influenced by general ideological and strategic dispositions, as well as their individual careers and selective perception of the organization.

Statistical analysis can help us disentangle cognitive and normative cues in the militants' assessments. In Table 5, a significant share of the variance in the militants' view of membership lethargy and elite control is explained by membership in Agalev or in Ecolo. If Agalev is truly more subject to elite control than Ecolo and has fewer problems of membership lethargy, then the explanation of interparty variance should be independent of the attributes, beliefs, and political wants of individual party militants. In other words, the fact that one of the parties had more 'radicals' or more 'moderates' should not affect the perception of party oligarchy. My key question, then, is: Will party membership still explain perceptions of oligarchy, once we hold constant for individual-level variables that may shape the intellectual frame which governs militants' evaluations?

Militants who attribute great importance to elite control, but discount membership lethargy and/or transaction costs, adopt a position which comes close to Rosa Luxemburg's radical intellectual frame. I will therefore select indicators of 'radicalism' that are independent from views of the party organization, but could serve as predictors of interpretations of oligarchy. In this respect, the Agalev and Ecolo survey provides data on the militants' radicalism in (1) programmatic, (2) strategic and (3) tactical respects.[23]

Programmatic radicalism is measured by self-placement on a left-right scale.

About half of the Agalev and Ecolo militants' place themselves on the far left or the left, the other half on the centre left and in the centre. R-L self-placements are highly correlated with ideological beliefs (cf. Kitschelt and Hellemans 1990). Militants who place themselves on the left are more strongly opposed to capitalist institutions of economic governance and to a liberal individualism against which they set a new 'post-modern' sense of communal solidarity and participatory self-organization.

Strategic radicalism concerns the militants' willingness to advocate policy concessions that their party should offer in order to gain votes or enter government coalitions.[24] In the language of European ecological politics, 'fundamentalists' reject strategic compromise, while 'realists' welcome them. Strategic radicals also harbour the greatest anxieties about government coalitions with other parties. Because they feel that political office is a powerful temptation for party leaders, they may endorse theories of elite control more than do other activists. In the Agalev and Ecolo survey, militants placed themselves in a fundamentalism-realism scale. Moreover, they were asked whether they would support the ecologists' entry into a coalition government if the parties gained votes in the 1985 elections. Taking both items together, I constructed an index of organizational radicalism. In both parties, majorities support comparatively moderate positions. Whereas in Agalev, however, one-third of the respondents supports strategic radicalism, the same is true for only one-seventh in Ecolo.

Tactical radicalism refers to the militants' willingness to contribute to spontaneous techniques of interest mobilization and disruptive protest. Radicals are more likely to engage in 'unconventional' participation, such as demonstrations or sit-ins. Barnes and Kaase et al. (1979) found protestors to be more leftist, more post-materialistic, more educated, and younger than the average population. What characterizes protestors in general are attributes typical of Agalev and Ecolo activists (cf. Kitschelt and Hellemans 1990, Chs. 5 and 6). While all party militants should thus be predisposed towards protest politics, there may be variations between moderates and radicals. Radicals are especially protest-oriented and suspicious of institutional channels of interest representation. Therefore, they may also be most attentive to and critical of party leaders. In the survey, Agalev and Ecolo militants indicated in how many of six specific protest events of the Belgian peace, environmental, women's and working class movements they had participated. In Agalev, the average was 2.4 events, in Ecolo 2.1.

Since intellectual frames may also be based on the militants' selective perception of party politics, three further control variables will be considered. Empirical research found that 'middle level' activists involved in national party affairs, but not belonging to the elected party leadership, are especially radical, while militants involved in local party politics or party leaders are more moderate (see Eldersveld 1964, Ch. 8; Whiteley 1983). Various mechanisms of differential recruitment into parties, organizational screening, and political socialization explain these differences of organization.[25] Activists involved in different arenas of party politics may therefore also hold different views on party oligarchy. Empirically, we can divide the Agalev and Ecolo militants into 'localists' who are primarily concerned with municipal politics, 'middle level activists' who usually attend party conferences, but have no office, and members of the party executive.

We are now ready to examine the associations between the normative and experiential framework of party activists, on the one hand, and their evaluations of party oligarchy on the other. Table 6 provides zero-order correlations for these variables. Programmatic radicalism is clearly unrelated to evaluations of oligarchy theories. Yet, in both parties, strategic radicals are more willing to support elite control theory than are other militants. Since there are relatively more strategic radicals in Agalev than in Ecolo, this suggests that the militants' personal political dispositions, rather than factually greater elite control in Agalev, explain difference in the evaluation of oligarchy by Agalev and Ecolo activists.

Strategic radicalism is also related to membership lethargy, yet only in Agalev. Here, the trade-off between evaluations of membership lethargy and elite control appears that is so typical of radical theories of party organization in Rosa Luxemburg's tradition. Strategic radicals endorse elite control theory, but tend to reject the significance of membership lethargy as an impediment of democracy. Since no equivalent trade-off appears in Ecolo, evaluations of membership lethargy seem to be based on an interaction effect between strategic orientation and party membership. Hence, both cognitive perceptions, indicating a true difference between the parties, and normative cues, originating from the militants' strategic views, contribute to the evaluation of lethargy theories.

Next, the tactical dimensions of radicalism is associated with the theory of elite control. In Agalev, frequent protest involvement influences evaluations of elite control theory positively, yet this association is absent for Ecolo. Again, there appears to be an interaction effect between intellectual frames and the objective power relations in the parties. In both parties, tactical radicalism is negatively related to assessments of membership lethargy, yet the correlations are too weak to be statistically significant.

Political experiences inside the parties, finally, have little predictive power for evaluations of oligarchy theories. Only middle level activism shows some of the linkages that the theory of curvilinear disparity predicts. In both parties, middle level activists are distinctly less willing to support the theory of transaction costs than other activists. In Agalev, middle level activists also tend to reject membership lethargy as an obstacle to party

Table 6 Ranking of the three theories of party oligarchy intellectual frames, and party experience

		Transaction Costs	Membership Lethargy	Elite Control
1 Programmatic radicalism	Agalev	+0.08	−0.03	−0.05
leftist self-placement	Ecolo	+0.05	−0.16	+0.13
2 Strategic	Agalev	−0.07	-0.19**	+0.24***
radicalism	Ecolo	−0.07	+0.11	+0.22*
3 Tactical radicalism: protest	Agalev	+0.03	−0.08	+0.19**
involvement	Ecolo	0.00	−0.13	+0.02
4 Political experence 1:	Agalev	−0.13	−0.04	+0.03
localists	Ecolo	−0.04	+0.04	−0.01
5 Political experirience 2: middle level	Agalev	-0.17**	−0.20*	+0.04
activists	Ecolo	-0.24**	+0.06	+0.08
6 Political experirience 3: membership in the	Agalev	+0.11	−0.02	−0.08
party executive	Ecolo	−0.09	−0.04	+0.17

* $p \leq 0.05$ ** $p \leq 0.01$ *** $p \leq 0.001$

democracy. In neither party, however, is there a significant positive association with elite control theories. Overall, these data lend little support to the theory of curvilinear disparity, particularly in Ecolo.[26]

My preliminary finding, then, is that the normative orientations and the political practices that shape the militants' intellectual frames do make a difference for their evaluations of oligarchy theories. In particular, the greater strategic radicalism in Agalev explains why there is more support in this party for elite control theory than in Ecolo. This suggests that the 'objective' interpretation of power structures is vindicated, once we control for the militants' political radicalism.

To clarify the relative share of variance in the evaluation of membership lethargy and elite control that is explained by party affiliation, strategic radicalism, and tactical radicalism, we have entered variables with significant bivariate correlations in Table 6 into multiple regression equations (Table 7). The regression of intellectual frames and party

Table 7 Evaluating Michels' oligarchy theory: subjective political orientations VS objective power relations

A. Elite Control

	B	Beta
1. Strategic radicalism	+0.10	+0.20**
2. Protest involvement x Party Membership	+0.09	+0.15*
3. Agalev party member	+0.46	+0.15*
Adjusted R²:	0.13***	
	(N=202)	

B. *Membership lethargy*

(1)	B	Beta	(2)	B	Beta
1. Strategic radicalism	−0.04	−0.08 (p=0.23)	1. Strategic radicalism x party membership	−0.05	−0.15 (p=0.13)
2. Middle level militants	−0.04	−0.08 (p=0.27)	2. Middle level miltants x party membership	−0.04	−0.12 (p=0.11)
3. Agalev party member	−0.16	−0.20**	3. Agalev party member	−0.28	−0.08
Adjusted R²:	0.05** (N=204)		Adjusted R²:	0.07*** (N=204)	

$^*p \leq 0.05$ $^{**}p \leq 0.01$ $^{***}p \leq 0.001$

membership on elite control theory now shows clearly that most of the differences between Agalev and Ecolo are probably due to the individual activists' political dispositions (Table 7A). Agalev attracts more radical militants than Ecolo.

Matters are somewhat different with respect to the perception of membership lethargy in Agalev and Ecolo. In equation 7A where no interaction effects between party membership and intellectual frame has been entered, party membership remains clearly the dominant factor accounting for differences between Agalev and Ecolo. Once we model interaction effects, no single variable reaches an acceptable level of significance, although the explained variance of the equation increases (7B). This equation, too, suggests that we have identified real rather than purely ideological differences between the two parties. These conclusions are, of course, consistent with my 'objective' analysis which found that Agalev mobilizes more activists in its internal decision making process, both in absolute and relative terms. Thus, there are objective reasons for Agalev's militants to support membership lethargy theory less than their colleagues in Ecolo.

How can we explain the variance in Agalev and Ecolo's true power structures and in the perception of party militants? As I indicated in my discussion of Michels' theory, the 'law' of oligarchy may have to be restated as a contingency relationship. One of the predictors of greater or lesser oligarchy, then, is the ideological outlook and mobilization of a party's constituencies. In the case of ideology parties, the more environmental and other social movements (anti-nuclear, women's, peace movements) are mobilized, the greater may be the intensity of demands for participatory democracy. Such demands are communicated into ecology parties through the recruitment, internal socialization, and external exposure of party militants to the social movements. As an array of data can demonstrate, Flanders experienced a greater mobilization of social movements and protest activities feeding into ecology parties during the 1970s and early 1980s than Wallonia (Kitschelt and Hellemans 1990, Ch. 2). For this reason, it is not surprising that Agalev includes more radicals among its party membership and has committed itself to an overall more radical programme and strategy than Ecolo.

My analysis appears to contain a glaring contradiction which I would like to address briefly. In the preceding section, I employed the militants' perceptions of party oligarchy as an indicator of actual power relations, whereas this section showed that normative cues, rather than cognitions and experiences, may be responsible for militants' interpretations. After emphasizing the importance of the subjective construction of social reality early in this paper, have I not now returned to a purely 'objectivist' analysis that does not consider the Thomas-theorem according to which what (wo)men define as reality has real consequences? Have I not revealed subjective interpretations as pure 'false consciousness' that contributes nothing to our understanding of party organization?

First of all, we should not ignore that there remains considerable convergence between 'subjective' and 'objective' assessments of Agalev's and Ecolo's power structures. Where objective and subjective analyses converge, confidence in the findings is considerably strengthened. Inconsistencies between the two modes of analysis appear only at the margins. Convergence applies, for example, to the actual activism of party members and the militants' assessment of the theory of membership lethargy. Agalev members are more active, and the interviewed Agalev militants are generally less inclined to believe that membership lethargy is a serious obstacle to democracy than their counterparts in Ecolo. Convergence also applies to the general assessment of the the elite control theory of oligarchy, where reputational, decisional, and positional analysis are consistent with the party activists' subjective interpretations insofar as also a majority of the latter in both parties rejects the strong oligarchy theory Michels had made the centrepiece of his reasoning. The one inconsistency between subjective and objective power analyses concerns the *relative share* of Agalev and Ecolo militants endorsing elite control theories of oligarchy.

Second, however, even where the observers' and the participants' interpretations of oligarchy diverge, it is possible to reconstruct a logic in these findings that makes them compatible with each other: subjective interpretations may 'cause' the very objective patterns that are - at first sight - inconsistent with the militants' own definition of the situation. In the case of assessing elite control in Agalev and Ecolo, the underlying rationale may be simple: a greater number of radical militants enters Agalev than Ecolo. One important element of their green radicalism is suspicion of hierarchy and leadership and the insistence on an open grassroots democracy inside the party organization. They tend to believe that participatory democracy is always endangered by an oligarchy of self-interested leaders. This belief itself may have the practical consequence of weakening the party leadership which is gradually 'worn out' by having to justify itself to a distrustful audience of party militants for every step it undertakes! In-depth interviews reveal bitter complaints of many Agalev party leaders about the excessive mistrust that party militants express vis-à-vis office holders. As a consequence, frustration among the leadership runs high, causing rapid turnover in office and a general unwillingness to stake out political positions that may be rejected by the rank-and-file. This process holds at bay the distancing of the leadership from the militants and *falsifies* the radical militants' interpretations of the situation as strong party oligarchy. Nevertheless, these interpretations themselves are causally responsible for bringing about their own falsification. Ecology party organization, in this sense, operates on the basis of a *self-destroying prophecy*. This self-destroying prophecy is stronger in Agalev than in Ecolo where leaders encounter less mistrust and enjoy more freedom of action.

It is questionable, however, whether party militants are able to subscribe to the logic of self-destroying prophecies consciously and rationally. Can we intentionally engage in wishful thinking (or more to the point: imaginations of the evil) in order to bring about beneficial results that falsify our beliefs? Such a thought process would involve the logical contradiction that individuals believe and do not believe in what they say at the same time. This contradiction rules out that rational militants could consciously bring about the virtuous consequences of false beliefs. The self-destroying prophecy is a by-product of action which cannot be rationally created (Elster 1983). At the same time, the existence of this 'hidden hand' causal mechanism shows that studying actors' beliefs about the dynamics, of organizations is vital to scholarly investigation, even where 'objective' and 'subjective' interpretations, when taken at face value, yield diverging findings.

Conclusion

In this article I have established that the Belgian ecology parties in the mid 1980s were not 'strong' oligarchies in the sense suggested by Michels. Moreover, I have shown that there is systematic variance in the *degree* of oligarchy across parties and that this variance can be explained in terms of the mobilization of social movements (ecology, women, peace, etc.) whose participants support ecology parties. Of course, my analysis has not disproven the broader claims of Michels' theory and I will address how they might bear on the future of ecology parties in this conclusion.

Michels proposes a life-cycle theory of party organization, according to which oligarchy is gradually institutionalized with the growing age, electoral support and institutionalization of elites in a party (see also Robertson 1976, pp. 101–5). For this reason, findings on ecology parties cannot be easily generalized, not even for the same family of leftist and libertarian parties. Including the social movement organizations from which Agalev and Ecolo emerged in the late 1970s, the parties were only twelve years old in 1985 and still relatively small. Nevertheless, we may challenge whether ecology parties will ever go through the same life-cycle that Michels attributed to the parties of his own age. Also older parties that appeal to the same left and libertarian sentiments as the Belgian ecologists, such as the Dutch Socialist Pacifists, the Dutch Radical Party, or the Danish Socialist People's Party, have a very low member/voter ratio compared with the establishment conservative or social democratic parties. Moreover, with age challenges to the party leadership and a centrifugal, decentralizing dynamic of power, relations appear not to subside in these and other left-libertarian parties (cf. Kitschelt 1990).

Moreover, the social base of ecology and other left-libertarian parties and the ideas they express may preclude a dramatic transformation of their goals and organizational structure. The parties involve mostly young intellectuals with university degrees. Most studies of political participation have found that personal resources, such as cognitive skills, facilitate political involvement and increase the demand for participation.[27] Hence, I suggest that *ideas will continue to count* and reduce the impact of a life-cycle mechanism. The radical egalitarian and participatory thrust expressed by ecology party militants translates into a more open, fluid party organization than what is typical of the ideologically more collectivist, organizationally more formal, and hierarchical socialist and conservative Belgian political parties.

The limits of Michels' 'iron law' of (strong) oligarchy could be further explored through more systematic cross-national comparison of ecology and other parties. The extent of hierarchical control of party strategy varies with a number of contingencies. I have emphasized the *mobilization of the political cleavage* on which a party is built. It can be easily shown that left-libertarian parties, immersed into an environment with higher cleavage mobilization than either in Wallonia or in Flanders, such as the West German Greens, tend to have more fluid, decentralized, disjointed power structures (Kitschelt 1989a). In a similar vein, *political institutions* do matter for the organization of parties (cf. Harmel and Janda 1982). The Belgian ecology parties operate in a multi-party system where parties can lose voters and militants by moving to moderate as well as more radical policies. In these circumstances, party leaders face fewer incentives to abandon their core constituencies and loyal militants than in two-party systems with plurality vote where marginal voters in the centre of a competitive space gain extraordinary importance.

Finally, the extent of oligarchy may vary with the *electoral competitiveness* of a party: do small differences in electoral support translate into large differences in party power (seats in parliament, strategic influence over government formation, impact on public policy)? Where competitiveness is high, party leaders may be more tempted to distance themselves from their rank-and-file militants and form strong oligarchies. Yet, even in this instance, the evidence of ecology parties is ambiguous. In the West German Greens, for example, the party's entry into government coalitions at the state level was triggered and fully supported by a massive mobilization of rank-and-file militants, whereas certain leadership circles insisted on the ideological purity of the party (Kitschelt 1989, Ch. 9). In a similar vein, the entry of the Dutch and Danish left-libertarian parties into government coalitions in the late 1960s and 1970s did not reinforce a party oligarchy intent on cooperation with moderate parties, but led to a process of radicalization and party splits that eventually drove the parties from power (Kitschelt 1990).

The ideas of ecological politics, as well as the multiple contingencies in the environment of party organization, make it likely that ecology and other left-libertarian parties will not become strong Michelsian oligarchies controlled by status-quo oriented elites. As long as participatory and left-libertarian ideas run high in the parties' constituencies and give them a *raison d' être* they must face the productive dilemma of reconciling imperatives of participatory democracy with the exigencies of intraparty cooperation and strategic choice in a competitive party system.

NOTES

1 This property of scientific evidence has given rise to epistemological debates about the testability and commensurability of different scientific theories. The best-known examples for this controversy is probably Lakatos and Musgrave (1970).

2 The epistemologically most powerful statement of this research perspective was provided by Alfred Schütz in numerous articles. See e.g., Schütz 1960).

3 See especially Cicourel (1964) on measurement in the social sciences, Alan Blum (1970) on 'theorizing' as a practical activity and Mehan and Wood's (1975, Chs. 3 and 4) review of ethnomethodological reconstructions of social reality.

4 Habermas (1970) still provides the best survey of these developments in the social sciences.

5 This is one of the main criticisms that has been advanced against ethnomethodology as the purest form of sociological idealism. Cf. Attewell (1974), Bauman (1973) and Goldthorpe (1973).

6 In conventional Marxist terminology, this is the problem of 'false consciousness': individuals perceive social reality in a way that systematically distorts or neglects important aspects of it. Marxists have tried to explain this distortion itself as a consequence of an objective social structure.

7 The classic most rigorous empirical exploration of Michels' law which employs an 'objectivist' methodology is Lipset, Trow and Coleman (1956) study of the American printers' union. The most thorough study of party oligarchy with an 'objectivist' methodology is probably Eldersveld's (1964) analysis of Democratic and Republic party organization in Wayne County. For a more recent empirical analysis using the Swedish labour unions as an example, see Lewin (1980). Incidentally, all these studies reject or qualify Michels' oligarchy theory.

8 The extension beyond Pareto's and Mosca's elite theory has been emphasized by Beetham (1977, p. 14). Hands (1971, p. 159) also points out that Michels gives the notion of oligarchy two different meanings.

9 Wippler (1984, pp. 117-24) and Eldersveld (1982, pp. 159-61) offer lucid schematic reconstructions of the different theoretical arguments in Michels' account of oligarchy.

10 Even radical democrats like Barber (1984, pp. 245-51) recognize the problem of transaction cost, but are much less willing to subscribe to the inevitability of mass lethargy or elite control. A useful survey of major objections to Michels' theory, particularly the conception of 'strong' oligarchy, can be found in Beetham (1981).

11 As comparative studies of participation and factionalism in parties see Beller and Belloni (1978) and Raschke (1977).

12 Michels found, for instance, that intellectuals tended to be more radical than leaders with working class origin in the German Social Democratic Party (Michels 1911, pp. 294-7).

13 For Michels, most material benefits were dispensed by the party and union bureaucracy, providing well-paying long-term jobs. Historical studies show, however, that these political bureaucracies were very small and showed little tendency to grow relative to the size of the rank-and-file (Lehnert 1979; Schoenhoven 1980).

14 This point has been worked out in detail by May (1965, pp. 423-9).

15 For this reason, opinion differences between party leaders and rank-and-

file militants have been demonstrated most frequently for British and US parties. For a review of the literature see May (1973, 139-43) and Pierre (1986, pp. 469-70).

16 For a reconstruction of her theory of organization, see Kitschelt and Wiesenthal (1979).

17 In the recent literature, the most scholarly statement of a voluntarist theory of 'strong oligarchy', applied to a broad scope of voluntary political associations is probably Piven and Cloward (1977). In the European party literature, left critics of social democratic parties have often seen party leaders as the villains who abandon their followers and become supporters of the system. See most recently Panitch (1986) and Keane (1988, pp. 126-30).

18 As general statements of this conflict, compare McKenzie (1955) and Kevenhoerster (1975).

19 This proposition and the analytical underpinnings of conservative views of party democracy (rank-and-file radicalism) are also shared by many rational choice theorists (Wellhofer and Hennessey 1974; Robertson 1976) whose models usually build on the Anglosaxon two party systems. For a more guarded, but still unsatisfactory, conceptualization of the relationship between rank-and-file militants and party leaders in the rational choice school see the otherwise highly sophisticated contributions by Aldrich (1983, pp. 980-3) and Schlesinger (1984, p. 385).

20 For a comprehensive analysis of the data, see Kitschelt and Hellemans (1990).

21 An exception is Janda's (1980, pp. 108-17) data bank on political parties around the world. Unfortunately, Janda is forced to rely on the formal structure and statutes of parties as the primary indicators of power centralization as well as case studies of varying quality. Thus, the comparability and validity of the data are questionable.

22 See Kitschelt (1989a, chs. 4-8) who compares the Belgian and the West German ecology parties and primarily uses a decisional and a reputational approach as well as Kitschelt and Hellemans (1990, Ch. 7) on Agalev and Ecolo with data on the scope and structure of intraparty participation and the power reputation of various party organs.

23 A detailed description of the various measures of programmatic, strategic, and tactical radicalism can be found in Kitschelt and Hellemans (1990, chs. 3 and 4).

24 Strategic radicalism is only moderately related to anti-capitalism, opposition to liberal individualism or R-L self-placements. It measures indeed a different dimension of political beliefs than attitudes about public policies.

25 Compare May (1973). For a qualification and restatement of May's 'law of curvilinear disparity' see Kitschelt (1989b). Like Michels' 'iron law', May's law also must be formulated as a relationship that is contingent on contextual factors (the nature of a party constituency, institutional rules, a party's competitiveness) as well as the organizational structure of a party itself.

26 Other individual level variables, such as education, gender, age, or income reveal no statistically significant relations to the evaluation of oligarchy theory.

27 In Agalev and Ecolo, about 40 per cent of all surveyed activists had university degrees and another third had graduated from a technical college. In the overall Belgian population, less than one-fifty attain these levels of educational accomplishment (cf. Kitschelt and Hellemans 1990, Ch. 5). Also Lipset et al. (1956) emphasize high skills in the American printers'

union as a facilitator of intra-organizational democracy. Similarly, studies of participation in political parties have always found that better educated party members are more active. See, e.g., Barnes (1967) and Stern et al. (1971) on the Italian Socialists.

REFERENCES

Aldrich, J. (1983). 'A Downsian spatial model with party activism', *American Political Science Review*, Vol. 77, pp. 974-90.
Attewell, P. (1974). 'Ethnomethodology since Garfinkel', *Theory and Society*, Vol. 1, pp. 179-210.
Barber, B. (1984). *Strong Democracy*. Berkeley CA.: University of California Press.
Barnes S. H. (1967). *Party Democracy: Politics in an Italian Socialist Federation*. New Haven CT: Yale University Press.
Barnes, S. H. and Kaase, M., et al. (1978). *Political Action: Mass Participation in Five Western Democracies*, Beverley Hills, CA: Sage.
Bauman, Z. (1973). 'On the Philosophical status of Ethnomethodology', *The Sociological Review*, Vol. 21, pp. 5-23.
Beetham, D. (1977). 'From socialism to fascism: The relation between theory and practice in the work of Robert Michels', *Political Studies*, Vol. 25, pp. 3-24 and 161-181.
Beetham, D. (1981). 'Michels and his Critics', *Archives Europeenes de Sociologie*, Vol. 22, pp. 81-99.
Beller, D. C. and Belloni, F. P. (1978). *Faction Politics: Political Parties and Factionalism in Comparative Perspective*. Santa Barbara, CA: ABC-Clio.
Blum, A. F. (1970). 'Theorising', in Douglas, Jack D. (ed.), *Understanding Everyday Life*. Chicago IL: Aldine, pp. 301-19.
Ceulers, J. (1977). 'De lijstensamenstelling in de Belgische Socialistische Partij', *Res Publica*, Vol. 19, pp. 411-21.
Cicourel, A. V. (1964). *Method and Measurement in Sociology*. New York: Free Press.
De Winter, L. (1981). 'De parteipolitisering als instrument van particratie. Een overzicht van de ontwikkeling sinds de Tweede Wereldoorlog', *Res Publica*, Vol. 23, pp. 53-107.
Eldersveld, S. J. (1964). *Political Parties: A Behavioural Analysis*. Chicago IL.: Rand McNally.
Eldersveld, S. J. (1982). *Political Parties in American Society*. New York: Basic Books.
Elster, J. (1983). *Sour Grapes*. Cambridge: Cambridge University Press.
Goldthorpe, J. H. (1973). 'Review article: A revolution in sociology?' *Sociology*, Vol. 7, pp. 449-62.
Habermas, J. (1970). *Zur Logik der Sozialwissenschaften*. Frankfurt am Main: Suhrkamp.
Hands, G. (1971). 'Roberto Michels and the study of political parties', *British Journal of Political Science*, Vol. 1, pp. 155-72.
Harmel, R. and Janda, K. (1982). *Parties and their Environments: Limits to Reform?* New York: Longman.
Heider, K. (1984). 'Party power: Approaches to a field of unfilled classics', *Scandinavian Political Studies*, Vol. 7, pp. 1-16.
Hofstetter, C. (1971). 'The amateur politician: A problem in construct validation', *Midwest Journal of Political Science*, Vol. 15, pp. 31-56.
Janda, K. (1980). *Political Parties: A Cross-National Survey*. New York: MacMillan.
Janda, K. and King, S. (1985). 'Formalizing and testing Duverger's theories on political parties', *Comparative Political Studies*, Vol. 18, pp. 139-69.
Keane, J. (1988). *Democracy and Civil Society*. London: Verso.
Kevenhoerster, P. (1975). *Das imperative Mandat: Seine gesellschaftspolitische Bedeutung*. Frankfurt am Main: Herder & Herder.

Kirkpatrick, J. (1976). *The New Presidential Elite: Men and Women in National Politics.* New York: Russell Sage Foundation.

Kitschelt, H. (1988). 'Organisation and strategy in Belgian and West German Ecology parties: A new dynamic of party politics in Western Europe?' *Comparative Politics,* Vol. 20, pp. 127-54.

Kitschelt, H. (1989a). *The Logics of Party Formation. Ecological Politics in Belgium and West Germany.* Ithaca, N.Y.: Cornell University Press.

Kitschelt, H. (1989b). 'The internal politics of parties: The law of curvilinear disparity revisited', *Political Studies,* Vol. 37, pp. 400-21.

Kitschelt, H. (1990). 'New social movements and the decline of party organization', in Dalton, R. J. and Kuechler, M. (eds.), *Challenging the Political Order.* New York: Oxford University Press pp. 179-208.

Kitschelt, H. and Hellemans, S. (1990). *Beyond the European Left: Ideology and Political Action in the Belgian Ecology Parties.* Durham, NC Duke University Press.

Kitschelt, H. and Wiesenthal, H. (1979). 'Organization and mass action in the political works of Rosa Luxemburg', *Politics and Society,* Vol. 9, pp. 152-202.

Lakatos, I. and Musgrave, A., (eds.) (1970) *Criticism and the Growth of Knowledge.* Cambridge: Cambridge University Press.

Lehnert, D. (1979). 'Zur politischen Transformation der deutschen Sozialdemokratie: Ein Interpretationsversuch für die Zeit des Übergangs zum organisierten Kapitalismus', in Bergmann, J. Megerle, K. and Steinbach, P. (eds.) *Geschichte und politische Wissenschaft.* Stuttgart: Klett-Cotta, pp. 279-314.

Lewin, L. (1980). *Governing Trade Unions in Sweden.* Cambridge, MA: Harvard University Press.

Lipset, S. M. (1962). 'Introduction', in Michels R., *Political Parties.* New York: Free Press, pp. 15-30.

Lipset, S. M., Trow, M. A. and Coleman, J. S. (1956) *Union Democracy.* New York: Free Press.

Luxemburg, R. (1971) *Selected Political Writings.* ed. D. Howard. New York: Monthly Review Press.

Luxemburg, R. (1974). *Gesammelte Werke* Berlin: Dietz.

May, J. D. (1965). 'Democracy, organization, Michels', *American Political Science Review,* Vol. 59, pp. 417-29.

May, J. D. (1973). 'Opinion structure of political parties: The special law of curvilinear disparity', *Political Studies,* Vol. 21, pp. 135-51.

McKenzie, R. T. (1955). *British Political Parties: The Distribution of Power Within the Conservative and Labour Parties.* London: Heinemann.

McKenzie, R. T. (1982). 'Power in the Labour Party: The issue of intraparty democracy', in Kavanagh, D. (ed.), *The Politics of the Labour Party.* London: Allen & Unwin, pp. 191-202.

Mehan, H. and Wood, H. (1975). *The Reality of Ethnomethodology.* New York: Wiley.

Michels, R. (1911). *Political Parties.* English Edition 1962. London: Collier-Macmillan.

Panitch, L. (1986). *Working Class Politics in Crisis: Essays on Labour and the State.* London: Verso.

Payne, J. L. (1968). 'The oligarchy muddle', *World Politics,* Vol. 20, pp. 439-53.

Pierre, J. (1986). 'Attitudes and behaviour of party activists: A critical exmination of recent research on party activists and "middle level elites," ' *European Journal of Political Research,* Vol. 14, pp. 465-79.

Piven, F. and Cloward, R. (1977). *Poor People's Movements.* New York: Random House.

Raschke, J. (1974). *Innerparteiliche Opposition : Die Linke in der Berliner SPD.* Hamburg:

Hoffmann and Campe.

Raschke, J. (1977). *Organisierter Konflikt in westeuropäischen Parteien*. Opladen: Westdeutscher Verlag.

Robertson, D. (1976). *A Theory of Party Competition*. London: Wiley.

Schlesinger, J. A. (1984). 'On the theory of party organization', *Journal of Politics*, Vol. 46, pp. 369-400.

Schoenhoven, K. (1980). *Expansion und Konzentration: Studien zur Entwicklung der Freien Gewerkschaften im wilhelminischen Deutschland, 1890-1914*. Stuttgart: Klett-Cotta.

Schütz, A. (1960). 'The social world and the theory of social action', *Social Research*, Vol. 27, pp. 203-21.

Stern, A. J., Tarrow, S. and Williams, M. F. (1971) 'Factions and opinion groups in European mass parties: some evidence from a study of Italian socialist activists', *Comparative Politics*, Vol. 3, pp. 529-59.

Wellhofer, I. S. and Hennessey, T. M. (1974). 'Models of Political Party Organization and Strategy: Some analytic approaches to oligarchy', in Crewe, I. (ed.), *Elites in Western Democracy*, London: Croom Helm, pp. 279-316.

Whiteley, P. (1983).*The Labour Party in Crisis*. London: Methuen.

Williamson, O. (1975). *Markets and Hierarchies: Analysis and Anti-Trust Implications*. New York: Free Press.

Wilson, J. Q., (1973). *Political Organizations*, New York: Basic Books.

Wippler, R. (1984). 'Het oligarchieprobleem: Michels' ijzeren wet en latere probleem-oplossingen', *Mens en Maatschappij*, Vol. 59, pp. 115-41.

5. Environmental Crisis, Green Party Power: Chernobyl and the Swedish Greens[1]

ANTHONY DESALES AFFIGNE
Department of Political Science, Brown University
Providence, Rhode Island, USA

Introduction

When the 1000-megawatt nuclear reactor at Chernobyl exploded, on 26 April 1986, particles from its burning core lofted to an altitude of one kilometre, and blew north by northeast toward Sweden, where they were first detected during heavy rainstorms on 28 April. With shifting winds, large radioactive clouds soared into central Europe, then south to the Mediterranean (Silver 1987, p. 73).

Near the reactor in the Soviet Union, at least 31 people died, 237 were hospitalized, and more than 24,000 exposed to 'significant' levels of radiation.[2] In terms of immediate casualties, the scale of the disaster was almost unimaginable: during the previous 42 years of the atomic age, 284 accidents had killed 33 people and significantly exposed 620 (Mould 1988, p. 152). Estimates of the total release of radioactive material range from 50 to 70 million curies, with 4-5 tonnes deposited within 20 kilometres of the plant and another 2-3 tonnes at greater distances (Mould 1988, p. 118). In Sweden the fallout totalled about 9 kilograms of various radioactive isotopes (SSI 1986).

In view of the magnitude and transnational impact of the accident at Chernobyl, we might reasonably wonder what role the catastrophe played in subsequent environmental politics in countries most affected by the airborne fallout. In particular, because a key feature of European politics since the mid 1970s has been the growth of small, environmentally radical political parties, we might ask whether an environmental crisis like Chernobyl further stimulated partisan realignments represented by these new parties. Looking toward the future, we might also wonder whether or not increasing frequency and severity of ecological problems portends continued growth of the 'Greens' in Western Europe and elsewhere. Chernobyl was an environmental disaster, by any measure, and Sweden, home to a nascent but struggling Green party, was the most severely affected of all the Western democracies.

This study investigates the case of Chernobyl and the Swedish Greens to help answer questions about the relationship between objective environmental conditions and contemporary politics. What, in general, is the impact of ecological crisis on political change? What, in particular, was the impact of Chernobyl on the fortunes of the Swedish Miljöpartiet de Gröna, the Green Environmental Party, which first entered the Parliament in 1988, two years after the accident? Can lessons from this incident help political analysts build a general model of political ecological crisis?

Value Shift, Linkage Failure, Opportunity Structures

European green parties and their growth have attracted a fair amount of scholarly attention in recent years, based primarily on Inglehart's identification of the materialism-postmaterialism dimension in social and political values (Inglehart 1977, 1981). This approach depicts the greens as both proponents and beneficiaries of a post-war decline in public affinity for 'materialism', including the continuous expansion of industrial production and global political-economic conflict between the superpower blocs. From this perspective the growth of postmaterialist values within Western mass publics has fractured political alignments along a new dimension: a spectrum of noneconomic values perpendicular to the traditional left-right (class conflict) axis, which has long dominated electoral politics in the West. In industrialism's later years, goes the argument, affluence and education conjoin to foster postmaterialist values among the new middle class, values include environmentalism, egalitarianism, opposition to nuclear power, pacifism, women's rights, consumerism, and support for limits to economic growth. Movements advocating these new concerns reflect 'a long-term shift in the value priorities of Western publics'(Inglehart 1984, p. 25).

Because there is general symmetry between green party programmes on the one hand and the repertoire of postmaterialist values on the other, Inglehart's value change perspective has borne much fruit, and fostered numerous related arguments about the class base (or lack thereof) and the (middle) class interests of the green parties.[3]

In an extension of this approach, the relationship between postmaterialist values and structural features of democratic systems has been specified, by Lawson and others, using the concept of electoral linkage failure. In this view, green parties are the progeny of a failed marriage between traditional party systems and the postmaterialist social movements.[4] Unable to accommodate new demands within existing ideological alignments, party systems may fracture. Dalton, Flanagan and Beck depict the resulting partisan realignment in one of two ways: existing parties expand their issue portfolios to incorporate new elements; or one or more new parties form to 'represent new issue interests'.

In a third analytical current, Kitschelt has argued that the existence of postmaterialist values alone would not result in the formation of new, 'left-libertarian' parties. Agreeing that postmaterialist parties *may* form when existing political institutions are unresponsive, he argues that this realignment is *likely only* when pressure for change 'coincides with favorable *political opportunities*' (Kitschelt 1988a, p. 215). Key 'political opportunity structures', he suggests, include affluence; high levels of social security; corporatist labour and economic systems; leftist parties which have been integrated into mainstream politics and government; and a strong anti-nuclear movement.

Somewhat surprisingly, none of these contemporary approaches provides a central theoretical role for general environmental conditions, let alone ecological crisis - despite the fact that the objects of interest are political parties whose ideologies are explicitly environmental. Against the theoretical backdrop of *value shifts, linkage failure,* and *opportunity structures* using new evidence from Sweden, this study will test a fourth possibility: that much of the political change represented by green party growth may be directly related to conditions of *ecological crisis.*

Green Politics in Sweden, 1976-88

In Sweden the current shape of environmental politics was introduced in the national election of 1976, when the *Centerpartiet* (Centre Party), the former Agrarian Party, campaigned strongly against nuclear power, promising to phase out fission entirely by 1985. When the Centre Party launched its anti-nuclear gambit, five political parties dominated Swedish politics. Two parties of the 'socialist bloc' and three of the non-socialist 'bourgeois bloc' competed for control of the Swedish parliament, the *Riksdag;* the Social Democratic Workers Party (*Socialdemokratiska Arbetarepartiet*) and Left Communists (*Vänsterpartiet kommunisterna*) made up the socialist bloc, while the Centre Party, the Moderate Party (*Moderata Samlingspartiet*), and the People's Party (*Folkpartiet*) formed the non-socialist bloc.

The environmental gambit succeeded: for the first time since 1932, the Social Democrats lost control of the government, as they and their Left Communist allies were defeated at the polls. Sweden's three non-socialist parties - the Centre, Moderate, and People's parties - gained a 180:169 edge over the socialists in parliament, and formed a centre-right coalition government under the leadership of Centre Party chief Thorbjörn Fälldin.

Unfortunately for the coalition, the Moderate and People's parties strongly *favoured* nuclear power, creating an energy and environmental policy stalemate which forced the government's collapse just two years later. For one year the People's Party ruled with a minority government.

In 1979 the non-socialists again outpolled the socialists, this time gaining only a slim, one-seat parliamentary majority.

Before the 1979 election, however, a major accident at the Three Mile Island nuclear plant near Harrisburg, Pennsylvania, had forcefully reshaped the nuclear power debate, in Sweden as elsewhere.

The accident at Three Mile Island and a revitalized Swedish anti-nuclear movement convinced the Social Democrats - who, having presided over the development of Sweden's nuclear power industry, were advocates of 'safe' nuclear energy - to shift position somewhat. In April 1979 the Social Democrats joined the anti-nuclear Centre and Left Communist parties in calling for a national referendum, after the autumn elections, on phasing out nuclear power in Sweden.

The 1980 referendum turned out to be a defeat for anti-nuclear forces. The ballot included three options, two of which provided for the construction of six additional nuclear plants *before* a permanent moratorium took effect. The third, an absolute ban on nuclear expansion, was narrowly defeated.

Environmentalists who had supported the Centre Party in 1976 and 1979, as well as those who held faith with the dominant Social Democrats, were disillusioned and discouraged by the referendum results. The Centre Party, after campaigning on a strong anti-nuclear platform, then had compromised repeatedly with its pro-nuclear partners in order to maintain a two-year hold on the national Government. Under these conditions it was impossible for the Centre Party to fulfil its promises to phase out nuclear power entirely by 1985. The Social Democrats, having paid lip-service to anti-nuclear politics, then helped orchestrate a nominally anti-nuclear referendum which actually allowed the nation's nuclear capacity to double. This was a classic case of electoral *linkage failure*, in which the Centre party failed when in power to respond to the 'ecological, particularly anti-nuclear, views' of its new supporters (Vedung 1988a, p. 101).

In response, on 19 September 1981 a group of disillusioned anti-nuclear activists founded the Miljöpartiet, the Environmental Party. In the spring of 1982, some public opinion polls showed that 6 - 7 per cent of the electorate might vote for the new party in the autumn parliamentary elections. By the time of the elections, however, most of that new support had evaporated. The Greens polled just 1.7 per cent nationally, ranging from 1 per cent of the vote in northernmost Norbottens Län, to a high of 2.3 per cent on the Baltic Sea island of Gotland. The results meant the new party would have no seats in parliament, no public subsidies, and limited access to national public media.

Three county council seats - one on the island of Gotland, and two in the city of Göteborg - were the party's most significant victories, as 1.9

Table 1 Miljöpartiet electoral trends, 1982-8

	1982	1985	1988
Total votes cast for Miljöpartiet	91787	83645	296935
Share of national Vote	1.7%	1.5%	5.5%
Range: Läns	1.0-2.3%	0.8-2.5%	3.6-7.9%
Range: Municipal districts	0.5-4.9%	0.3-3.7%	2.1-15.3%
Seats in Parliament	0	0	20
County council seats	3	6	101
Municipal council seats	129	237	698

Sources: Riksskatteverket (National Tax board); Statistisk Årsbok för Landsting, Landstingsförbundet (Federation of County Councils); Gustafsson, 1988; Ragnar Aagard, Miljöpartiet de Gröna National Office, Stockholm.
Note: Totals and percentages are for votes cast in elections to the Riksdag. Votes for Län (county) and kommun (municipal) elections are cast and counted separately and were not used for this report.

per cent of all Swedish voters cast ballots for the Environmental Party in county-level (Län) polling. There were a total of 1,927 county council seats chosen in the 1982 election.[5]

At the municipal (kommun) level, however, the Environmental Party was able to gain representation in one-third of the country's local elections, winning 129 municipal council seats in 96 of 284 municipalities, with 1.6 per cent of the total municipal-level vote. Its highest municipal percentages were 5.8 per cent in Haninge, 5.2 per cent in Nynäshamn and 5.2 per cent in Lund (Vedung 1988a, p. 105).

In an election featuring primarily economic concerns, including a highly charged conflict over labour-controlled capital investment pools, the 'wage-earner funds,' Swedish voters in 1982 returned the Social Democrats to power after six years of non-socialist rule. During these six years two centre-right coalition governments had collapsed, in 1978 when the Centre Party left the Government, and in 1981 when the Moderates walked out. Amid the 1982 power struggle and return to socialist rule, the Greens gained no more than a foothold in municipalities, and a toehold in the counties (see Table 1).

In the 1985 elections a slight increase in support at the county level, from 1.9 per cent to 2.0 per cent, earned the Environmental Party three additional county council seats, again in Gotland (two) and Göteborg (one), for a total of six. In the municipalities, support for the Greens increased from 1.6 per cent to 2.5 per cent, yielding 108 additional seats, to a new total of 237 seats in 148 communities (Gustafsson 1988, p.111). But, in contrast to these improved results at the county and town levels, the Greens' share of the national (Riksdag) vote declined to 1.5 per cent, ranging once more from a low in Norbottens Län (0.8 per cent) to a high in Gotland (2.5 per cent). With this poor showing the Greens again gained no seats in Parliament, demonstrating the problems faced by a new party, lacking 'a "hot"new politics issue that could have helped it gain a solid electoral foothold' (Poguntke 1987, p. 86).

Poguntke's assessment, while ignoring the Environmental Party's steady growth in the municipalities, was nonetheless a fairly accurate picture of the situation facing the Swedish Greens in early 1986. Judging by the 1982 and 1985 parliamentary elections Swedish voters were not yet ready to send the environmentalists to the national government. Only their growing support in local jurisdictions gave any indication that, with major changes in the Swedish political landscape, the Greens might someday vault the 4 per cent threshold, enter parliament, and join their more successful ecology party peers already seated in West Germany, Belgium, Austria, Switzerland, Luxembourg, Italy, Finland, and the European Parliament.

Thus, the political situation in Sweden before the spring of 1986 was one of apparent stability, with the Rikdag's five-party dominance secure, the traditional near-balance between socialist and bourgeois blocs intact, and the previously crucial questions of nuclear power and wage-earner funds receding in importance. On the nuclear issue, in fact, some suggested that the 1980 referendum phasing out nuclear energy (by 2010) should be reconsidered, arguing that 'scrapping an energy technology as beneficial as nuclear power was madness, at least in economic terms' (Dyring 1987, p. 2).

The apparent calm would not last, however. The first shock of 1986 struck Sweden on 28 February, when Prime Minister Olof Palme was assassinated on a Stockholm street, leaving the field of Swedish politics to a new generation of leaders.

Then, on 26 April, a massive steam explosion blew apart the Chernobyl No. 4 nuclear power station, near Kiev in the Soviet Ukraine. Radioactive debris pummelled adjacent buildings and streets, a raging fire was ignited by a second explosion of hydrogen gas, and a plume of radioactive particles rose 1200 metres into the air. On 27 April the nearby town of Pripyat (population 49000) was abandoned, and by 7 May a 30 km-diameter 'Forbidden Zone' was established around the devastated reactor. Within the zone Soviet authorities evacuated 135000 people from the large towns of Pripyat and Chernobyl (population 12000), dozens of smaller villages and farming collectives. In subsequent months fire brigades, the Air Force and the Army were pressed into service decontaminating the earth and entombing the hot reactor beneath a 400000-tonne concrete sarcophagus (Mould 1988, p. 152).

Clouds over Sweden

When the explosion at Chernobyl drenched Europe in radioactive iodine, cesium, plutonium, strontium and other isotopes, it was the atomic power station at Forsmark, Sweden which detected the accident and sent alarms ringing across the globe.[6] Dry winds had carried a cloud of radiation 800 miles north of Kiev, until heavy rains across the Baltic Sea sent radioactive particles to earth in Sweden, Norway, and Finland, with an estimated one-tenth of all Chernobyl cesium precipitating over Sweden alone (Sweden Now, No.1 1987).

The town of Gävle learned from the World Health Organization that, outside the ghost towns of the Forbidden Zone, it was the most radioactive community on the planet, each square metre of its fields, flowers, and homes emitting up to 137000 becquerels (Bq) of cesium-137. Locations in Bavaria recorded 35000 Bq/m^2 and Trondheim, Norway, 13000 Bq/m^2 (Mosey 1986, p. 9). Cesium-137 is the most troubling component of Chernobyl's fallout, with a long half-life of 30 years. About 1 kg of cesium is estimated to have fallen on Sweden (Edin 1987, p. 3).

Data collected by Sweden's Statens Strålskyddsinstitut (National Institute Of Radiation Protection, SSI) show that the distribution of long-term contamination was extremely variable. Wind, rainfall, and geologic patterns created a situation in which communities separated by a few kilometres measured very different radiation levels. The pattern of fallout is depicted in Figure 1.

As can be seen in the illustration, ground-level cesium contamination was most intense immediately around Gävle and, further up the eastern coast, around Sundsvall. At these locations, ground activity exceeded 85000 Bq/m^2, in some spots reaching 200,000 Bq/m^2. The hardest-hit counties, with large areas registering more than 30000 Bq/m^2, were Gävleborg, Västernorrland, Uppsala, Västermanland, and Södermanland. Significant amounts of radiation (7000-30000 Bq/m^2) were also deposited on Östergötland, Kalmar, Västerbotten, Jämtland, and Gotland. Two smaller 'hot spots' with this level of radiation were detected in Halland and Malmohus (SSI 1986, p. 4).

Norbotten was virtually untouched, as were much of Värmland and Kronoberg. Other sections of the country, including the three largest population centres of Stockholm, Göteborg and Malmö, received moderate amounts of radiation (3000-7000 Bq/m^2).

To protect its citizens from the effects of radiation in the food chain (primarily a greater long-term risk of various cancers), the Swedish government imposed a foodstuff limit for cesium of 300 Bq/kg. As a result, mushrooms and berries in high-radiation areas were declared unsafe for consumption. The Sami (Lapps) were especially hard-hit, as

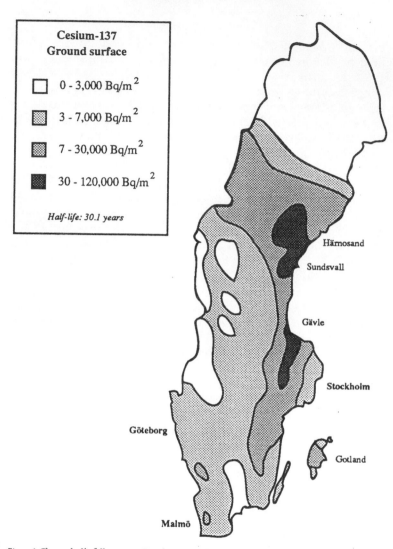

Figure 1 Chernobyl's fallout over Sweden, 1–23 May 1986 (*Sources*: Statens Strålskyddsinstitut, Chernobyl – its impact on Sweden, SSI Rapport 86-12. Stockholm: National Institute of Radiation Protection. Measurements by Sveriges Geologiska AB. Illustration by the author)

their culture and economy depend on fishing and reindeer herding. In mountain lakes of northern Sweden fish exceeded the limit and could neither be eaten nor sold.

In June and July [1986] meat from reindeer that had grazed in the northern part of the province of Jämtland and in southern Lapland was found to contain several thousand Bq per kilo... During October, 21,000 reindeer were slaughtered in Sweden and only a quarter of them were within the acceptable limit. The rest were bought by the state and fed to mink... Chernobyl is estimated to have cost the counties of Norbotten, Jämtland, Västernorrland, Västmanland, Västerbotten, Uppsala and Gävleborg something like SEK 200 million, primarily in the form of losses to the food retail and tourist trades (Dyring 1987, p. 5).

As part of the government's aggressive policy response, imports into Sweden of Soviet meat, fish, potatoes and vegetables were prohibited on 30 April. On 5 May milk products, cheese, and fresh fruit were added to the list of banned imports. A broad range of other foodstuffs were tested for radioactivity, as was human breastmilk.

Mother's milk from the Stockholm region (27 April-4 May) showed 8-25 Bq/l. Deposition of iodine-131 [on outdoor surfaces] varied between 6000 and 170000. Bq/m^2, with the highest values in northern Sweden...Iodine-13 1 concentration, in milk varied from 2-70 Bq/l, except on the island of Gotland where 700 Bq/l was measured. In raw milk on this island, 2900 Bq/l was measured (Mould 1988, p.128).

Later scientific assessments would indicate that stringent foodstuff limits set by the Swedish government were justified, although, by some accounts, somewhat strict.[7] The National Institute for Radiation Protection estimated that, during 1986, many Swedes living in regions of highest contamination received a dose of radiation equal to 4 millisieverts (mSv), about four times the normal yearly exposure from the Swedish natural environment (SSI 1986, p.10). For the country as a whole, radiation exposure for all of 1986 averaged the equivalent of one stomach X-ray: about 1 mSv. Swedish workers routinely exposed to radiation, by contrast, are allowed doses of 50 mSv annually, ten times the highest amount recorded among the Swedish populace in 1986 (Edin 1987, p. 6). This compares to the area just around Chernobyl itself, where more than 25000 people may have received doses of 350-550 mSv.

As the months passed and immediate fears generated by the accident subsided somewhat, the quiescent debate over nuclear power in Sweden resumed. Swedes began to look around them at the country's twelve operating nuclear stations, wondering whether potential Chernobyl-style disasters weren't much closer than Kiev. On the anti-nuclear side, the People's Campaign Against Nuclear Power re-emerged and demanded the immediate closure of all Swedish reactors (Edin 1987, p. 5).

On the opposite side, the nuclear industry adopted a new, more 'realistic' approach to the public debate. Following two major accidents in less than ten years – Three Mile Island and Chernobyl - the industry's earlier assertions that the technology was nearly risk-free were no longer credible. The new emphasis was on costs and benefits of nuclear power relative to other energy sources, and the technology now available for limiting effects of any mishaps. A public relations effort began in earnest, including guided tours of reactors, well-publicized safety drills, and stacks of colored brochures touting the benefits of nuclear energy (Dyring 1987, p. 5).

As the election of 1988 approached, the government's response, in a general climate of uncertainty and resurgent debate, was to convene an Energy Council to consider the implications of Chernobyl and the future of nuclear power in Sweden. With representatives from industry, environmental groups, the trade unions, and all political parties, the Council was ordered to bring recommendations to Parliament in the spring of 1987. A year after the Energy Council report was issued, the Government responded with legislation to accelerate the nuclear phase-out and close two plants before 2010: Barsebäck in 1995 and Ringhals in 1996.

The 1988 Elections

In the months leading up to the 1988 election, Swedish political observers found much to talk about: speculation centred on whether the squabbling Left Communists would fall below the 4 per cent threshold, depriving the Social Democrats of the Riksdag votes necessary to form a government. At the same time, the possibility that the 'non-aligned' Greens might surpass 4 per cent was taken seriously, fostering uncertainty about the future of the traditional party blocs and the balance of power in Parliament (Lagercrantz 1988, p. 9). By most accounts, the central issues in the 1988 elections were environmental. With a stable economic situation, Swedish media and voters were free to concentrate on an unprecedented rash of bad news on the environmental front.

> During the campaign, the Swedish people were bombarded with news about toxic algae, acid rain destroying our forests, dioxin in milk and, above all, the summer's mass deaths of sea lions in the Kattegat, an area of the North Atlantic off Sweden's southwest coast (Vedung 1988b, p.7).

Not surprisingly, then, the Greens' primary campaign effort was to promote an aggressive environmental programme. This platform included the complete shutdown of all Swedish nuclear power plants by 1991; tougher anti-pollution laws using special taxes on air pollutants and toxic substances; within three years, full disclosure of ingredients in all chemical products; a 1 per cent of GNP investment in the environment; within ten years a 90 per cent reduction of agricultural chemical use; in the same period, the transfer of half of all long-distance roadway freight transport to railways; increased rail subsidies combined with penalties for motorists and trucking firms; rural development subsidies; and, within 25 years, the elimination of fossil fuel use in Sweden (Mosey 1988, p. 22; Strandberg 1988, p. 10).

The other opposition parties staked out environmental positions as well: the Left Communists proposed a phase-out of nuclear power within twelve years; the replacement of coal and oil consumption by greater use of wind, solar and geothermal power; intensive locally-financed development of natural gas and rail transport modernization; and limits on allowable distances for truck transport.

Among the non-socialists, the Centre Party advocated similar approaches to energy policy and rail transport (albeit with market and not state control); lower highway speed limits; further development of ethanol fuel; and limitations on the use of farm chemicals. The Liberals proposed a broad system of surcharges to stimulate environmentally benign production and consumption habits, and proposed new efforts to preserve Sweden's remaining wilderness areas. The Moderates found it difficult to project any environmental programme at all, finding themselves in opposition to most of the other parties' initiatives: they favoured nuclear and opposed hydro-electric power, as well as further state-sponsored wilderness conservation, environmental surcharges, restrictions on road transport, and plans to supplant private motoring with public transit! The best the conservatives could manage in this 'environmental election' was a proposal to offer grants to motorists retro-fitting catalytic converters on older cars, and tax concessions to corporations that reduced harmful emissions.

In March the Social Democratic government presented its own wide-ranging programme for environmental protection. Minister of Environment and Energy, Birgitta Dahl was quoted to the effect that her government was now attacking environmental problems with the vigour socialists once reserved for social reform. In addition to the early closing of Barsebäck and Ringhals, the government proposals included strict limits on the use of ozone-depleting chlorofluorocarbons (CFCs); cuts in marine emissions of cadmium and mercury; restrictions on farm discharges of nutrients; firmer penalties for environmental 'criminals'; tighter emission standards for buses and trucks; and reduced levels of chlorine discharge from pulp mills (Smith 1988, p. 19; Strandberg 1988, p. 7).

Just as all this environmental politicking was getting underway, however, newspaper reports sparked a political scandal involving Social Democratic Justice Minister; Anna-Greta Leijon, which immediately joined environmental issues at the top of the campaign agenda. Frustrated by slow progress in the official investigation into Olof Palme's assassination, Leijon had authorized a publishing executive, Ebbe Carlsson, to conduct a secret inquiry. The exposé which followed revealed numerous violations of Swedish law, including an attempt to import illegal electronic surveillance equipment. Leijon was forced to resign, tarnishing the image of politicians in general and Social Democrats in particular.

On 18 September, after a long campaign dominated by scandal and environmental policy one-upsmanship, Swedish voters finally went to the polls. The results confounded nearly everyone's prognostications. The Greens did nearly quadruple their previous showing, polling 5.52 per cent and gaining representation in the Riksdag, but this was a lower figure than many had expected. Far from being knocked out of the Riksdag, the Left Communists delivered their own surprise by managing to increase vote totals and pick up two additional seats in Parliament. And the Social Democrats, rather than losing control of the Government, ended up stronger than before: though the ruling party lost three Riksdag seats, the opposition Moderates lost ten. the Liberals seven and the Centre two, leaving Social Democrats with more seats than the three bourgeois parties combined. With 21 seats now held by Left Communists, the socialist bloc established a comfortable 177:152 margin over the centre-right parties. Thus, while the Greens gained 20 seats, they were denied a power-broking role between the two main blocs.[8]

In addition, at the same time they established a parliamentary presence, surpassing the 4 per cent threshold in 26 of 28 jurisdictions, the Greens made major gains at the important county and municipal levels. To understand the significance of these local victories, it is important to realize that many activities which in other nations are assigned to private agencies or federal and state governments are in Sweden the responsibility of municipalities and counties. Municipal councils provide child care as well as pre-school, primary and secondary education. They finance social assistance and elderly care, subsidize housing, and manage land use; supervise publicly owned utilities, including water, gas, electricity and sanitation, regulate environmental and health hazards, and direct cultural and recreational programmes including sports facilities, gymnasia, parks, public baths, ice rinks, and art galleries.

Sweden's 26 county councils have primary responsibility for the nation's system of public health services and medical care. They manage a national system of local, county, and regional hospitals, as well as schools, support services and employment programmes for the disabled. The counties provide all public dental care services. All of Sweden's nursing education, and about one-third of all other post-secondary programme, primarily in technical fields, are sponsored by the county councils. Finally, these mid-level governments manage Sweden's public transit systems, conduct regional development programmes, and are among the nation's biggest consumers of art, operating a range of cultural institutions from museums to music festivals (Landstingsförbundet 1989; Gustafsson 1988).

Thus can be seen the significance of Miljöpartiet success at the municipal and county levels. In 1988 the Greens were elected to 101 county council seats (compared with six in 1985), and are now represented in all 26 regional governments. Moreover, for the first time they hold the swing votes in nine counties, able to tip the balance of power to either the socialist or non-socialist blocs. The picture is similar in the municipalities, where the Greens now hold 698 seats in 260 municipalities, far more than the 1985 total of 237 seats in 148 municipalities.

How did this situation come about? What can account for the quadrupling of support for the Greens between 1985 and 1988?

Conventional wisdom held that the ecologists benefited from two features of the 1988 elections. First, this was finally the 'environmental' election which failed to materialize in 1982 or 1985, an ideal opportunity for an explicitly environmental political party. Secondly, the Ebbe Carlsson affair may have discredited the 'professional' politicians of the dominant parties and disillusioned many voters, providing smaller opposition parties, including the Greens, with both campaign issues and a luster of innocence with which to approach voters.

Additionally, Vedung (1988b) reports that in many of the 148 municipal councils where Greens won seats in 1985 the Miljöpartiet faction had often sided with the non-socialists. This may have helped the Greens calm fears about their intentions and gain support among 'bourgeois' voters in 1988, perhaps in the hope that the Greens would help form a non-socialist government.

Taking these three possibilities in reverse order: Vedung's proposal is plausible and is not contradicted outright by electoral data, which show that the greatest increase in support for the Greens did come in districts and counties previously dominated by the bourgeois parties. Yet, of the nine counties where Greens now hold the balance of power, six were until 1988 controlled by the non-socialists, and only three by the socialist coalition. In fact, between 1982 and 1985 the non-socialists had wrested power from the socialists in three county councils, to gain control of eleven, only to see the Greens rob them of their majorities in six and the socialists reclaim one (Malmö) in 1988! (See Figure 2) Among the 14 subnational districts showing the greatest increase in Green vote share from 1985 to 1988, only five were dominated by the socialist bloc, while nine were bourgeois-controlled. Following the Green successes of 1988, the non-socialists have retained outright control of just two (Halland and Kristianstad). Thus, if voting for the Greens was a strategic move on the part of bourgeois party supporters, it was a spectacularly self-defeating strategy.

As for the Carlsson affair, there may very well have been a disillusionment factor in 1988, when turnout nationally declined from 89.9 per cent to

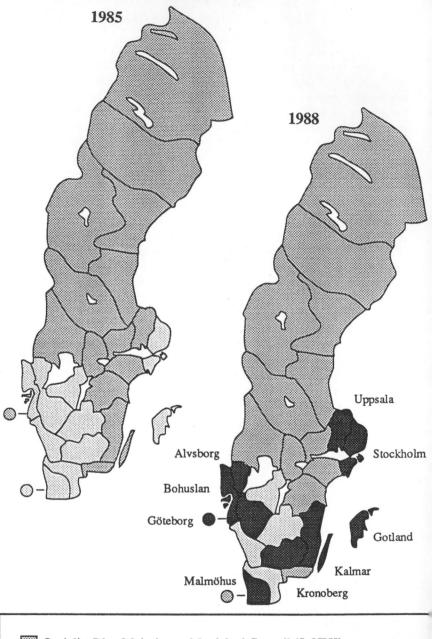

1985

1988

Uppsala

Alvsborg

Bohuslan

Stockholm

Göteborg

Gotland

Kalmar

Malmöhus

Kronoberg

Socialist Bloc Majority on Municipal Council (S, VPK)

Bourgeois Bloc Majority (M, C, Fp)

Green Party Holds Balance of Power between the Two Major Blocs

Figure 2 The balance of power in Sweden's county councils (*Sources: Statistisk Årsbok för Landsting*, Stockholm: Federation of County Councils. Illustration by the author)

86.0 per cent, its lowest level since 1964. As a group the small parties were somewhat more successful in 1988 than in earlier elections, especially the Christian Democrats (Kristdemokratiska Samhällspartiet,KdS), who rose from 2.5 per cent in 1985 to 2.9 per cent in 1988. In county council elections the KdS picked up twenty-one additional seats for a total of forty one. Among the larger parties, only the Centre was able to increase its vote share at all, gaining 1.4 per cent in Riksdag balloting and adding five county council seats.

Even the Left Communists, who increased vote share and seats in Parliament, nonetheless lost ground at the county level. However, to say that 'small parties' did better in 1988, while large parties did more poorly, does not explain why the Greens did so much better than the rest.

In Riksdag voting, the Miljöpartiet increase in vote share was ten times that of either the Communists or the Christian Democrats, and 20 times that of the other small parties. In the counties, the Christian Democrats gained 21 seats; the Greens 95. In Malmö the small Skånepartiet dropped from five seats to three, while the Greens gained three where they had none before. In Göteborg the Hisingens kommunala väljare (HKV) lost its two seats and disappeared altogether, while the Göteborg Greens increased their representation from three to nine seats.

Finally, then, we return to the environment, what Koblik called the 'one undeniable feature of the...election' (Koblik 1988, p. 4). Anecdotal and journalistic accounts of the campaign, at least, suggest that the environment was the key issue of the election, and was recognized as such by both voters and the political parties. An empirical indicator leading to the same conclusion is the fact that all four of the parties which increased vote shares in 1988, the Centre, Left Communists, Christian Democrats and Greens, were solidly opposed to nuclear power, and the party most identified with anti-nuclear politics - the Miljöpartiet - experienced the most dramatic and politically significant electoral growth.

In 1988, the toxic algal bloom and viral plague among seals were recent reminders that Sweden faced ongoing environmental problems. But in the period since the 1985 elections, the most serious of environmental issues was the accident at Chernobyl. 'It is hard to say what direct impact [Chernobyl] had on the outcome of this year's election,' wrote one analyst, 'but the results...were certainly a great success for the groups which had opposed nuclear power in the 1980 referendum' (Bergström 1988, p. 9). To Chernobyl, then, we now return.

ANTHONY D. AFFIGNE

Analysis: Radiation Impacts and Green Party Electoral Trends

If an ecological crisis like Chernobyl can change public attitudes enough
to stimulate political change, we may identify the process empirically by
examining the voting behaviour of populations most directly affected by
the crisis. Chernobyl's sole physical impact on Sweden was in the form of
radioactive fallout, impossible to see and impossible to stop - but not impossible to identify and measure. It was exactly such radiation measurements which informed the Swedish government's response to the crisis.
Because of this response, it is evident that Swedes living in areas of heavy
fallout were subject to more discomfort, uncertainty and fear - sparked by
restrictions on food, outdoor activity, and commerce.

One way to investigate Chernobyl's impact, then, is to analyse fallout
patterns and electoral trends, to see if there is a discernible relationship
between levels of radiation impact and subsequent voting behaviour in
affected regions. To begin this analysis, official measurements of fallout
levels were obtained from the National Institute of Radiation Protection
(SSI), the government agency with central responsibility for emergency
planning outside the country's nuclear power plants. Following the
detection of fallout on 28 April, continuous radiation readings were taken
by SSI and the National Defence Research Institute (FOA). Measurements
were taken by SSI at 25 permanent monitoring stations, built in 1957 to
monitor American and Soviet atomic weapons tests, and by FOA at another
system of seven air-sampling stations. Using these ground stations and
specially equipped aircraft, SSI was able to map fallout deposition patterns
as well as changes over time in radiation intensity.

While high levels of extremely toxic iodine-131 were initially detected,
this isotope has a relatively short half-life of eight days and, beyond the
first days of the emergency, attention focused instead on levels of cesium-
137 (Cs-137). Its long half-life of 30 years, and its easy entry into the food
chain through contaminated vegetables and fodder, made cesium fallout
the most serious problem facing Sweden as a result of Chernobyl. Because
cesium levels dictated the imposition of long-term agricultural and food
retail restrictions by the Swedish Government, and because cesium
contamination has had the most enduring impact on the country, the
choice of cesium for this analysis is justified both in terms of technical
import and policy impact.

Cs-137 deposition patterns reported by SSI were used to classify
municipalities according to levels of fallout. The country's 362 municipal
election districts were divided into three groups: high, medium and low
impact. Towns classified as high impact were those which showed levels
of Cs-137 greater than 7000 Bq/M^2. Medium impact areas had levels
between 3000 and 7000 Bq/m^2 while low-impact regions were under

3000 Bq/m². These break points were based on expected food chain impacts. 3000 Bq/m², for example, was thought to be the ground contamination level below which grass eaten by cows would yield safe levels of cesium activity in milk. Areas with cesium levels higher than 7000 Bq/m² have yielded game, produce and livestock with contamination levels higher than the permissible 300 Bq/kg, and are thus classified as high-impact regions. (A fourth, highest impact designation was also established for the 14 areas where Cs-137 levels exceeded 30000 Bq/m². These communities near Gävle, Sundsvall and Härnosänd were subject to especially intense – albeit temporary – radiation monitoring and food restrictions).

The grouping by fallout levels resulted in the classification of 58 districts as high impact (including fourteen in the highest group), 30 as low-impact, and the remainder as medium-impact areas. The smallest amount of fallout was deposited in the sparsely populated far north and mountainous West, while the populous regions of Stockholm, Malmo and Göteborg were spared heavy deposits and are classified into the medium impact category.

The first part of the analysis was conducted by calculating trends in electoral support for the Miljöpartiet in all 88 municipalities. Electoral data were obtained from the Riksskatteverket (the National Tax Board, the Swedish agency which conducts elections), for Riksdag elections of 1982, 1985 and 1988. The results for 58 high-impact and 30 low-impact municipalities were compared. A second comparison was performed, this time limiting the groups to the 14 highest impact municipalities and the 14 municipalities of Norrbottens Län, the least-affected area in Sweden (see Table 2).

Table 2 Miljöpartiet electoral trends and Cs-137 fallout impact regions

Municipalities, by radiation impact group	1982	Change 1982-5	p-value	1985	Change 1985-8	p-value	1988
				Votes cast for Miljöpartiet (%)			
High group (N=58)	1.49	-0.08		1.41	3.51		4.92
			0.425			0.022	
Low group (N=30)	1.13	-0.09		1.04	3.12		4.16
Highest group (N=14)	1.45	-0.13		1.32	3.34		4.66
			0.302			0.003	
Lowest group (N=14)	0.96	-0.16		0.80	2.61		3.41

Sources: Statens Strålskyddsinstitut (National Institute of Radiation Protection)
Riksskatteverket (National Tax Board)

ANTHONY D. AFFIGNE

The mean increase in Green Party share for municipalities in high-radiation areas was found to be 3.51 per cent. For municipalities in 30 low-radiation areas the mean increase was 3.12 per cent. The difference in mean scores was statistically significant (p = 0.022)

In the second comparison, the mean increase in Green Party share for districts in the highest-radiation areas was found to be 3.34 per cent, while in 14 lowest-impact municipalities, the mean increase was just 2.61 per cent. Again statistical testing indicated that the difference was significant, with a p-value of 0.003.

To check the meaningfulness of these results, a similar analysis was conducted for the period prior to Chernobyl, using election trends between 1982 and 1985, in the same 88 municipalities. For the larger groups of 58 high-impact areas and 30 low-impact communities, the mean differences in Green party vote shares between 1982 and 1985 were -0.08 per cent and -0.09 per cent respectively. With a p-value of 0.425, comparison of these two means appears to indicate no significant difference between the groups. The two sets of municipalities showed about the same degree of change (decline) in vote share for the Miljöpartiet between 1982 and 1985.

For the smaller groups at the extremes of radiation impact, the picture is similar: between the 1982 and 1985 elections, vote share for the Greens in the 14 highest-impact communities declined by 0.13 per cent while for the 14 lowest-impact communities the decline measured 0.16 per cent, an insignificant difference yielding a p-value of 0.302.

To summarize the results:

When communities at the extremes of radiation impact are compared, the highest-impact areas show an additional measure of growth in vote share for the Greens, above that seen in the lowest impact areas, amounting to just over 21 per cent of the total increase.

Subjecting the earlier period (1982 to 1985) to the same analysis suggests that, whatever differences existed between the two groups of communities in 1988, differences which resulted in a measurably different rate of growth for the Miljöpartiet, did not appear until after the 1985 election. Before 1988 the difference in Miljöpartiet growth trends between the two groups was not significant.

How can these results be interpreted? The selection into comparison groups was neither random nor arbitrary, but was based on empirical evidence regarding the impact of an objective event. Chernobyl exploded, fallout travelled across Europe, and was deposited on different parts of Sweden; the pattern of fallout was mapped, and based on that mapping 88 municipalities were classified into high- and low-radiation groups. Between the two groups, a difference in growth rates for the Environmental Party was observed, and the difference appears to be a real one.

Are there important differences between the two groups of communities, other than Chernobyl impact, which could result in this pattern? What politically significant factors might there be which suppressed Green Party growth rates in one group more than the other?

As we have seen, the Miljöpartiet appears to have had its greatest success in areas where the socialist parties are weaker, perhaps because the socioeconomic profile of Green supporters is more like those of the bourgeois parties than those of the Social Democrats or Left Communists.[9] Traditionally, northern Sweden has been a socialist stronghold, and, because of the way fallout was deposited, 16 of 30 low-impact munici-palities are located in that region, as are all 14 lowest-impact districts.

Thus it is possible that socialist strength in the north may be suppressing Green party growth rates in the lowest-impact areas, irrespective of external factors, ecological or otherwise. To check this possibility, vote share distributions by party and bloc (socialist/bourgeois) were calculated for both the highest and lowest groups, in 1982, 1985 and 1988. In all three years the magnitude of socialist dominance is measurably greater in the lowest impact areas, due largely to greater prominence of the Left Communists in those areas (see Table 3).

But, the apparent impact of this difference in socialist vote share is limited by the fact that in other respects, partisan structure and trends in the two groups are very similar. The mean Social Democratic shares are well over 50 per cent in both areas: no coalition on the left is required to maintain Social Democratic power, which is assured. The rank ordering of the bourgeois parties is consistent throughout: Centre with the most

Table 3 Vote share distributions and trends by partisan blocs and Cs-137 fallout impact regions

Partisan bloc:	Bourgeois		Socialist		Green		Other	
Highest (H) and lowest (L) groups:	H	L	H	L	H	L	H	L
Vote share (%) in 1982	38.6	28.6	59.9	70.4	1.4	0.9	0.1	0.1
Change, 1982-5	+0.7	+0.5	-0.8	-0.7	-0.1	-0.1	+0.2	+0.2
Vote share (%) in 1985	39.3	29.1	59.1	69.7	1.3	0.8	0.3	0.4
Change, 1985-8	-2.6	-2.3	-1.0	-1.0	+3.4	+2.6	+0.3	+0.7
Vote share(%) in 1988	36.7	26.8	58.1	68.7	4.7	3.4	0.6	1.1
Net change, 1982-8	-1.9	-1.8	-1.8	-1.7	+3.3	+2.5	+0.5	+1.0

Party blocs:
Bourgeois bloc: Moderate, Centre, People's and Christian Democratic parties
Socialist bloc: social Democratic and Left communist parties
Green: Environmental Party
Other: small parties, generally regional and primarily socialist
Note: H and L are the 14 (H)ighest and 14(L)owest radiation impact municipalities, ranked by Cs-137 fallout levels.

Table 4 Vote shares (%) by party and Cs-137 fallout impact regions

	M	C	Fp	KdS	Mp	S	VPK
Highest-impact areas				%			
(N=14)							
1985	13.8	14.0	10.8	(a)	1.3	53.9	5.2
1988	10.9	13.6	9.8	2.4	4.7	52.3	5.8
Change, 1985-8	-2.9	-0.4	-1.0	–	+3.4	-1.6	+0.6
Lowest-impact areas							
(N=14)							
1985	10.2	11.8	7.1	(a)	0.8	58.5	11.2
1988	7.8	10.1	6.5	2.4	3.4	57.5	11.2
Change, 1985-8	-2.4	-1.7	-0.6	–	+2.6	-1.0	0.0

Party abbreviations:
M Moderate   KdS Christian Democrats   Mp Environmental Party
C Centre Party   S Social Democratic Workers Party
Fp People's Party   VPK Left Communist Party
(a) In 1985 the KdS and Centre parties campaigned jointly, an alliance which dissolved by 1988.

votes, then Moderate, then Liberal.

In the 1988 election, the bourgeois and socialist blocs lost a combined 3.6 per cent share in the highest-impact group, with 3.4 per cent of this going to the Greens and the rest to smaller parties. In the lowest-impact group, the main blocs lost a similar 3.3 per cent with 2.6 per cent going to the Greens and 0.7 per cent to 'other'. Insignificant proportions of vote share had changed hands between the 1982 and 1985 elections.

As for the Greens, they are the only party to show growth in mean share in both the lowest- and highest-impact groups in the 1988 election (see Table 4). The Left Communists showed no change in share in the lowest-impact group, but were the only party other than the Greens to show growth in the highest-impact municipalities; while among the larger parties, all of which lost share, the Centre Party fared the best, declining just 0.4 per cent on average in the 14 highest-impact communities.

Furthermore, in 1988 the Christian Democrats split from their 1985 coalition with the Centre, so that much of the Centre Party decline is attributable to votes which shifted back to the Christian Democrats. Added to the Centre Party's share, the 2.4 per cent earned by the Christian Democrats would have given the Centre Party 2.0 per cent increase in the highest-impact regions and a 0.7 per cent increase in the low-impact areas.

Based on these observations, the partisanship patterns we see in the test groups have two implications for the analysis of Miljöpartiet growth rates:

Firstly, partisan alignments are visibly different in the two groups, with socialist strength in the lowest-impact regions significantly greater than in the highest, greater even than in the country as a whole. The possibility that variations in levels of Miljöpartiet growth are due to partisan structural factors, and not to impacts from Chernobyl, is therefore plausible and cannot be ruled out without further study. Neither, however, does the evidence rule out the possibility that public reaction to Chernobyl's impact was responsible for the greater increase in Green Party share, in the group subject to the highest levels of radioactive fallout.

Secondly, it appears that the national pattern of partisan shifts in 1988 was generally reflected in both the highest- and lowest-impact groups: all of the major parties lost vote share to the Miljöpartiet (and the Christian Democrats), with the notable exception of the Left Communists whose share was unchanged in the lowest-impact areas and grew slightly in the highest-impact region. Among the large parties, the Centre fared the best in the highest-impact districts, declining just 0.4 per cent on average.

The evidence further shows that all four of the anti-nuclear parties - the Greens, the Centre the Christian Democrats and the Left Communists - fared better in the highest-impact group than in the lowest.

The most important remaining puzzle is that nothing in the comparison of electoral trends in high- and low-impact regions has explained why both groups had a growth rate lower than the country as a whole. For all of Sweden, the Miljöpartiet electoral share increased from 1.5 per cent to 5.5 per cent between 1985 and 1988, a rise of 4.0 per cent.

When mean percentage gains for Green party vote share are calculated, the high-radiation-impact group does appear to have a greater rate of increase than the low-impact group; but why did the 14 communities with the highest levels of radiation only average a 3.34 per cent increase, as far below the national rate as it is above the lower group?

And, when 44 communities with somewhat lesser radiation levels are added to the pool of high-impact districts. why does the mean increase in Green Party share go up 4 to 3.51 per cent? If increases in vote share are related to intensity of fallout impact, as they would appear to be from a comparison between the highest and lowest impact regions, then the same relationship should generally hold between other groups of communities, even within the high-impact area

Finally, even if we accept at face value the finding that,in regions greatly affected by fallout, the Greens' electoral showing was greater by about one-fifth, what would account for the other four-fifths? In terms of explaining the electoral fortunes of the Miljöpartiet de Gröna analysis of Chernobyl's fallout impact on Sweden leads us to puzzles as significant as the answers it apparently provides. To help resolve these issues, and shed more light on the growth of the Miljöpartiet de Gröna, we now turn to public opinion data collected in Sweden during the period 1986-88. Perhaps here we shall find more clues about the general question of ecological crisis, and its impact on political change.

Public Opinion and the 'Environmental Election'

When a valve at the Three Mile Island (TMI) nuclear plant malfunctioned, sending radioactive steam drifting across central Pennsylvania farmlands, support for nuclear power in the United States suffered a setback from which it has never recovered. Opinion polls measured a decline of as much as 20 percentage points in the number of US citizens who favoured any further nuclear development.[10] No new plant has been ordered in the United States since the accident, and 69 planned facilities have been cancelled. While the decline of nuclear power in America must be attributed primarily to economic factors, the important role played by public fears and the dramatic shift in public opinion after TMI is undeniable.

In Sweden, the Chernobyl accident had a similar effect on public opinion, and appears likely to contribute to an even worse fate for the nuclear power industry there. In the 1980 referendum, 39 per cent had voted for Option 3, calling for an immediate end to nuclear expansion, and the closing of all existing plants within ten years, while better than 60 per cent supported continued operation of 12 plants. Polls taken shortly after Chernobyl found these figures reversed: opposition had risen to 60 per cent and support fallen below 40 per cent (Mosey 1986, p. 11).

Two years later, in March 1988, a national poll conducted by the Swedish Institute for Opinion Research (SIFO) found the public to favour a Social Democratic proposal to close two existing plants, in 1995 and 1996, by a margin of 47 per cent to 37 per cent.[11] As in the United States, support for nuclear energy has not recovered since the disaster. In November 1988 SIFO found the government's current programme to close all of Sweden's plants by 2010 was endorsed by 55 per cent of the respondents. This represented an erosion of only five points from the highest level of opposition just after Chernobyl.

In Swedish politics, the Miljöpartiet is closely linked to the anti-nuclear movement and its umbrella organization, the People's Campaign Against Nuclear Power, and in 1986 the two groups shared a storefront headquarters in Stockholm. In the new climate of general hostility to nuclear power following Chernobyl, it would be reasonable to expect the Miijöpartiet to benefit politically.

Such a result, however, is anything but automatic. Opinion polls, as we have seen, indicated a dramatic shift against nuclear power plants located in Sweden following the Chernobyl accident, despite a strong lobbying effort by the industry's supporters. And, from its inception after the 1980 referendum, the Miljöpartiet has been the party most strenuously opposed to nuclear energy. None the less, neither fact could be expected to alter Sweden's remarkably stable partisan alignments, unless significant portions of the voting public viewed environmental issues as central, and the

Miljöpartiet programme as both politically competent and environmentally sound. An informed and fully mobilized electorate like Sweden's will not easily shift support to a new party, simply on the basis of one lesser issue: votes in this tightly balanced partisan system are not 'wasted' lightly (see Vedung 1988a).

Surveys conducted between 1986 and 1988 show that on these two key points – the importance of the environment as a political issue, and perceptions of the Miljöpartiet – public views strongly favoured a breakthrough by the ecologists. Even before Chernobyl, of course, the environment was important to Swedish voters, in recent years ranking second only to unemployment as the nation's top political question. In a poll conducted by SIFO for Volvo just before the accident, in the four industrial cities of Göteborg (the country's second largest), Olofström, Skövde and Uddevalla, 42 per cent of 2500 respondents ranked unemployment as one of the top two issues while 34 per cent named the environment.

Before the end of 1986, however, the environment surpassed unemployment to become the single most important political issue in Sweden. A national SIFO poll conducted in December 1986 for the national Industry Association found 64 per cent naming the environment as one of the three top issues, ahead of unemployment at 58 per cent and taxes at 35 per cent. Publication of the SIFO results in early 1987 – made more dramatic by charges that the study was 'secret' – helped lift environmental policy to the top of the parties' agendas for the 1988 election. 'For the first time now', wrote a SIFO pollster, 'it became generally known in the media that the environment was the most important political question for the general public. Leaders of the political parties began to talk even more about the environment' (Sjöström 1989, p. 9).

Later in 1987 another poll reaffirmed the environment's position at the top. Asked which one political question would be most important for the new government after the 1988 elections, 27 per cent named the environment, should a bourgeois government come to power, while 33 per cent said the environment, should the socialists retain control. The second most important issue was thought to be taxes for a bourgeois government (23 per cent), and unemployment for a socialist regime (19 per cent).

Public perceptions and awareness of the Environmental Party also improved in the months following Chernobyl. In the 1986 SIFO/Volvo poll, between 11 per cent and 14 per cent had named the Greens as the party they trusted most on the environmental question, compared with 17-22 per cent for the Social Democrats and 15-22 per cent for the Centre. In the same poll 23 per cent felt a new environmental party was necessary, that none of the existing parties (including the Miljöpartiet) could solve the environmental problem. 'This question may now seem interesting', wrote

Sjöström, 'but as late as the spring of 1986 the Environmentalist Party did not seem a realistic alternative to the established parties...[and] was written about very seldom in the newspapers' (Sjöström 1989, p. 8).

In November 1986 SIFO surveyed Swedes to find out how well known the nation's small parties were among the public. Three parties not represented in Parliament were recognized by the electorate: the *Arbetarepartiet kommunisterna* (Communist Labour Party, APK) was familiar to 8 per cent, the *Kommunistiska partiet marxist-leninisterna* (Communist Party, Marxist-Leninist, KPMLR) to 10 per cent, and the *Miljöpartiet de Gröna* to an astounding 61 per cent. As a result SIFO changed the way it conducted its periodic 'electoral barometers', giving the *Miljöpartiet* separate standing from the other small parties.

The very next survey, in January 1987, found the Greens with support from 3.0 per cent of the nation's prospective voters. In November 1986, using an earlier, cumbersome method in which respondents were required to write in small party names, while larger parties were selected with colour-coded envelopes, the Greens scored 1.6 per cent - with much of the difference attributed by SIFO to the change in method (Sjöström 1989, p. 10). In the next survey (February 1987) the Greens passed the critical 4.0 per cent threshold, reaching 4.5 per cent. Thus, during the 13 months between January 1986 and February 1987, support for the Greens *more than tripled* from less than 1.5 per cent to 4.5 per cent. For the first time SIFO, Sweden's most experienced survey research organization, announced that the Green Environmental Party had acquired sufficient support among the voters to gain seats in the *Riksdag* (see Figure 3).

Between February 1987 and the end of the year support for the Greens increased less rapidly, to stand at 4.9 per cent in the January 1988 barometer. After January, however, the final months of the campaign saw another period of rapid increase like that of 1986 and early 1987. In a June 1988 party preference poll by Statistics Sweden (SCB), 6.5 per cent said they planned to vote for the Greens. Then, in one of the final polls before the election, SIFO found in August that 8 per cent of those who did not think the Greens were the best party were considering voting for them anyway.

Polls show that the Greens' credibility regarding environmental policy was also on the upswing. In May 1988, 50 per cent of the respondents in a national poll named the *Miljöpartiet* as the party with the best ideas for solving the environmental problem, compared with 12 per cent for the Social Democrats, 10 per cent for the Centre, and less than 5 per cent for each of the other parties - and compared with the Greens' own 11-14 per cent in the April 1986 SIFO/Volvo survey.

Finally, in the August SIFO poll, 50 per cent indicated their belief that, if the *Miljöpartiet* entered the *Riksdag*, it would lead to a renewal (*förnyelse*) of parliament, a figure identical to an earlier reading in June; while the

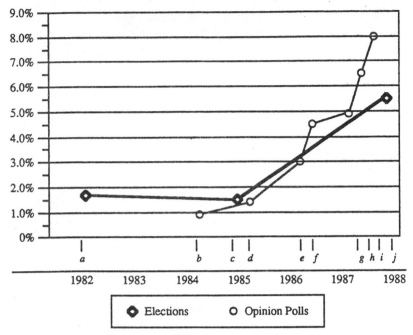

Figure 3 National trends, support for the Miljöpartiet, 1982–8
a. National Riksdag election, September 1982.
b. SIFO election barometer, January 1985 (see note, below).
c. National Riksdag election, September 1985.
d. SIFO election barometer, January 1986 (see note, below).
e. SIFO election barometer, January 1987.
f. SIFO special survey, February 1987.
g. SIFO election barometer, January 1988.
h. Party preferences survey, Statistics, Sweden, (SCB), June 1988.
i. SIFO special survey for Aftonbladett newspaper, August 1988.
j. National Riksdag election, September 1988.
Note: Before the election barometer of 1987, SIFO's surveys grouped the Miljöpartiet
with other small parties. In the 1985 survey these parties showed a combined support of
1%, and in 1986, 1.5%. The graph uses estimates for the Miljöpartiet of not more than
0.9% and 1.4% in those two years. The true figures are lower.

percentage who expected the Greens to bring chaos (primarily Moderate
Party supporters) declined from 32 per cent in June to 24 per cent in
August.

Between early 1986 and late 1988, then, two trends in public opinion
appear to have increased support for the Miljopartiet de Gröna: the environment
during 1986 became the nation's top political issue, a standing it did not
relinquish throughout 1987 and 1988; and the public came to view the

Greens as having the best ideas for addressing environmental problems, while bringing 'renewal' to the Riksdag. The combined effect was to increase rapidly and steadily the numbers of voters who would support the Greens in 1988, at what may someday be seen as a turning point in Swedish politics.

The Politics of Ecological Crisis

'There would be no environmental politics, and no green parties, without the existence of environmental problems' (Lowe and Rüdig 1986, p. 536).

The preceding discussion of the Swedish Miljöpartiet de Gröna, using an analysis of Chernobyl's radiation impact, in the context of public opinion shifts between 1986 and 1988, suggests a number of conclusions regarding the Chernobyl accident's role in shaping subsequent political events in Sweden. The study's findings may be summarized in the following way.

¶ Swedish communities subject to the highest levels of radioactive fallout from Chernobyl showed an additional measure of growth in vote share for the ecologically radical Green Environmental Party, above that seen in the lowest-impact areas, amounting to just over 21 per cent of the total increase.

¶ Whatever factor led to this difference between the highest- and lowest-impact regions appears not to have been effective before 1985: analysis of trends in the earlier 1982-5 period does not reveal the same difference between the two regions.

¶ As possible explanation of the variation in Green Party growth trends, differences in partisan alignments were compared, and it was found that in the areas showing lower radiation impact and lesser Green Party growth, the socialist bloc did enjoy a larger margin vis-a-vis the non-socialist parties. In other ways partisan structures in the regions were very similar, and showed nearly identical patterns of partisan change in the period 1982-8, making it impossible to accept confidently or rule out this alternative.

¶ In both the areas of highest radiation impact and those of lowest, all the major parties lost vote share to the Green Environmental Party and, to a smaller degree, to the Christian Democratic Party; with the notable exception of the Left Communist Party whose share was unchanged in the lowest-impact region and grew slightly in the highest-impact areas. In the 1988 election the Left Communist and Green Environmental parties' environmental programme were very similar, although the two parties differed substantially on labour and economic policy.

¶ Among the large parties, the anti-nuclear Centre Party fared the best in the highest-impact regions, declining just 0.4 per cent on average. Had its 1985 electoral coalition with the Christian Democrats continued into the 1988 election, it seems likely the Centre would have been the only major party to gain vote share in both the highest-

and lowest-impact regions.

¶ All four of the anti-nuclear parties - the Greens, the Centre, the Christian Democrats and the Left Party Communists – fared better in the highest-impact group than in the lowest.

¶ It was also observed, but not explained, that the growth in Green Party share was lower in both the highest and lowest-radiation-impact regions than in Sweden as a whole.

¶ Public opinion polls for the period 1986-8 were analysed, and it was found that, after the Chernobyl accident, opposition to nuclear power in Sweden rose to 60 per cent, receding to 55 per cent by November of 1988. These figures compare with the 39 per cent in 1980 who voted for Option 3, the anti-nuclear choice, in a national referendum on Sweden's nuclear development policy.

¶ Surveys revealed that some time between April and December 1986 the environment became Sweden's single most important political question, rising above unemployment and taxes for the first time.

¶ In almost the same period, between January 1986 and February 1987, electoral support for the Green Party, as reflected in opinion polls, rose from less than 1.5 per cent to 4.5 per cent after hovering between 0.9 per cent and 1.5 per cent for at least two years, and probably much longer.

¶ Between April 1986 and May 1988, public estimation of the Green Environmental Party's environmental programme improved dramatically, until 50 per cent of the voters of all parties believed the Greens to have the best ideas for solving environmental problems.

¶ Finally, surveys revealed that, in addition to confidence in the Greens' environmental programme, the Swedish voting public also felt that the ecologists' entry into parliament would revitalize the Swedish legislature.

The stories told by radiation impact analysis, public opinion data, and the outcome of the election itself all point to Chernobyl. Some time between the national elections of 1985 and 1988, two groups of municipalities which had shown similar trends in support for the Environmental Party between 1982 and 1985 took different paths. In one, the growth of support for the Greens was measurably greater than in the other. The municipalities in question were selected for comparison not by size, nor by partisanship, nor by demographics: they were classified into one group or the other based on levels of fallout received from the most serious nuclear plant accident since the harnessing of atomic power four decades earlier. Something happened between 1985 and 1988 to shape political change in those communities in this particular way.

In early 1986 the environment ranked second on the priority list of Swedish public issues, while by the end of the year it had become the most important single political question. In preparation for the 1988 election, Sweden's political parties virtually tripped over one another to get on the environmental bandwagon. The Social Democratic government announced plans for an early shutdown of two operating nuclear plants, despite opposition from industry and several of the most powerful labour groups. The other parties adopted competing environmental programmes, with proposals ranging from grants for catalytic converters, to penalties on truck transport, and the elimination of fossil fuel use by the year 2013. Something happened in 1986 to shake up the Swedish public and political establishment and raise environmental issues to the very top of the national agenda.

Finally, at some point in time between January 1986 and February 1987, public support for the Green Environmental Party began a sharp upward trend which persisted throughout 1987 and 1988, carrying the small, seven year old ecology party into Parliament, all twenty-six regional governments, and 260 of 284 municipal governments as well.

These trends all suggest very strongly that the accident at Chernobyl was a precipitating crisis: after Chernobyl, Swedish public opinion, environmental politics, and partisan alignments all manifested measurable and dramatic change, the end results of which have been considerable strengthening of environmental protection policies, the likely demise of nuclear power, and an opportunity for the Miljöpartiet de Gröna to prove itself (or not) at the national level. It is true that environmental disasters after Chernobyl, including the bloom of toxic algae in the North Sea, the subsequent deaths of millions of fish, and the unrelated lethal plague among Kattegat harbour seals, were important as well, coming as they did in the Summer months just before the election; they may have been responsible for the second sharp upswing in support for the Greens during 1988, and for the high percentages the Greens gained in communities along the western coast.

Yet, the evidence evaluated here suggests that the most important shifts in environmental opinion and support for the Miljöpartiet de Gröna came earlier, beginning in the spring of 1986 - at just the time of the Chernobyl disaster. Like the first great tremour of an earthquake, Chernobyl shook the foundations of Swedish politics. Later aftershocks, including the algae, the seals, and the Ebbe Carlsson affair, helped guarantee the house would never lean quite the same way again - but it was almost certainly Chernobyl which sparked the great initial change in public opinions, government policies, and electoral politics.

Political Analysis and Green Politics

The evidence about Chernobyl's impact on Sweden's 1988 election suggests that in the analysis of democratic politics, in Europe and elsewhere, a greater role must be ascribed to objective ecological conditions, at least where the 'new politics' parties are concerned. Prevailing currents in the study of ecological politics – *value shifts, linkage failure,* and *opportunity structures* – fail otherwise to explain the rise of the Swedish Miljöpartiet.

For example, the overtly postmaterialist values and corresponding policy goals of Environmental Party activists had failed before 1988 to attract broad electoral support, even among Sweden's large, affluent and educated 'new class'. In the absence of evidence that postmaterialist value shifts within the general Swedish public accelerated rapidly after 1985, the 1988 election results must be explained in some other way. And, even if such a value shift were identified, the task of explaining its emergence would remain. Are we to believe that Sweden became significantly more affluent, or the 'new class' significantly more active politically, during these three years? In the light of this study's findings, it seems more plausible to conclude that what changed between 1985 and 1988 was not the public's underlying attitudinal alignment along a materialist-postmaterialist dimension, but rather, its perception of very real ecological threats and its distribution along the range of preferred environmental policy alternatives.

In fact, the Swedish case implies that environmentalism can become mainstream politics, given sufficiently powerful ecological crises as a precipitate. For this reason the appearance of postmaterialism, a catch-all designation for 60s and 70s-style values and social movements, seems less than sufficient explanation for Green Party growth, if over time one of the key colours in the postmaterialist rainbow - ecology green - can become part of dominant politics as it did in Sweden. Materialists and postmaterialists alike became convinced that environmental protection was an important political issue, and environmental opinions were arrayed across the partisan spectrum just like opinions in any other policy category. It was not postmaterialism *per se* which lifted the Swedish Greens into national prominence. Rather, widespread fear and uncertainty, sparked by ecological crisis of unimaginable scale, seem to have been the powerful motivators for ideological realignment regarding environmental politics, a realignment for which the Greens were the primary, though not the only, electoral beneficiaries.

Secondly, while the failure of Sweden's existing parliamentary parties to link sufficiently with the early environmental movement helped create founding conditions for the Miljöpartiet, by 1988 all parties from left to right (with the possible exception of the reluctant Moderates) were making extraordinary efforts to ride the newest wave of environmental sentiment – or at least not be swamped by it. It appears that, because the stakes were high enough (and public attitudes insistent enough), the Swedish party system was compelled to build linkages to the renascent environmental movement, in order to limit political damage. These efforts were not enough, it turned out, to keep the upstart Greens out of the *Ridsdag*; and not enough to prevent the worst election in recent memory for the bourgeois parties; but enough at least to preserve the existing Social Democratic regime and deprive the Greens of the balance of power.

In this case electoral success by the ecology party *and* relatively successful mainstream party linkage were found to coexist. We cannot simply assert that the Miljöpartiet success reflects a linkage failure, unless we are willing to ignore the fact that the Swedish partisan landscape in 1988 was littered with bountiful evidence of aggressive linkage efforts by all seven parties: environmental handbills, position papers, and official pronouncements. Again, our explanation is improved when we include consideration of the ecological context in our assessment of political change, even from the perspective of linkage failure, and recognise that the credibility and effectiveness of partisan linkage efforts - vis-a-vis environmental politics and ecology parties - will ultimately depend on the public's perception of actual environmental conditions and risks.

Finally, using Kitschelt's political opportunity descriptors, Sweden, characterized by affluent welfare state corporatism, socialist dominance, and early opposition to nuclear power, appears an ideal candidate for the emergence of a green party, satisfying all five of his structural preconditions. Yet, the five existed in Sweden long before the Greens entered Parliament. It was not until the single Kitschelt predictor which is environmental in nature - the conflict over nuclear power - reached crisis proportions following the Chernobyl accident, that the Swedish Greens were able to overcome existing structural constraints and make the final breakthrough into the Riksdag. Once again, analytical efforts are enhanced when they provide a central role for objective environmental conditions.

Several other analysts, uncomfortable with the absence of the environment from explanations of ecological politics, have recently attempted to focus attention on objective ecological problems. Two such efforts are those of Eckersley (1989) and Rohrschneider (1988).

Eckersley, for instance, argues that much of the postmaterialism literature, especially its 'class-interest' variant, is devoid of ecological crisis, while in fact 'the present scale and gravity of environmental degradation is the worst that the planet has known, and much of this degradation has taken place in the latter half of this century' (Eckersley 1989, p. 220).

Eckersley's project — explaining why the leadership of the ecology movement comes largely from the 'new class' of well-educated, generally public service, professionals — ends with observations that:

> the new class...[is] likely to be more aware of the scale and depth of the social and ecological problems facing the modern world and more able and motivated to become politically engaged in over-coming them...the actual, multi-faceted social and ecological crises facing the world today are the *sine qua non* of the green movement.

This crucial fact is downplayed by proponents of the class-based argument and ignored by Inglehart. My own conclusion is that the green movement ought to be accepted as a rational response to these objective crises...(Eckersley 1989, p. 223).

Analysing a similar question, the 'selfishness' of the ecology movement, Rohrschneider criticized simple psychological models ('postmaterialism' and 'self-interest') for failing to 'link environmental concerns to the true state of ecological affairs' (Rohrschneider 1988, p. 347). Using a 1982 Eurobarometer survey, Rohrschneider found that opinions about environmental crisis were shaped both by internal psychological structures and by reactions to perceived external conditions. These inner and outer measures he divided into three parts: postmaterialist value preferences, the inner factor, and two outer factors - perceptions of environmental damage to the nation and ecological threats to the self. Of the three dimensions, he found that the one showing the strongest effect on overall environmental opinion was concern for the national environment. 'These findings suggest', he wrote, 'that citizens hold favourable attitudes toward environmental protection because their value priorities have changed, and because they are worried about the true state of ecological problems' (Rohrschneider 1988, p. 363).

My analysis of Chernobyl and the Swedish Green Party lends further support to Eckersley's views regarding the 'rationality' of the green politics response to ecological crisis; and to Rohrschneider's findings that attitudes toward environmental protection are based most directly on perceptions of objective ecological problems. Additionally, while my analysis focused on local impacts in affected regions, Rohrschneider's emphasis on perceptions of the national environment may help explain why the increase in Miljöpartiet vote share was greatest in populous regions far from the areas of greatest radiation impact.

Based on the findings of this study it may be possible to sketch out a preliminary model for understanding how objective ecological crisis can affect political change, with a framework for analysing crises as they occur.

A Model of Ecological Crisis

To model the logic of a relationship between ecological crisis and political change, we need symbols for the objective crisis (either chronic or sudden in nature), the socially generated information which describes the crisis, social capacity for response, social impact, and finally, political effect deriving from the social impact.

For the sake of argument, of course, we could assert that there is no relationship in the first place: we might claim that the physical condition of the European environment was a factor in none of the region's elections since 1986, although, observing that ecology parties during these years have mounted their most successful campaigns ever, in Austria, West Germany, Switzerland, Finland, Italy, Ireland, the United Kingdom, France, Sweden, and the European Parliament, we might make such a claim with hesitation.[12] We would then be required to argue that the Chernobyl accident had little impact on later political events in Sweden.

Considering the *prima facie* evidence of the formation and growth of explicitly ecological political parties, as well as the evidence offered by this study of the Swedish case, the argument that objective environmental problems are unrelated to political events seems highly implausible. A more useful approach would be to describe how the relationship between eco-crisis and political change might work; to conceptualize possible interactions between physical environmental events, institutional frameworks mediating political impacts, and the political change we ultimately observe (see Figure 4).

Beginning with an ecological crisis we can conceive of how physical impacts may immediately be subject to mediation, depending on the quality of *social information*. In other words, some social impacts (in the short term) may be affected by the means available for detecting, measuring, and publicizing hazards which, as with radiation, can be invisible without specialized equipment. The crisis or event is thus politically potent (again, in the short term) only when it is known, when the scope of the problem can be assessed by officials, the public, or both.

Policy responses, broadly defined to include information policy (private and public) as well as technical, public health, and environmental practices, help process the way social information about a crisis shapes *social impact*. For nuclear accidents, policy responses might centre on public information and technical advice, including the establishment of food chain and personal exposure thresholds; on radiation monitoring; and on decontamination projects. At this stage interactions between past and present policy choices are significant: the quality of information available in the current crisis, and the consequent response options, depend on prior, anticipatory policies. An example from the Swedish case would be the creation in 1957 of a national radiation monitoring network, without which Sweden's response to Chernobyl's public health threat would have been much more difficult.

In some cases, when ecological damage is especially acute or broadly visible, policy responses may be less important in determining whether an impact is felt. As a case in point, it is clear that following the massive *Exxon Valdez* oil spill, the impact of biological and economic catastrophe would have been felt by managers, workers, clients, and neighbours of Alaskan fish hatcheries - even without mediating policy responses by corporate, federal, and state agencies. Dead hatchlings simply cannot be

Figure 4 Logic model: political impacts of ecological crisis

Ecological crisis	Social information	Policy response	Social impact	Political change
Nuclear accident	• Intensity • Toxicity • Distribution	• Public information • Food chain thresholds • Exposure thresholds • Monitoring • Detoxification	• Visible damage to environment • Cultural dislocation • Public health threat • Economic losses • Public opinion shift	• Change of government • Partisan realignment • Environmental policy shift
Chernobyl fallout over Sweden	High intensity Known Positive toxicity Known Wide distribution Known	Accident announced immediately Thresholds lowered and enforced Monitoring expanded Decontamin-ation ordered, implemented	Cultural dislocation *Severe* Environmental opinions *Intensified* Visible damage *Limited* Economic losses *Significant* Health threat *Uncertain* Current pathologies *Minimal*	Social Democrats remain in power, non-socialists lose ground Greens enter Riksdag with twenty deputies Regional governments imbalanced All parties shift environmental policies

released or harvested, no matter what the government says or does. As it was, of course, policy response mediated those potential effects. In the same way, public knowledge about the spill did not depend on special detection equipment or policies, although testing and official reports have shaped subsequent debates over the spill and clean-up. At least for residents of the area, the scope of the crisis was all too visible with the 'naked eye'.

In other types of crises, however, including long-distance fallout incidents like Chernobyl, many social effects, especially economic losses, will depend to a great extent on existing public policies, and on how agencies react to the crisis. If, for instance, minimum contamination levels for foodstuffs were not set and enforced, the economic impacts of a nuclear accident at a geographically distant location would be minimal.

The final step in the logic model is to conceptualize how social impacts - scenic despoliation, cultural dislocation, economic losses, public health effects - lead to *attitudinal shifts*, and thence (in democratic systems) to *political change*. While the role played by political mobilization or partisan and policy preferences will vary from system to system, attitudinal factors will be of *some* importance everywhere. The model incorporates the premise, derived from this study of Chernobyl and Sweden, that given sufficiently powerful social effects and, in democratic systems, attitudinal shifts, an ecological crisis can trigger political change, by forcing economic, energy, environmental and public health policy adjustments, by government and/ or opposition; or by sparking partisan realignment with or without a change in regime.

As we saw in Sweden, the 1988 elections manifested both of these political effects: although the Social Democratic hold on state power was strengthened and the national formation of socialist and non-socialist blocs preserved, the *Miljöpartiet de Gröna*, the Green Environmental Party, entered the *Riksdag*, the first new party to do so in seventy years; all seven major parties moved toward more protective environmental policies; and, at the important local levels of government, the Greens gained enough seats to hold the balance of power between the socialist and non-socialist blocs, in many municipalities and in nine of 26 counties.

The case of Chernobyl and the Swedish Greens tells us that environmental crisis can affect political change, and suggests that techniques for modelling its impacts should be part of our political analysis toolbox. As Chernobyl, *Exxon Valdez*, and other crises around the globe will continue to remind us, ecological disasters may become the most permanent legacy of the twentieth century. Our survival into the twenty-first may depend on understanding all we can about how these crises shape our lives, our communities and our politics.

NOTES

1   An earlier version of this chapter was presented at the Annual Meeting of the American Political Science Association, Atlanta, Georgia, on 1 September 1989. I am indebted to the A. Alfred Taubman Center at Brown University, which provided material support throughout the preparation of this paper. Professor Thomas J. Anton, director of the Center, deserves special credit for encouraging my interest in European politics, assisting with English translations, and for many other services only a gracious and helpful colleague can provide. Alf Sjöström at the Swedish Institute for Public Opinion in Stockholm kindly provided survey data, as well as excerpts from his book on the 1988 Swedish elections. Finally, Marna Feldt and the Swedish Information Service in New York proved to be extremely

helpful local resources in my navigation of Swedish government agencies.

2 Western experts are sceptical about these official Soviet figures for casualties and radiation exposure levels. Actual figures are surely somewhat higher, although there is no doubt that early Western reports of thousands dead and injured were erroneous (see Maples 1986, pp. 130-41 and Marples 1988, pp. 32-7). In any case, the largest number of casualties probably will occur in the future, as victims succumb to 'excess cancers' spawned by the fallout.

3 For applications of the postmaterialist values-green politics approach, see, for example, Poguntke 1987 or Schoonmaker 1988. Von Beyme (1985) argued that the ecology movement does not *have* a unified class base; Lowe and Rüdig (1986) that radical political ecology runs *contrary* to the class interests of its adherents; and Frankel (1987), that postmaterialists will *never* challenge economic interests of the 'new class,' namely, the welfare state's public service bureaucracies which employ many who are of postmaterialist inclination.

4 Lawson and Merkl's entire volume (1988) is dedicated to this approach (see also Lawson 1980). Others who have focused on the interaction between traditional party systems and the new parties, although not necessarily calling it *linkage failure* include Kolinsky (1987) and Daalder (1987). Rüdig also argued that the 'failure to penetrate existing party politics was one important, if not the most important, input into the formation process of separate ecological or green parties' (Rüdig 1988, p. 33).

5 According to Swedish electoral law, the 4 per cent threshold which governs apportionment of seats in the *Riksdag* does not apply to smaller jurisdictions. There is no hurdle at all in municipal elections, and county council elections require only 3 per cent of votes cast in order to gain seats.

6 Outside the Soviet Union between 28 April and 2 May 1986, fallout was detected in Sweden, Finland, Poland, Denmark, Norway, Austria, Hungary, Italy, Yugoslavia, East Germany, West Germany, Turkey, Switzerland, France, the United Kingdom, the Netherlands, Belgium, and Greece. Wind patterns would have also deposited some radiation in Czechoslovakia, Romania, Bulgaria, and Albania (Mould 1988, p. 43). In Sweden, deposited isotopes included, in order of magnitude, cesium-137, iodine-131, tellurium-132, cesium-134, barium-140, neptunium-239, tellurium-129, ruthenium-103, molybdenum-99, cesium-136, niab-95, zirconium-95, cerium-141 and -144, ruthenium-106, plutonium-241, curium-242, plutonium-239, plutonium-240, americum-241, plutonium-238, and curium-244. In all rutenium-103, barium-140, cerium-141, tellur-132, lautan-140, cirkonium-95, niab-95, and strontium-90 (SSI 1986, p. 14).

7 The Swedish government's rationale for setting the 300 Bq/kg limit was based on the maximum dosages thought safe for young children, the persons most at risk from long-term exposure. 'For cesium, then, an annual dose of 5 mSv would correspond to a daily intake of 137 Bq. Assuming an intake of some 0.3 kg per day (for a 1-year-old) and rounding off, gave the activity limit of 0.3 kBq [300 Bq] per kilogram (liter)...'(SSI 1986, p. 8).

8 Even without a permanent swing position between the two blocs, the Greens' new parliamentary role would prove to be crucial in February 1990, when their refusal to support a Social Democratic austerity plan finally forced that Government's resignation. Failing to win VPK support for a strike-ban proposal, the Social Democrats had turned to the Greens, whose 20 votes were sufficient to preserve the plan - and the Government.

But negotiations with the Greens broke down the weekend of 10-11 February, the Social Democrats lost the critical 15 February vote in the *Riksdag*, and the Government was forced to resign.

9 For instance, surveys from the 1985 election showed that 36 per cent of the Green electorate came from the ranks of blue-collar and lower-level white-collar workers, exactly the same proportion as for the Liberals and Christian Democrats, and comparable to the Centre's 40 per cent and the Moderates' 31 per cent. For both the Left Communist and Social Democratic parties, the percentage of supporters who are blue-collar and lower-level white-collar was 75 per cent (*Svenska Institutet* 1987, p. 2).

10 A national poll taken on 15-18 March 1979 showed 72 per cent of Americans favoured further nuclear plant construction, while 22 per cent were opposed (Opinion Research Corporation). Two weeks later just after the 28 March accident, support had fallen to 52 per cent, while opposition had increased to 42 per cent (ABC News/Louis Harris). For surveys questioning support for nuclear plants *near the respondent*, favourable sentiment fell from 55 per cent before the accident to 30 per cent afterwards (CBS News/New York Times; Institute for Survey Research, Princeton University).

11 A gender gap strongly affected the results of this national poll: Swedish women favoured the accelerated phase-out proposal, by a margin of 59 per cent to 27 per cent, while men *opposed* the proposal 60 per cent to 37 per cent.

12 The prominence of environmental formations in the Eastern European and Soviet mobilizations of 1989 and 1990 provide further evidence that political responses to objective ecological conditions must be viewed as important elements of contemporary political analysis.

REFERENCES

Bergström, H. (1988). 'Social democrats still going strong - incorporating the green wave?' *Current Sweden*, No. 367, 10/88.

Daalder, H. (ed.) (1987), *Party Systems in Denmark, Austria, Switzerland, the Netherlands and Belgium*. New York: St Martin's Press.

Dalton, R. J., Flanagan, S.C., and Beck, P. A. (1984). *Electoral Change in Advanced Industrial Societies: Realignment or Dealignment?* Princeton N.J.: Princeton University Press.

Dewachter, W. (1987). 'Changes in a Particratie: The Belgian party system from 1944 to 1986' in Daalder, 1987, pp.285-363.

Dyring, E. (1987). 'Sweden after Chernobyl: Revival of the nuclear power debate', *Current Sweden*, No. 354, 3/87.

Eckersley, R. (1989). 'Green politics and the new class: selfishness or virtue?' *Political Studies*, Vol. 36, pp. 205-23.

Edin, K. (1987). 'Sweden after Chernobyl: Consequences of the nuclear accident', *Current Sweden*, No. 353, 2/87.

Frankel, B. (1987). *The Post-Industrial Utopians*. Madison, Wi: University of Wisconsin Press.

Gustafsson, A. (1988). *Local Government in Sweden*. Stockholm: Svenska Institutet.

Inglehart, R. (1977). *The Silent Revolution: Changing Values and Political Styles among Western Publics*. Princeton N.J.: Princeton University Press.

Inglehart, R. (1981). 'Post-materialism in an environment of insecurity', *American Political Science Review*, Vol. 75, pp. 880-900.

Inglehart. R. (1984). 'The changing structure of political cleavages in Western society', in Dalton, *et al*. 1984, 25-69.

Kerr, H. H. (1987). 'The Swiss party system: Steadfast and changing', in Daalder 1987, pp. 107-192.

Kitschelt, H. P. (1988a). 'Left-Libertarian parties: Explaining innovation in competititve party systems', World Politics, Vol. 40, pp. 194-234.

Kitschelt, H. P. (1988b). 'Structure, interests, and ideas in the analysis of political parties: Reconstructing the experience of European ecology parties' presented at the 1988 Annual Meeting of the American Political Science Association, Washington, D.C.

Koblik, S. (1988). 'Predicting the great one', Political Life in Sweden, No. 26, 12/88.

Kolinsky, E. (ed.) (1987). Opposition in Western Europe. New York: St Martin's Press.

Lagercrantz, A. (1988). 'The political scene in Sweden prior to the autumn parliamentary elections', Current Sweden, No. 360, 4/88.

Landstingsförbundet. (1982, 1985, 1988). Statistisk Årsbok för Landsting (Statistical Abstract for County Councils). Stockholm: Federation of County Councils.

Landstingsförbundet. (1989). The County Councils in Sweden - their Responsibilities and Activities. Stockholm: Federation of County Councils.

Lawson, K. (1980). Political Parties and Linkage: A Comparative Perspective. New Haven CT: Yale University Press.

Lawson, K. and Merkl, P. H. (eds.) (1988). When Parties Fail: Emerging Alternative Organizations. Princeton N.J.: Princeton University Press.

Lowe, P. D. and Rüdig, W. (1986). 'Political ecology and the social sciences - the state of the art', British Journal of Political Science, Vol. 16, pp. 513-50.

Marples, D. R. (1986). Chernobyl and Nuclear Power in the USSR. New York: St Martin's Press.

Marples, D. R. (1988). The Social Impact of the Chernobyl Disaster. New York: St Martin's Press.

Mosey, C. (1986). 'We are not as radioactive as you've been led to believe', Sweden Now, Vol. 20, No. 4., pp. 7-13.

Mosey, C. (1988). 'Socialists hold Greens in check', Sweden Now, Vol. 22, No. 6, pp. 20-3.

Mould, R. F. (1988). Chernobyl: The Real Story. Oxford: Pergamon Press.

Poguntke, T. (1987). 'New politics and party systems: The emergence of a new type of party?' West European Politics, Vol. 10, pp. 76-88.

Riksskatteverket. (1982, 1985, 1988). Riksdagsvalet kommunvis (Election to Riksdag by municipality). Stockholm: The National Tax Board.

Rohrschneider, R. (1988). 'Citizens' attitudes toward environmental issues: selfish or selfless?' Comparative Political Studies, Vol. 21, pp. 347-67

Rüdig, W. (1988). 'Peace and ecology movements in Western Europe', West European Politics, Vol 11, No. 1, p. 26-39.

Sainsbury, D. (1986). 'The 1985 Swedish election: The conservative upsurge is checked', West European Politics, Vol. 9, pp. 293-7.

Schoonmaker, D. (1988). 'The challenge of the Greens to the West German party system', in Lawson, and Merkl, 1988, pp. 41-75.

Silver, L. R. (1987). Fallout From Chernobyl. Toronto: Doneau.

Sjöström, A. (1989). The Environmental Question in the Election. Stockholm: Svenska Institutet för Opinionsundersökningar (Swedish Institute for Opinion Research, SIFO).

Smith, G. H. (1988). 'Green is go', Sweden Now, Vol. 22, No. 3, pp. 18-20.

SSI (1986). Chernobyl - its impact on Sweden. SSI-Rapport 86-12 Stockholm: Statens Strålskyddsinstitut National Institute of Radiation Protection.

Strandberg, H. (1988). 'Time for an environmental election?' Current Sweden, No. 362, 5/88.

Svenska Institutet. (1987). 'The Swedish political parties', *Fact Sheets on Sweden*, No. 16, 8/87.

Vedung, E. (1988a). 'The Swedish five-party syndrome and the environmentalists', in Lawson, and Merkl, 1988, pp. 76-109.

Vedung, E. (1988b). 'Green light for the Greens', *Inside Sweden*, No. 3-4, 12/88, pp. 67.

Von Beyme, K. (1985). *Political Parties in Western Democracies.* New York: St Martin's Press.

6. The Italian Ecology Movement: From Radicalism to Moderation

MARIO DIANI
Istituto di Economia Politica
Università Bocconi, Milano, Italy

Moderate and Radical Actors in the Italian Ecology Movement

In this chapter I aim to provide a reconstruction of the main events that the Italian ecology movement has gone through since early environmentalist organizations began to exert some (very limited) influence in Italian society in the late 1950s/early 1960s. In doing so I adopt a specific perspective, focusing upon major changes in patterns of alliances within the movement. In Italy, as well as in other countries such as Britain (Lowe and Goyder 1983) and Germany (Rucht 1989), environmental issues have been represented both by actors (individuals, groups and organisations) with moderate political orientations and by actors supporting far more radical world-views. Their patterns of interaction and alliance building have rarely been steady over time. Rather, linkages have been quite occasional in certain phases, quite intense in others. In Italy, political ecology groups which emerged out of previous social movements in the mid 1970s showed very limited connections to the already existing organisations devoted to nature protection. It was only in the early 1980s that cooperation tended to become more stable and frequent, and conflicts about different approaches to the environmental question gave way to more pragmatic attitudes. Indeed, in recent years alliances between moderate and radical sectors of the movement have become so frequent that one may legitimately speak of a highly unified movement.

The major questions I want to address in this chapter are precisely why reciprocal mistrust has been to a large extent overcome and why differences in sets of beliefs between environmental organisations, which still persist, are no longer a strong cause of fractionism. The problem of alliance building has not been at the core of environmental movement scholars' interest in recent years (but see Rucht 1989). On the contrary, the rise and development of environmental, ecology and anti-nuclear movements in the western world since the 1960s has largely been analysed as one of the most relevant and interesting aspects of the wider phenomenon which is usually labelled as 'new politics': new political issues and cleavages, new patterns of political behaviour, broader processes of value change. The 'newness' aspects in recent political and social movements have usually been emphasized, often in association with the leading role played in them by the so-called 'new middle class': young, well-educated people, active mostly in the services and information sectors as well as in the field of intellectual production. Some have even postulated (a) that the social and political changes currently in the making will eventually produce one or more new central cleavage(s), able to replace the more conventional ones, and to revitalize Western 'frozen' political systems; (b) that in the new era the new middle class is going to take up the role played by the working class in the bourgeois era. Moreover, conflicts and disputes about environmental issues will be of the utmost relevance in the new scenario.[1]

Although I am far from denying the 'newness' in the mobilizations of the last few decades, I think that concentrating exclusively upon it has been somewhat misleading. The reason is that contemporary mobilization processes are the product of 'old' and 'new' actors, interacting and exchanging with each other. If we assume that a social movement is an action system (Melucci 1989), whose collective identity and structure are not a mere 'precondition' for action, i.e. a datum, but the product of a social process which is worth investigating in depth, then we understand why it is important to look at the role played in new social movements by different social actors who are active on the same issues, or, at least, share some concern about them.

All this fits better possibly to the environmental movements than to other kinds of new social movements. Whereas the role of traditional, politically moderate actors in, say, the women's or the youth movements may either have been limited or have developed along different lines from the role of the 'new politics' actors, the same does not hold, rather, does not always hold, for the campaigns for environmental preservation, started in several western countries in recent years. As I have already remarked, environmental and ecology movements have quite often seen some sort of interaction between activists and constituents from moderate, traditional organisations and from radical ones, although with changing outcomes in terms of environmental politics: in some cases, (seemingly) long-lasting alliances have been established; in other cases, only sporadic contacts have been set up; in other cases still, patterns of interaction seem to have been changing substantially over time.

In my effort to describe and later explain such processes, I shall put a special emphasis upon changes in alliances between the most relevant ecology organisations. More specifically, I shall focus upon the relationships between the two basic sectors in the Italian ecology movement: the 'conventional ecology' sector, the organisations of which are more frequently supported by activists with moderate political orientations and weaker contacts with the overall social movement sector; and the 'political ecology' sector, which looks more likely to adopt unconventional styles of action and radical sets of beliefs. In particular, I intend to show how the original 'segmentation' of the movement in two rather self-centered and non-communicating sectors has slowly given place to a more unified and connected structure, with the leadership of the movement being held jointly by the most relevant organisations from different sectors. Drawing upon a simplified theory of action I shall try to explain changes in the relational structure of the movement in terms of three basic factors: (1) quality and quantity of resources available to social actors; (2) cultural frames (Gamson 1988; Snow and Benford 1988) adopted by actors in order to interpret and analyse their own situation; (3) external factors, such as 'political opportunity structure' (Tarrow 1983), 'facilitators' (see, e.g., Rüdig 1990) or, in the words of the organizational theory, 'systemic constraints' (see Scott 1981 for an overview). Availability or shortage of resources for action may push the actors to choose either more instrumental and goal-oriented patterns of action or more radical and expressive ones. The nature of cultural frames available to actors in a given society at a given time may have a long-lasting influence upon the way they frame reality and give an answer to the fundamental question, which puzzles any social movement: 'Who are *we*, who are *they*, *what* are we struggling for?' Finally, such frames can be developed in a more radical or reformist direction according to the degree of responsiveness of the established political actors (parties first) to the new issues; to the salience of other cleavages (especially the class cleavage); to the openness/ closedness of institutional channels for transmission of new demands. In the Italian case, I shall maintain particularly that the current, relatively unified structure of the ecology movement may be largely due to the substantial changes in political cultures that have occurred in Italy since the 1970s, and to the impressive increase in opportunities for environmental action in the Italian political system as well as to changes in Italian public opinion.

The Italian Ecology Movement: Patterns of Development across Time

Two basic, different cultural and political traditions can be pointed out within the Italian ecology movement: *conventional ecology* and *political ecology*.[2] The former represents the traditional approach, putting the accent on the strenuous defence and protection of the surviving natural environment and the artistic and architectural masterpieces. The peculiarities of Italian society, i.e. a poor tradition of commitment to political life by the moderate sectors of the middle class, make the activists of conventional ecology much more likely to engage in educational activities aimed at nurturing a positive attitude to environmental defence in young people; or in voluntary work (e.g., cleaning gardens, looking after animals, etc.), than to take an active part in the political debate. This does not imply, of course, that conventional ecology groups do not promote or join campaigns aimed at obtaining political outcomes; or that they do not get involved in disputes and, sometimes, confrontations with public authorities. It simply means that the attitude towards political activity, easily confused (in Italy) with partisan politics, has been over time a major obstacle to a strengthening of links and cooperations between the most traditional environmental groups and the political ecology organisations. The growth of a political ecology sector in Italy has followed the rise and fall of antagonistic movements of the late 1960s and early 1970s. Rather than the protection of nature, political ecologists gave priority to a wider transformation of the capitalist social structure, without which no real environmental preservation could occur. Opinions about the most suitable strategy for ecology action (defence vs social change) are therefore another core factor for the distinction between conventional and political ecology currents (the first being the positive/negative attitudes to political activity). I am going to show later how such factors dividing the movement have been changing during the years, and under what circumstances they no longer seem to constitute a real threat to the (relative) unity of the movement; or, better, how their persistence does not prevent at least the major organisations in different sectors from cooperating regularly with each other.

Although there has not yet been a systematic effort to count the ecology groups and associations currently active in Italy, it seems plausible to estimate no less than 2000 groups (either autonomous or local branches of national organisations), many more if the smallest neighbourhood groups and committees are included (Diani 1988, pp.56-57). Among the biggest and most influential organisations in the conventional ecology sector are Italia Nostra (founded in 1955, with a current membership about 15 000); the Italian branches of WWF (World Wide Fund for Nature, 1966, 200 000) and Friends of the Earth (1977); some animal rights groups like LIPU (Italian League for the Protection of Birds, 1966, 20 000) and LAC (League for the Abolition of Hunting, 1978, 1000). The most important organization in the political ecology sector is by far the Lega per l'Ambiente (League for the Environment), set up in 1980 by ecology activists who were sympathetic either to 'old' or 'new' left parties and collateral associations. In spite of getting significant support even from the more traditional currents of the movement, the Liste Verdi (Green Lists) can also be considered a relevant component (there are currently over 200 local lists) of the political ecology sector.[3]

Ecology action before 1968

The first big challenge to intellectuals and citizens concerned with the preservation of nature and historical masterpieces in Italy took place in the late 1950s, when an impressive and sustained economic growth affected drastically the organization of the urban areas as well as the countryside (Cederna 1975).

The actions of economic groups and speculators, who did not care about environmental risks associated with massive urbanization processes and the rise of mass tourism, were not faced by large-scale opposition from public opinion. In fact, the 'political opportunity structure' was totally unfavourable for the development of environmentalist action at that time. The vast majority of the Italian people and politicians looked at fast economic growth as the only way to overcome the historical backwardness of the country. Lifestyles and patterns of consumption, formerly exclusive to the upper class, were just extending to the middle and the lower middle classes. For these reasons, there was a widespread and indiscriminate consensus for mere quantitative growth, and no attention was paid to opinions and analyses which questioned that notion of 'development' and pointed at its devastating impact on the environment.

Moreover, class cleavages were by far the most relevant ones in Italian society in the late 1950s and early 1960s, in spite of a rather low degree of explicit social and political conflict. Socioeconomic status was the main criterion for interest aggregation; most associational activities, not only partisan participation, took place within the framework of the two great political subcultures which have marked Italian history in the twentieth century; the 'white' (i.e. catholic) subculture and the 'red' (socialist and communist) one. As a consequence, very few resources were available for other forms of social and political participation, including environmentalist action, which could not be easily reduced to class (or, eventually, religious) terms.

Environmental concerns remained therefore a question for restricted intellectual and scientific elites, who played a central role in the foundation of associations like *Italia Nostra* (in 1955) or the *Federazione Pro Natura* (in 1959). Although the former paid more attention to the defence of urban areas from widespread land speculation, and the latter to the preservation of the natural environment, they shared a basic conservationist approach, emphasizing the need for public authorities to take up a more rational and long-sighted perspective, by regulating the economic growth and related transformation processes. A few years later, the setting up of the Italian branch of WWF (in 1966) and of LIPU was inspired by similar principles.

No real environmental movement was active in that phase, however. The few conventional ecology associations had to cope with a low mobilization potential, as there was no environmental consciousness among the public. Therefore, these associations acted mainly as small public interest lobbies, trying to influence the media and public authorities by the individual prestige and social connections of their most prospective members. Grassroots participation by citizens, either through local committees or through local branches of organisations with a national-scale structure, was virtually nonexistent.

The contentious 1970s

The current expansion and influence of the ecology movement is undoubtedly grounded in the 1970s. However, that decade did not start very promisingly for the ecology groups. The impressive outburst of class conflict, especially in the years 1968-72 (Pizzorno et al. 1978; Tarrow 1989), did not set the proper conditions for the growth of actions on environmental issues. In spite of a more positive attitude to participatory and grassroots politics, public opinion was much less sensitive to environmental issues than to classic 'materialist' (Inglehart 1977) issues, such as concern about economic crisis, or the defence of public order, shaken by street clashes between demonstrators and police, and, later, by the rise of terrorism (della Porta 1990). Political parties and New Left organisations did not show real interest, either. Political debate was about the legitimization of the Communist Party and of the Left as a whole to rule the country, putting an end to the thirty years domination by the Democratic Christian Party; or about the need/opportunity for social movement organisations to look for direct political representation in the elective assemblies.

In spite of a persisting shortage of favourable political opportunities, some preconditions for the successive emergence of the ecology movement began to develop precisely at that time. New forms of class conflict took place both within and outside the factories. Outside industrial plants, activists from urban social movements, community action groups and popular committees raised, in most cases for the first time, issues strongly linked to environmental protection: they fostered opposition to industrial pollution, to the degrading quality of life in the metropolitan areas, to segregation of members of the lower classes in the most deprived suburbs. Within factories, workers' action stressed the quest for wider control over the production cycle rather than for mere rises in wages, paying special attention to dangers connected with the organization of work and to protecting workers' health. Mobilizations against the Montedison chemical plants in Marghera (Venice) provide a good example of both tendencies. In the same period, some scientists put into question the supposed 'objectivity' of scientific research, and criticized its subordination to the interests of the ruling class. In some cases, alliances between scholars and politically active workers were set up: for example, in the Consiglio di Fabbrica (Workers' Council) of the Montedison plant in Castellanza (Milan); in the editorial boards of militant journals like *Sapere* and *Ecologia*; in organisations like *Medicina Democratica* (Democratic Medicine), founded in 1976, or *Geologia Democratica* (Democratic Geology), founded in 1973. Such small working groups were possibly the first organizational structures of what was going to become the political ecology sector.

In spite of the persisting influence of Marxist political theory on most political activists, a new concept of 'social' and 'political' ecology was in the making. On the one hand, it urged the lower classes to mobilize not only on strict wage grounds, but for a wider defence of some natural resources, such as air and water, the pollution of which was alleged to be just the last step in systematic exploitation of the working class by the bourgeoisie. On the other hand, it emphasized the connections between the environmental crisis and other social and urban dynamics, instead of identifying the ecosystem with the natural environment only. A further contribution to the growth of environmentalist consciousness among activists and supporters of radical social movements came from the spread of counterculture in the Italian society. Neo-oriental religious groups, youth subcultures, anarchist and libertarian currents all showed strong interest in the body–mind relationship, in the refusal of an anthropocentric approach to life, in the quest for an anti-authoritarian and self-regulated society. Even if such tendencies did not build up a specific 'alternative sector' as they did in Germany (Tarozzi 1982; Papadakis 1984), they affected in many ways the cultural orientations and lifestyles of the wider public. They were, for instance, a major channel for diffusion of alternative foods and body practices, like yoga, in Italian society.

The slow and difficult emergence of a political ecology sector from the new social movements was not the only innovation in the environmentalist area, however. Even conventional ecology associations went through impressive changes. The conflictual political culture of the day permeated in some ways even the most moderate groups, who took up a more critical attitude to public authorities or polluting firms, and showed some interest in playing a more direct role in the political arena. A strong drive towards a modernization of patterns of participation by the old (as well as by the new) middle class came from the Radical Party.[4] The Radicals modernized Italian politics by introducing both new issues (e.g., campaigns they run for divorce and abortion) and new repertoires, typical of single-issue politics and of anglo-saxon political cultures: referendum, petitions, sit-ins, non-violent direct action. They were also the first political party to pay careful attention to environmental preservation, either by starting specific campaigns or promoting the setting up of environmental associations with formal (now suppressed) ties to the party, such as *Friends of the Earth* or the LAC. Their rejection of marxist frameworks marked a substantial difference from the early political ecology groups. In spite of being in principle closer to conventional ecology organisations, 'Radical sympathizing' associations were also innovative from that side. In fact, they take the biggest credit for introducing grassroots participation and unconventional, although peaceful, techniques of action among groups who previously had mainly conceived of their action in strict lobbying terms.

The Seveso accident and the anti-nuclear struggles in Montalto di Castro

The spectrum of organisations engaged on environmental questions in Italy was much wider and more heterogeneous in the mid 1970s than before. However, as yet no regular ties existed between the various sectors of the movement. The lack of coordination within the environmentalist world was made evident by the Seveso accident. On 10 July 1976 a large amount of dioxyn gas came out from the Icmesa chemical factory located in Seveso, a small town about 30 kilometres north of Milan. A wide surrounding area was badly affected, and partially evacuated. The Milan political ecology groups played an active role, jointly with some new left groups, in setting up a local committee, aimed at exerting some citizens' control over public authorities concerned with the question. However, they proved unable to cope with moderatism of the conventional ecology associations and the local population, who were both reluctant to engage in a campaign which had been radicalized since the very beginning (see Lodi 1988).

It did not take too long, however, for a first, although temporary and mainly localistic, joint action to be promoted by the ecology movement. In 1977, the Italian parliament eventually passed a revised version of the National Energy Act, planning the construction of twenty nuclear power plants, to add to the Caorso plant, the only one in operation at that time. Fierce criticism of the project came from a very heterogeneous milieu, ranging from the moderate reformism of Italia Nostra to the radicalism of revolutionary left groups, not to speak of the opposition of local people. The opposition was, of course, motivated on different grounds: the conventional ecology associations did not oppose nuclear power in principle, but were rather sceptical about the reliability of safety measures adopted by the state agencies, and the latter's capacity to enforce them; at the other extreme, New Left organisations fought nuclear energy policies as the latest and more authoritarian response to the oil crisis, being pursued by the ruling capitalist class; local people, and especially farmers, public employees, shopkeepers and members of the tourism industry, were frightened by possible risks both to their health and to their activities, and did not seem to be concerned about wider 'ecologist' concerns. Different opinions about what repertoires of action should be legitimate played a role in splitting the movement, too. Also, as happened around the same time in France, after clashes in Creys-Malville, and in Germany, after Whye and Brokdorf (see Rüdig 1986), rejection not only of violence, but even of 'unorthodox political behaviour' by the conventional ecology groups was another major point of disagreement with political ecology sectors. It is therefore fully understandable why the efforts to start a national and unified campaign, supported by the globality of the ecology movement, ended up in failure, in spite of some occasional unified mobilization at the local level (for example, 20000 people marched on 20 March 1977 in Montalto di Castro, a country village on the borders between Lazio and Tuscany).

Other impressive mobilizations against nuclear plants were held in late 1978, when Friends of the Earth collected signatures asking for a referendum, aimed at abolishing the 1977 Energy Act (their effort was to be cancelled in 1981 by the Corte Costituzionale, the Italian Constitutional Court, which rejected as 'inappropriate' the quest for referendum); and on 19 May 1979 when political ecology and new left groups gathered 50 000 people in Rome for a national demonstration against the Energy Act.[5] In spite of the poor support from the conventional ecology sector, the anti-nuclear movement of the late 1970s was important for further developments of the ecology movement in many respects. First of all, failure in overcoming completely differences between the different currents must not hide the evidence that local united mobilizations were possibly one of the earliest examples of leftist and moderate activists working together on specific issues. Moreover, anti-nuclear initiatives provided the recently constituted political ecology groups and committees a first chance to set up a national network and to strengthen their bonds, thus increasing their political influence. On that occasion, a major coordinating role was played by the Comitato per il Controllo Popolare delle Scelte Energetiche (Committee for People's Control over Energy Policies), composed of prominent members of the radical sectors of scientific intelligentsia (including the current Green MPs Gianni Mattioli and Massimo Scalia) and of various political ecology groups, but not Friends of the Earth who opted for a full autonomy of action.

The successful 1980s

Both social and political factors contributed to create new opportunities for environmentalist action in the early 1980s. The drastical reduction in industrial and class conflict came along with a wider transformation in the social structure, with a large share of employment in the industrial sector being cut down and replaced with new jobs and functions in the tertiary and service sector. The fast trend towards 'post-industrial' society implied at least two important consequences for the green movement: (a) the class cleavage lost visibility and relevance in Italian political debate; (b) the growth of professional groups in the service sector enlarged what is usually considered to be the constituency par excellence of the new social movements (i. e. the new middle class). A better economic situation and the defeat of terrorist groups also encouraged the Italian public to give up typical 'materialist' issues such as rising prices or public order and to put greater emphasis upon 'post-materialist' values such as quality of life or self-realization (Biorcio 1987 and 1988c). Such a shift was contemporary to the expansion of a generic 'need for nature', which took the most heterogeneous forms: development of alternative tourism, especially in the countryside; increasing popularity of 'natural medicine', 'herbalist medicine', 'macrobiotics' and so on; the expansion of 'open-air' sports such as cross-country skiing, canoeing, free-climbing (see, e. g., Sabani 1987).

Some political factors are also to be taken into account. Growing disenchantment with conventional politics, and political parties in particular, set a favourable ground for new groups to arise, adopting 'unconventional' (i.e., innovative and informal, rather than violent) patterns of political action and giving priority to single-issue mobilization (Lodi 1984; Grazioli and Lodi 1984). Finally, the almost total disappearance of the political organisations created in the 1970s by the New Left (with the obvious exception of Workers' Democracy), and the Trade Unions' crisis, both had among their outcomes a great number of experienced grassroots activists, giving up their former memberships and becoming available for new commitments. There is empirical evidence that the large majority of them eventually joined some political ecology organization (Diani and Lodi 1988; Biorcio 1988a).

The factors I have outlined above account for the early 1980s being a 'turning point' for the Italian ecology movement. Both long-established organisations and more recent ones went through an impressive expansion of their structure, raising their capability to attract consensus and activists. The *League for the Environment* doubled their members from 1983 to 1986 (15 000 to over 30 000); the growth of *WWF* was even more impressive (30 000 to about 200 000 from 1983 to 1989). The only exception was, not surprisingly, *Italia Nostra*, which has always shown little or no interest in mobilizing mass support, giving priority to attracting members with specific experiences or qualifications (Sabani 1987). The number of small grassroots groups also increased, although no estimation of rates of growth has been attempted at a national level. However, research conducted in the Milan area revealed that 64 per cent of the environmental groups and associations active in 1985 had been set up not earlier than 1982 (Diani 1988, Ch. 3).

The quantitative growth of the movement since the early 1980s, and the end of the cycle of anti-nuclear mobilizations which had started in 1977, made it necessary to set up some new coordinating body, especially within the political ecology sector. Both the establishment of the *League for the Environment* in 1980, and *Arcipelago Verde* (Green Rainbow) in 1981 were a step in that direction. The former is an umbrella-organization which coordinates grassroots groups active mainly on a local basis. It was set up as a formal branch of ARCI, the cultural and leisure time association which is jointly run by the Communist and the Socialist Parties. Membership of this group was to be harshly criticized by other sectors of the environmental movement, especially by those activists who were closer to the Radical Party. They charged the League of being a mere instrument of the Communist Party (PCI), by which it would increase its influence on the environmental movement. However, and in spite of the existing overlappings between the League and PCI,[6] there is no evidence that the former was ever significantly manipulated by the latter. In fact, the League for the Environment often took up stances conflicting with the PCI policies on several issues, such as nuclear energy policy and restrictions to hunting (which also brought about deep disagreements with another and more influential branch of ARCI, the Hunters' League). Only in recent times, and especially after Achille Occhetto replaced Alessandro Natta as general secretary of the Communist Party, has the gap between the two organisations been almost completely filled. Moreover, it is the Communist Party which seems to have gone through a deeper change of its former orientations and beliefs, rather than the League. Whatever conclusions one might draw about relationships between the PCI and the League for the Environment, everybody would agree that the setting up of the latter witnessed the rising interest in institutional politics among the political ecology grass roots groups. The role played by *Arcipelago Verde* was much more informal, although significant, consisting in the organization of periodic meetings joining together groups and associations from all currents of the movement (Barone 1984). Whereas the League for the Environment is still a major association in the ecology movement, meetings called under the heading *Arcipelago Verde* have tended since 1984 to overlap with assemblies promoted by the just constituted National Coordinating Committee of Green Lists.

Both the League for the Environment and the *Arcipelago Verde* experiences suggest that conditions existed in the early 1980s for development of exchanges and alliances within the movement. This was to overcome 'ideological' boundaries between the different sectors, too. The crisis of Marxism and workerism pushed the political ecology activists to define their collective and political identity in 'ecological', rather than in class or ideological terms. This also implied their availability to take up specific issues in the field of environmental protection, which they would have disregarded in the 1970s as irrelevant, in face of the ongoing processes of revolutionary social change. On the other hand, the 'long wave' of the 1970s eventually affected the conventional ecology associations, in most cases *via* the adhesion to them by younger activists who had been somewhat involved in new social movements or in New Left parties of the previous decade. As a consequence, conventional ecology associations became more likely to adopt unconventional repertoires of action (sit-ins, expressive and symbolic protest, etc.) and to engage in disputes, if not (in a few cases only) in confrontations, with public authorities. That meant that some former barriers to cooperation with political ecology groups were not as hard to overcome as they had been in the past.

New political opportunities interacted with weaker ideological cleavages to sustain the rise of a relatively unified ecology movement. Among the most impressive examples of intergroup cooperation were two campaigns for referendums against hunting and (again) nuclear power plants, jointly launched in 1986 by the most prominent ecology associations from all sectors (including Italia Nostra, WWF, League for the Environment and Friends of the Earth) and by some small political groups (including Workers' Democracy and the Radical Party). On that occasion. over one million people supported both referendums.

The unification process was undoubtedly hastened in many respects by the Chernobyl disaster.[7] It was not by chance that the first massive commitment of Italia Nostra to the anti-nuclear mobilization (via support for the 1986 referendum campaign) came after the accident in the USSR; on the same basis, some previously unconceivable alliances developed, including for instance the joint participation of moderate organisations (such as Italia Nostra) and leftist groups such as Lotta Continua per il Comunismo (Continuing Struggle for Communism) in the same referendum committee. Even the ability of ecology associations to mobilize their sympathizers increased substantially after Chernobyl. On 10 May 1986 over 150 000 people marched in Rome against nuclear power, whereas participation in another national demonstration a few months earlier had not reached 30 000. The nuclear accident in the Ukraine can therefore be viewed as a 'facilitating event', i.e. as a factor which interacted with a positive political opportunity and with weakening ideological disagreements to soften the persisting obstacles to inter-organizational, and especially inter-sectoral, cooperation.

The public's growing concern for environmental problems, the reluctance by most parties to take up environmental issues in a satisfactory way, the unease experienced by most ecology activists with traditional patterns of political representation, all worked for a direct participation of the ecology movement in political life. After occasional participation of Green Lists in local elections in 1980 and 1983, some national meetings in 1984 and 1985 organized much more widespread participation (about 150 local lists) in local elections held in May 1985. Results were rather encouraging: in spite of poor organizational resources, the Greens polled over 600 000 votes (with an average share of 2.1 per cent in the constituencies in which they actually stood), having 141 representatives elected in the local councils.[8] Success in local elections opened the way to participation in the campaign for the National Parliament two years later. The Greens did rather well even on that occasion, obtaining 2.5 per cent of the total vote and fifteen MPs: thirteen in the Lower House (*Camera dei Deputati*) and two in the Higher House (*Senato*). The June elections were followed by the referendum about nuclear power plants. Originally scheduled for Spring 1987, the polls had been postponed because of the governmental crisis and the call for new general elections. The citizens were asked to express their opinions about three questions, concerning different although related aspects of nuclear energy policy, without which no development of nuclear power in Italy would be possible. The anti-nuclear front won all three referenda, with a share of 80.6 per cent, 79.6 per cent and 72.3 per cent respectively. This decisive vote against nuclear power owed much to the late and tactical support given to the anti-nuclear front by most parties, including the Communists and even the Christian Democrats.[9]

After the 1987 elections and referenda, a new political phase opened, the outcomes of which are very difficult to envisage. I will emphasize here, among several major events concerning the ecology movement, the impressive growth of (mainly local) conflicts on industrial pollution. The risks and offences to the environment as well as to people's health, usually associated with some industrial plants, especially chemical plants, have faced stronger and stronger opposition by local populations. In Tuscany (against the Farmoplant factory of Massa Carrara), in Piedmont (against the Acna factory in Cengio), and in Puglia (against Enichem plants in Manfredonia), activists from the New Left and political ecology groups have joined politically moderate citizens, in many cases from the old middle class, in a common effort to stop what they viewed as a threat to the welfare of their community. In some cases, as in Massa Carrara or in Cengio, a new way of structuring conflict has emerged, where new middle class and old middle class activists and sympathizers faced the local workers,who were defending their jobs, with the regional and national trade unions taking a somewhat softer and more cautious position.

In brief, widespread conflicts on polluting industrial plants support the feeling that new alliances and oppositions have emerged, which are not easy to classify along the conventional right-left continuum. They also suggest that new cleavages could be in the making, a much more hypothetical suggestion, however. The same holds true for the Green Lists experience. In spite of a membership sharing leftist orientations and background in the majority of cases, the Green Lists have also been able to attract significant support from conventional ecology activists. Further-more, according to the most recent polls, their potential support among Italian voters is highly heterogeneous, cutting through traditional classes and status groups, as well as through ideological cleavages (see Diani 1989 and Biorcio 1988a). Even these latest events and related findings are therefore consistent with the picture of the ecology movement that I have tried to draw in this section: a collective actor which has proved able to overcome, at least partially, the deep ideological and cultural cleavages which in the 1970s reduced opportunities for different sectors and organisations to set up alliances and joint campaigns. I will turn now to a brief assessment of the main factors which facilitated such a shift and the emergence of a (relatively) unified ecology movement at the national level.

The 'Alliance' Between Moderate and Radical Currents in the Italian Ecology Movement: a Possible Explanation

If our reconstruction of the development of the Italian ecology movement is correct, then we can conclude that the distance between the different components of the movement has decreased impressively in recent years, at least concerning their participation in joint campaigns. There has always been some cooperation between the different currents, even when social conflicts were far more radicalized, and therefore the different approaches to the environmental question also looked highly incompatible. However, as what happened in Montalto di Castro in 1977 shows, such alliances between conventional ecology and political ecology were rather occasional, and short lasting, whereas they are now much more frequent and long lasting (Diani 1988). I shall propose now a possible explanation for putting together and summarizing some points which have just been introduced in the historical analysis above.

We have to look first at the substantial changes that occurred in Italy in the late 1980s, in political cultures as well as in patterns of political participation. The intensity of class conflict and of related class cleavages and political cultures (the socialist culture, the catholic culture, etc.) is now much lower than it was ten years ago. Whether we are witnessing a conjunctural phenomenon, or a long-term trend towards reduction of class conflicts in Italian society, may be disputable. What is worth stressing here is how such change affected alliances within the ecology movement. My general hypothesis is that the reduction of class conflict has opened new opportunities for the growth of new and unusual alliances, for three fundamental reasons:

(a) although it may look simplistic to place the different currents of the ecology movement along the right-left dimension, empirical analysis (Diani 1988; Biorcio 1988a) suggest that most political ecology activists are at the same time either activists or supporters or former members of the left organisations; and that the opposite holds for the 'conventional' ecologists. As a consequence, conditions for cooperation between ecology activists are likely to be more favourable when other possible sources of disagreement, related to their political opinions, are weaker;

(b) the new social movements of the 1970s, including the political ecology movement, substantially contributed to the larger effort by the Left to 'defreeze' the Italian political system and set the conditions for a political alternative at governmental level (see Melucci 1982; Martinelli and Pasquino 1978; Tarrow 1989). When such projects became less and less feasible in the early 1980s many social movement activists moved from a 'partisan' style of political participation to an 'issue-oriented' one. The large majority of them concentrated in particular upon ecology issues (Biorcio 1988a; Diani 1989);

(c) the crisis of traditional political ideologies has strengthened not only the shift from 'class issues' to 'new issues', but even the trend towards 'single-issue' participation. Even political ecology activists, who still emphasize the need to connect environmental protection to wider social change, are now more likely to engage in limited 'single-issue' campaigns, which would have been dismissed as 'short-sighted' and 'particularistic' some years before. In the previous decade, any specific action had to be interpreted through a wider ideological framework, in order to place it within a more general and long-term strategy for social change; it does not matter whether it was conceived of in revolutionary or reformist terms. Thus it was rather difficult, for early political ecology activists, to start alliances with the moderate conventional ecology groups, who shared a totally different political culture. On the contrary, opportunities are now better for cross-cultural cooperation, since the decreased relevance of ideologies has made it easier for both sectors to get in touch with each other on specific questions, in spite of maintaining different global perspectives and a different *Weltanschauung*.

Changes in political cultures have been paralleled by changes in the wider 'political opportunity structure': public concern for environmental issues has been growing steadily, as well as support for the environment and ecology associations (Biorcio 1987 and 1988c). Even the established political parties (mostly, but not exclusively, the left ones) have opened their lists to 'green' candidates, intellectuals and politicians who are sympathetic to the green cause. New opportunities have been created at the institutional level, for example through the foundation of the *Ministero dell'Ambiente* (Environment Department) in 1986, where the biggest ecology organisations have a consultative status, or through the so-called 'Galasso Act' (1985), which sets strict limitations on further offences against the environment and gives citizens the opportunity to react against them by addressing the law courts. Such positive changes, and the associated feelings of the ecology groups acting in a more favourable (social) environment, seem to have greatly contributed to a 'deradicalization' of cultural and ideological frames shared by the various ecologist currents, especially the leftist ones; and to have consequently fostered the growth of exchanges between them. This evidence thus confirms the thesis that the greater the societal closure towards new issues, the wider becomes the use of ideology as a major mobilization resource, and the less chance there is for cooperation between actors with conflicting, and often totally opposing, cultural and political backgrounds.

Finally, the growth of 'mobilization potential' (Klandermans 1988) for ecology action has not been followed by an equivalent capability of ecology organisations to convert such potential into actual support. The Italian ecology movement is not, therefore, facing a situation of social movement organisations competing for the same (narrow and poor) political market, as analysed in general terms, for instance, by Zald and McCarthy (1980). The lack of harsh competition, at least until now, implies that individual organisations are not really forced to stress their specificity in front of their competitors by reinforcing their ideological beliefs and cultural frames. That is even more true of the relationships between conventional ecology and political ecology groups, which are not really competing for grassroots support, as their potential constituents are substantially different in attitudes as well as in political background, if not in strict social class terms. Once again, we see how the (relative) absence of factors stimulating the rise of ideological conflict could have opened up new opportunities for different, and potentially antagonistic, organisations to work together in specific mobilization campaigns.

The Rise of the Italian Ecology Movement in Comparative Perspective: a Tentative Assessment

Some features of today's environmental and ecology movements are clearly cross-national, such as the withdrawal from a traditional left-right reading of political conflict, the stress placed upon post-materialist values, the significant role played in them by the new middle class. Other traits are not so common to all countries, however, and require more careful atten-tion from scholars. Among the latter I would include the patterns of rela-tionships that in different countries link together moderate and radical currents of those movements. Looking at the Italian experience, I have claimed that originally very different and conflicting sectors of environ-mentalist action have step-by-step strengthened their bonds, owing to a favourable evolution of the political cultures and the political opportunity structure. Any effort to generalize such experience, for instance on the grounds that sooner or later any radical movement has to become institu-tionalized and more open to cooperation with moderate organisations, would be misleading, however. In fact, relationships between moderate and radical sectors of ecology movements have a different form, as well as a different timing, in different countries. In some areas, they have resulted in new, quite well-established, collective actors, or in unusual coalitions; elsewhere, they do not seem to have produced any long-term innovation, either in patterns of collective action or in representation of political demands. Although very tentative, a look at two archetypal examples of environmental action in Europe, the German case and the British case, will help us to capture the specificity of the Italian experience, and at the same time to formulate some hypothesis for further analysis.[10]

In the early 1970s, the large 'social movement sector' in Germany was substantially deprived of any political representation and looked rather isolated from other social milieux; very limited links existed with other cultural, community and political organisations supported by the traditional middle class, including the numerous conservationist and protectionist associations which mobilized the environmental concerns among the most moderate sector of the German public. The development of Citizens' Initiatives (Bürgerinitiativen) was strongly innovative in patterns of social and political alliances, for they brought together activists from social movements and new left groups with moderate, and often conservative, citizens, in order to cooperate on particular issues. Although very few ties seem to have been activated between leftist groups and the conventional ecology associations, Citizens' Initiatives may be considered a major opportunity, and the starting point for a more influential role in German politics to be played by new social actors and their organisations. Moreover, as Citizens' Initiatives covered mostly environmental issues, they were one of the main channels through which an autonomous political ecology sector grew up. In the midterm, the ecology movement became a reference point for other social sectors engaged in forms of 'unconventional political participation' (squatters, feminists, anarchists, etc.). It seems plausible to assume that disputes about the environment, and related organisations, were the 'core' of new politics in West Germany in that period. Even the vexed question of guaranteeing to new radical demands some sort of political representation in a corporatist society was eventually, at least temporarily, resolved through an ecology-related 'medium', i.e. through the establishment of the Green Party. Whereas in the late 1970s and early 1980s the ties between political ecology groups and other social movement organisations became closer, and early successes by the Green Party forecasted the emergence of a new influential actor in national politics, connections with the moderate sectors of the environmental movements seem to have been steadily decreasing, as is witnessed by the crisis experienced by the Citizens' Initiatives in the early 1980s (Rucht 1989). Moreover, conventional ecology associations in Germany already had access to institutionalized channels for transmission of their demands, which made the setting up of a Green Party rather irrelevant to them. As a consequence, persisting differences in cultural background and orientations were not counterbalanced by calculations in terms of political opportunities, and provided a strong drive towards a new deep segmentation between the moderate and radical sectors of the ecology movement.

In brief, the development of the environmental and ecology movement in Germany seems to have followed a quite different path from that in Italy. In the 1970s, the Citizens' Initiatives' experience favoured several overlaps between moderate and radical activists, whereas in the 1980s, the consolidation of the alternative sectors and their political branches has resulted in a new separation. Environmental mobilizations and (mainly local and temporary) alliances within the middle class in the 1980s seem to have therefore provided the opportunities and the framework for the upsurge of a new and autonomous actor in German political life. In Italy, on the contrary, early phases of the ecology movement were marked by a great distance between moderate and radical sectors, a distance which has been reduced over time, up to the current unity of the movement.

Empirical evidence from the British case suggests a radically different picture. Some similarities with Germany can be found, indeed, in the strong institutionalization of the conventional ecology groups as well as in their connections to public authorities and to sponsoring departments, although the degree of institutionalization experienced by British associations for the preservation of nature has probably no equal in Europe (Lowe and Goyder 1983; see also Richardson and Watts 1985). The same does not hold, however, for the relationships between new social movements and the political system. Unlike in Germany, British social movements of the 1970s preserved, generally speaking, their class identity as well as activating globally strong bonds with the Labour Party and other organisations of the traditional left. Therefore, there was not in Britain such an impressive overlap between the ecology movement and other protest movements as in the German or even in the Italian case. One could also wonder whether it is legitimate to speak of an ecology movement in Britain. In fact, action on environmental issues in the 1970s and the 1980s seems to have developed along two different and parallel lines. Initiatives aimed primarily at the preservation of the natural environment and the education of public opinion have been organized almost exclusively by traditionally moderate associations. On the other hand, issues such as the localization of nuclear power plants or the lowering standards of quality of life in urban areas - in principle, 'core' questions for ecology action - have been dealt with through theoretical frameworks which stressed their relevance for social conflict, rather than for an environmentalist strategy of change. No relevant political ecology groups, nor an autonomous political ecology sector, seem to have emerged and consolidated. This does not mean that environmental issues have not played an important role in

British new politics since the 1960s: rather, the emergence of such issues does not seem to have affected the basic structure of cleavages in British society, which are still strongly centred on the left-right dimension.

In both the German and the British case, the 'protest cycle' of the 1970s does not seem to have introduced impressive changes in relationships linking the moderate with the new radical organisations, within the environmental movements as well as in other social movements. In Germany, the crisis of Citizens' Initiatives has determined again a situation of segmentation, with very few overlaps between the conventional ecology sector and the political ecology one. In Britain, we have just hinted that no real communication seems to have occurred between the traditional associations for the preservation of nature and the new social movement organisations concerned with the environmental crisis.

I would suggest that the Italian case looks somewhat more 'innovative' from this point of view. In the 1970s the Italian situation was rather different from the German or the British one. In spite of their ideological radicalism, social movements of the day had quite strong ties with the 'old' left parties, besides enjoying after 1976 a valuable direct political representation by the Workers' Democracy Party (*Democrazia Proletaria*) and the Radical Party. That made a strong difference compared with the 'exclusion' experienced by the German new social movements. Conventional ecology associations were at the same time rather weak and isolated in Italian society, in spite of the impressive intellectual resources they could rely upon, because of the lack of a tradition of 'public interest' lobbying in Italian politics, another substantial difference from the British, or even the German situation.

During the 1970s, mobilizations for the environment were in Italy almost as segmented as in Britain. Two important differences must be stressed, however: the old middle class sectors of the ecology movement lacked an autonomous capacity of action, comparable to the British conventional ecology associations; the radical approach shared by political ecology groups was to fade by the early 1980s which was not the case in Britain. We have already clarified how the 'crisis of ideologies' favoured the growth of 'inter-sectoral' cooperation within the movement: it remains to add that new alliances were also fostered by the rather poor capacity of the conventional ecology associations to act autonomously in the political arena.

The emergence of a new, autonomous political actor constitutes one of the main differences between the British and the Italian pattern of development of the environmental movement. On the other hand, the basic features of this new actor differentiate between the Italian and the German case: in Germany, earlier, although partial, alliances between moderate and radical sectors of ecology action have set conditions for the growth of a strong radical political actor. It has eventually provided the most radicalized sectors of the German population with a direct, if disputed, representation. In Italy, former obstacles to cooperation between moderates and radicals have at least temporarily disappeared and a rather unified central structure of the ecology movement has emerged. A further difference from the German situation consists of the different roles played by parties and public interest groups. In Germany, where interest groups, including those struggling for public interests like conventional ecology groups, are well established, the rise of a new party, able to challenge the prevailing mediatory approach to policy making, has been by and large the most relevant outcome of new politics today. In Italy, the existence of other leftist parties, and of an open multi-party system, makes the foundation of the Green Lists a less impressive, although important, event (see also Diani 1989). The greatest innovation seems to come, on the other hand, in the rise of a sector of public interest groups. In fact, growing cooperation between conventional ecology and political ecology organisations are among the first examples of large-scale and influential alliances, cross-cutting the traditional class cleavages in Italy. As such, they might anticipate a wider and deeper innovation in Italian politics, which will be worth careful monitoring in the coming years.

To conclude, the analysis of the Italian experience suggests that the role of the new radical actors (mostly from the new middle class) and related organisations within new social movements can be more adequately assessed if the role of other more moderate social groups and actors is taken into account; and provided that the specificity of national political systems and political cultures is not neglected. Although very brief, the final section should, it is hoped, have offered some good case for the development of a comparative approach to these topics.

NOTES

1 For an overview on 'new politics', 'new cleavages' and related themes, see among many others Barnes and Kaase (1979); Dalton et al. (1984); Fabbrini (1988, Ch. 5); Inglehart (1977, 1981, 1984 and 1985); Lowe and Rüdig (1986); Melucci (1985 and 1989); Müller-Rommel (1989); Offe (1985); Rochon (1983); Rüdig and Lowe (1991); Touraine(1978).

2 This is obviously just one of many possible partitions of the movement. In fact, in other works (Diani 1988; Diani and Lodi 1988) I have proposed a three-fold distinction between conservationism, environmentalism and political ecology. However, for the present purpose it seems convenient to consider the former two as specifications of a wider 'conventional' approach to the environmental question. For similar partitions see: Rucht (1989); Lowe and Goyder (1983). For a much more detailed and articulated, yet not alternative, analysis of cultural differentiations within the Italian environmental movement: Farro (1990).

3 See Diani (1988 and 1989); Farro (1989 and 1990) for further details.

4 Founded in the mid 1950s by a group of dissidents of the Liberal Party,

the Radical Party was unable to exert any influence on Italian politics until the late 1960s. Since then, its capacity to influence the political debate has grown drastically, as is witnessed by the successful struggle to introduce divorce in Italy. Yet, figures of electoral support have remained quite poor along the years, the peak having been obtained in 1979 national elections, when the party polled 3.5 per cent of the vote. For an introduction see Panebianco (1988).

5 See Diani (1991) and Farro (1990) for further informations about the anti-nuclear campaigns in Italy.

6 The former chairman of the League, M. Enrico Testa, had for instance been appointed at that position by the PCI, and is currently a communist MP.

7 Ceri (1987) analyses in depth the political outcomes in Italy of the nuclear accident in the USSR.

8 See Del Carria (1986) and Diani (1989) for more detailed information about local results of former Green Lists.

9 In fact, even the governative parties, with the exception of PRI (Republicans), decided eventually to support the anti-nuclear front. They justified their shift of perspective on the grounds that the specific rules, target of the referendums, were dated and to be changed in any case . In so doing, they presumably tried to prevent what would have been, according to all polls, a great success for the anti-nuclear front, from being attributed exclusively to the ecology movement and to its allies.

10 Major references for the reconstruction of the German case were Helm (1980); Müller-Rommel (1985); Papadakis (1984) Rucht (1989); Rüdig (1986). For the British case, see Lowe and Goyder (1983); Richardson and Watts (1985); Rüdig (1986); Rüdig and Lowe (1986); Saward (1987) See also Müller-Rommel (1989); Rüdig and Lowe (1991).

REFERENCES

Barnes, S.H., Kaase, M. *et al.* (1979). *Political Action: Mass Participation in Five Western Democracies.* Beverly Hills/London: Sage.

Barone, C. (1984). 'Ecologia: quali conflitti per quali attori ', in Melucci 1984.

Biorcio, R. (1987). 'Ecologia e politica nell'opinione pubblica italiana', *Polis*, Vol.1, pp.517-64.

Biorcio, R. (1988a). 'Ecologia politica e liste verdi', in Biorcio and Lodi 1988, pp. 113-46.

Biorcio, R. (1988b). 'L'elettorato verde', in Biorcio and Lodi 1988, pp. 181-208.

Biorcio, R. (1988c). 'Opinione pubblica, questione ambientale e movimento ecologista', in Biorcio and Lodi 1988, pp. 27-50.

Biorcio, R. and Lodi, G. (eds.), *La sfida verde.* Padova: Liviana.

Cederna, A. (1975). *La distruzione della natura in Italia.* Torino: Einaudi.

Ceri, P. (1987). 'Dopo Chernobyl: il nucleare come nuova frattura nella politica e nella societa' italiana', in Corbetta, P. and Leonardi, R. (eds.), *Politica in Italia. Edizione 1987.* Bologna: Il Mulino.

Dalton, R.J. (1988). *Citizen Politics in Western Democracies.* Chatham NJ: Chatham House.

Dalton, R. J., Flanagan, S. C. and Beck, P. A. (eds.) (1984) *Electoral Change in Advanced Industrial Democracies: Realignment or Dealignment?* Princeton N.J.: Princeton University Press.

De Meo, M. and Giovannini, F. (eds.) (1985). *L'onda verde: i verdi in Italia.* Roma: Alfamedia.

Del Carria, R. (1986). *Il potere diffuso: i Verdi in Italia.* Verona: Edizioni del Movimento Nonviolento.

della Porta, D. (1990). *Organizzazioni politiche clandestine: il terrorismo di sinistra in Italia durante gli anni Settanta*. Bologna: Il Mulino (forthcoming).

Diani, M. (1988). *Isole nell'arcipelago: Il movimento ecologista in Italia*. Bologna: Il Mulino.

Diani, M. (1989). 'Italy: The "Liste Verdi"', in Müller-Rommel 1989, pp. 113-22.

Diani, M. (1991). 'The conflict on nuclear energy in Italy', in Flam, H. (ed.), *Conflicts Over Nuclear Energy in Comparative Perspective*. (forthcoming).

Diani, M. and G. Lodi (1988). 'Three in one: Currents in the Milan ecology movement', in Klandermans *et al*. 1988, pp. 103-24.

Fabbrini, S. (1988). *Politica e mutamenti sociali*. Bologna: Il Mulino.

Farro, A. (1989). 'Cultural options in the Italian environmental movement', paper for the conference 'Environmental Constraints and Opportunities in the Social Organization of Space', ISA Working Group on Social Ecology, University of Udine, June.

Farro, A. (1990). *La rottura e l'equilibrio: cultura e politica ambientaliste*. Milan: Angeli (forthcoming).

Gamson, W. (1988). 'Political discourse and collective action', in Klandermans *et al*. 1988, pp. 219-46.

Grazioli, M. and Lodi, G. (1984). 'La mobilitazione collettiva negli anni Ottanta: tra condizione e convinzione', in Melucci 1984, pp. 267-314.

Helm, J. (1980). 'Citizen lobbies in West Germany', in Merkl, P. H. (ed.), *Western European Party Systems*. New York: Free Press, pp. 576-96.

Inglehart, R. (1977). *The Silent Revolution: Changing Values and Political Styles Among Western Publics*. Princeton N.J.: Princeton University Press.

Inglehart, R. (1981). 'Post-materialism in an environment of insecurity', *American Political Science Review*, Vol. 75, pp. 880-900.

Inglehart, R. (1984). 'The changing structure of political cleavages in Western Societies' in Dalton *et al*. 1984, pp. 25-69.

Inglehart, R. (1985). 'Perspectives on value change: Response to Lafferty and Knutsen, Savage, and Böltken and Jagodzinski', *Comparative Political Studies*, Vol. 17, pp. 485-532.

Klandermans, B. (1986). 'New social movements and resource mobilization: the European and the American approach', Paper for the workshop on 'Transformation of Structure into Action', Vrije Universiteit, Amsterdam, June.

Klandermans, B. (1988). 'The formation and mobilization of consensus', in Klandermans *et al*. 1988 pp. 173-196.

Klandermans, B., Kriesi, H. and Tarrow, S. (eds.) (1988) *From Structure to Action*. Greenwich, Conn: JAI Press.

Lewanski, R. (1981). 'Environmentalism and new values in Italy: new skin for an old ceremony?', paper for the workshop on 'Environmental Politics and Policy', ECPR Joint Sessions, Lancaster, April.

Lewanski, R. (1982). 'Comparative research on nuclear energy policy: A state of the art report, Italy', paper for the workshop on 'Comparative Research on Nuclear Energy Policy: The State of the Art', ECPR Joint Sessions, West Berlin, December.

Lipset, S. M. and Rokkan, S. (eds.) (1967). *Party Systems and Voter Alignments*. New York: Free Press.

Lodi, G. (1984). *Uniti e diversi: le mobilitazioni per la pace nell'Italia degli anni Ottanta*. Milano: Unicopli.

Lodi, G. (1988). 'L'azione ecologista in Italia: dal protezionismo storico alle Liste Verdi', in Biorcio and Lodi, 1988, pp. 17-26.

Lowe, P. D. and Goyder, J. M. (1983). *Environmental Groups in Politics*. London: Allen and Unwin.

Lowe, P. D. and Rüdig, W. (1986). 'Political ecology and the social sciences: the state of the art', *British Journal of Political Science*, Vol. 16, pp. 513-50.

Martinelli, A. and Pasquino, G. (eds.) (1978). *La politica nell'Italia che cambia*. Milano: Feltrinelli.

Melucci, A. (1982). *L'invenzione del presente. Movimenti, identita', bisogni individuali.* Bologna: Il Mulino.

Melucci, A. (ed.) (1984). *Altri Codici*. Bologna: Il Mulino.

Melucci, A. (1985). "The symbolic challenge of contemporary movements', *Social Research*, Vol. 52, pp. 789-816.

Melucci, A. (1989). *Nomads of the Present.* London: Hutchinson Radius/Philadelphia: Temple.

Menichini, S. (ed.) (1983). *I verdi: chi sono, cosa vogliono*. Roma: Savelli.

Müller-Rommel, F. (1985). "Social movements and the Greens: New internal politics in Germany', *European Journal of Political Research*, Vol. 13, pp. 53-67.

Müller-Rommel, F. (ed.) (1989). *New Politics in Western Europe: The Rise and the Success of Green Parties and Alternative Lists.* Boulder, Co./London: Westview Press

Offe, C. (1985). 'New social movements: Challenging the boundaries of institutional politics', *Social Research*, Vol. 52, pp. 817-68.

Panebianco, A. (1988). 'The Italian Radicals: New wine in old bottles?' in Lawson, K and Merkl P. H. (eds.) *When Parties Fail: Emerging Alternative Organisations*. Princeton, N.J.: Princeton University Press, pp. 110-136.

Papadakis, E. (1984). *The Green Movement in West Germany.* London: Croom Helm.

Pizzorno, A., Regini, M., Reyneri, E. and Regalia, I. (1978). *Lotte operaie e sindacato: il ciclo 1968-1982 in Italia.* Bologna: Il Mulino.

Richardson, J. and Watts, N. (1985). 'National policy styles and the environment: Britain and West Germany compared', Discussion paper 85-16. Berlin: International Institute for Environment and Society.

Rochon, T. R. (1983). 'Political change in ordered societies: The rise of citizens' movements', *Comparative Politics*, Vol. 15, pp 351-73.

Rokkan, S. (1970). *Citizens, Elections, Parties*, Oslo: Universitetsforlaget.

Rucht, D. (1989). 'Environmental movement organizations in West Germany and France: Structure and interorganizational relations', in Klandermans, B. (ed.), *Organizing for Change*. Greenwich, Conn: JAI Press, pp. 61-94.

Rüdig, W. (1986). *Energy, Public Protest and Green Parties*, unpublished PhD dissertation, University of Manchester.

Rüdig, W. (1990). *Explaining Green Party Development: Reflections on a Theoretical Framework*, (Strathclyde Papers on Government and Politics, No. 71) Glasgow: Department of Government, University of Strathclyde.

Rüdig, W. and Lowe, P. D. (1986). 'The "withered" greening of British politics: A study of the Ecology Party', *Political Studies*, Vol. 34, pp. 262-84.

Rüdig, W. and Lowe, P. D. (1991). *The Green Wave: A Comparative Analysis of Ecological Parties.* Cambridge: Polity Press. (forthcoming).

Sabani, P. G. (1987). 'Domande irrisolte della nuova cultura ambientale', *Censis. Note e commenti*, Vol. 23, n. 5-6.

Savage, J. (1985). 'Postmaterialism of the left and right: Political conflict in postindustrial society', *Comparative Political Studies*, Vol. 17, pp. 431-51.

Saward, M. (1987). 'Institutional cooption: Values, expertise and "insiders"', paper for the workshop on 'New social movements and the political system', ECPR Joint Sessions, Amsterdam, April.

Scott, R. W. (1981). *Organizations: Rational, Natural and Open Systems.* Englewood Cliffs, N.J.: Prentice Hall.

Snow, D. and Benford, R. (1988). 'Ideology, frame resonance and participant mobilization', in Klandermans et al. 1988, pp. 197-218.

Tarozzi, A. (1982). *Iniziative nel sociale*. Milano: Angeli.

Tarrow, S. (1983). 'Struggling to Reform', Western Societies Program Occasional Paper No. 15. Ithaca NY: Cornell University.

Tarrow, S. (1989). *Democracy and Disorder: Society and Politics in Italy 1965-1975*. Oxford: Clarendon Press.

Touraine, A. (1978). *La Voix et le Regard*. Paris: Seuil.

Zald, M. and McCarthy, J. (1980). 'Social movement industries: competition and cooperation among movement organizations', *Research in Social Movements, Conflict and Change*, Vol. 7. pp. 1-20.

7. Activists and Ideas in the Green Movement in France

BRENDAN PRENDIVILLE

Department of French Studies, University of Reading, UK

and TONY CHAFER

School of Languages and Area Studies, Portsmouth Polytechnic, UK

Introduction

This study of the green movement in France is based largely on the findings of a survey of activists which was undertaken partly at the Annual General Meeting of Les Verts (The Greens) in 1987 and partly by means of a question-naire sent out by post to 172 activists in Brittany in early 1988. In recent years a number of studies of the Greens' electorate have been published, while the activists who make up the movement and largely define its policies, strategy and campaigning priorities have been largely neglected. Being a new move-ment, the role of activists in this respect is probably even greater than in longer-established and more formally structured political movements. It is perhaps thus particularly surprising that so little work has been done on the movement's activists. It will be the intention of this chapter partly to fill this gap, first of all by establishing the age, social and political background, and socio-economic status of activists, and secondly by asking a range of questions about their political attitudes and the issues which concern them most.

The first part aims to set the movement in context by providing a brief historical overview of the emergence of the movement since the mid 1970s. The second part examines the background of activists and their attitudes on certain issues, in order to try to ascertain how the activists themselves situate the green movement in relation to other social and political movements. The third part then focuses on the ideological diversity of the movement, with four distinct, although frequently overlapping, currents being identified. Finally, while acknowledging the success of the movement in establishing itself as an independent organization, the question is posed whether the French green movement has the social and ideological cohesiveness which would be necessary for it successfully to be able to constitute itself as a fully fledged social movement. As we suggest in the concluding section, this task is a particularly difficult one given the rather uncongenial French institutional and ideological context in which the movement has to operate.

History of the Green Movement in France.

The emergence of the present-day French green movement may be traced back to March 1973 when the Alsace group *Ecologie et Survie* put forward a candidate at Mulhouse for the National Assembly elections of that year. This marked the entry of the ecologists into the arena of party politics and prepared the way for the agronomist René Dumont's campaign for the 1974 presidential elections. The announcement on 6 March 1974 by Prime Minister Pierre Messmer that France was to embark upon the world's most ambitious civil nuclear programme not only gave impetus to the anti-nuclear movement but was also a major underlying factor behind the recognition by many environmentalists of the need for specifically political action, as opposed to action purely at the level of civil society:

> Possibly the most important single factor in the shaping of the present movement is the battle and eventual victory of the ecologists over the environmentalists. The battle gave birth to political ecology (Prendiville 1981, p. 38).

Even if there was no hope of winning, as was the case in 1974, Dumont's election campaign provided a useful political platform for antinuclear and ecological issues. His relative success in obtaining over 300 000 votes, while giving impetus to the movement, also drew attention to splits within it.[1] These were to prove a major obstacle to the political unification of the movement, which was to take ten years, and the sources of which remain a central cause of divisions within the ecology movement today.

The most marked disagreements were largely over organization, leadership and strategy, rather than policy. The critique of productivism and consumerism, the demand for new forms of work, for a less wasteful and polluting style of life and for the achievement of a more balanced relationship between man and nature, based on conservation and the careful exploitation of the resources of the planet through the development of renewable technologies and energy sources, formed a somewhat diffuse, but nevertheless largely agreed, ideological basis for policy formation within the movement.

The ecology movement at this time consisted of three main groups, which frequently collaborated loosely at the time of elections. This happened for example at the 1977 and 1983 municipal elections and at the 1978 parliamentary elections. There was, however, no permanent coordination of their activity outside election times. The three groups were: the *Réseau des Amis de la Terre* (RAT: the French branch of the international Friends of the Earth movement, formed in 1970); the *Mouvement d'Ecologie Politique* (Movement of Political Ecology MEP), formed in 1979 partly out of the original *Mouvement Ecologique*; and *Les Verts-Confédération Ecologiste* (The Greens-Ecologist Confederation), formed at Cuizat (Aude) in December

1981 by members of the RAT and some former members of the former MEP, which had by now changed its name to Les Verts-Parti Ecologiste, (The Greens-Ecologist Party VPE).

It may seem at first sight somewhat strange to include the RAT here, as this organization might appear to belong more appropriately to the environmentalist wing of the movement. In France, however, the RAT from the outset combined pressure group activity and single-issue campaigns with other actions more commonly associated with a political movement. This was partly because leading figures in the Réseau, such as Brice Lalonde, did not eschew - and indeed actively sought - opportunities to take part in the electoral process.[2] It was also, however, a product of the increasingly overt political stance being adopted by the RAT, as for example at the 1978 parliamentary elections when it issued a statement favouring an electoral alliance between the ecologists, other social movements such as the women's and regionalist movement, and innovatory movements such as Lip.[3] One example of such an alliance was in Poitiers, where the local Friends of the Earth association, the Parti Socialiste Unifie (Unified Socialist Party PSU),[4] the Mouvement pour un Alternatif Non-violent (Movement for a Non-violent Alternative MAN), ex-members of the Comité de Larzac[5] and the Comité de Malville,[6] joined together to present a Convergence - Ecologie - Autogestion - Pouvoir Populaire (Convergence - Ecology - Self-determination - Popular Power) candidate at the 1978 parliamentary elections, the RAT, or at least certain parts of it, were thus to become important actors in the various attempts to integrate the different arms of the French ecology movement into a unified structure.

The formation of the MEP reflected a feeling shared by many activists that the ecologist movement needed a permanent and organized political arm if its interventions in the political arena were to be fully effective. However, the attempt to create a unified political movement based in Paris was viewed with suspicion by many members, who felt that a movement which was structured and controlled along such centralized and apparently hierarchical lines was contrary to the ideology and organizational principles of ecology. This feeling was reinforced by the decision of the movement to transform itself into a political party, the VPE, and was a major factor in the decision by a number of activists to create another organization, the Confédération Ecologiste, with a regionally-based federal structure. Rather than uniting the movement, this only served further to divide it. The VPE saw the Confederation as a challenge to them in the political field and the RAT withdrew in February 1982 after only one of their members was elected to the new organization's équipe confédérale (executive committee).

Unification was finally achieved in January 1984, when it became clear that a united organization would be necessary to fight the 1984 European elections. It was at this time that Brice Lalonde distanced himself formally from the political ecology movement by resigning from the executive committee of the RAT. He shortly afterwards announced his intention of participating in the formation of an independent green list to fight the elections.

From the outset many groups and individuals within the movement did not agree with the increasing emphasis that the ecology movement was attaching to interventions into the political arena at the expense, as they saw it, of other, more concrete and direct forms of activity at the level of civil society. These included, for example, support for local actions in defence of particular sites or landscape features, education of the public on ecological issues, encouraging people to live a more ecological lifestyle and, more generally, the building of a popular, grassroots, green movement. These individuals and groups largely refused to support Dumont's campaign, preferring either to concentrate on local action, for example against specific developments which they considered environmentally harmful, or on other forms of activity at the level of the individual or local community, rather than become part of an organized political movement with, as they saw it, all the disadvantages and constraints that implied. In addition to this division between what one could perhaps characterize as the 'political ecologists' and the 'environmentalists', there was a further line of disagreement between those who agreed about the necessity for political action about the need for a more coherently structured and coordinated political movement, but who nevertheless disagreed fundamentally about the political strategy and form of organization the movement was to adopt.

1984 saw the birth of a unified green movement in France. In January, at Clichy in Paris, the two principal wings, the Confédération and the VPE, merged to become Les Verts (The Greens), just five months before the European elections which were to be held under a system of proportional representation. The results of these elections were not particularly encouraging. Les Verts polled 678,826 votes (3.4 per cent) which compared rather unfavourably with the ecologists' results in the 1979 European elections (887, 863 votes, 4.4 per cent)

By way of an explanation of, and justification for, the drop in the overall vote, Les Verts themselves put forward three reasons: a high rate of abstention (43.30 per cent), the (too) recent structural unification, and the presence of the ex-ecologist leader, Brice Lalonde, at the head of a rival list, Entente Radicale Ecologiste (Radical Ecologist Concord ERE), which obtained 664, 403 votes (3.3 per cent). However, on a more positive note, for the first time in French ecology movements' history the organization that went into the elections came out of it intact!

Between their creation in 1984 and their spectacular arrival on the political stage in the Municipal elections of 1989, the French Greens went through a difficult period of self-identification and affirmation on the social and political scene.[7] This was a lean period for them as they struggled for recognition in a political system that largely ignores minorities. In order to illustrate the difficulties they faced we would cite three events from this period in which one might have expected the Greens to play a more prominent role than in fact they did.

The first of these was the sinking of the Greenpeace ship, *Rainbow Warrior*, in the port (Auckland) of a friendly country (New Zealand) by the French Secret Service in July 1985. This act of 'state terrorism' which saw the fall from grace of the then very much in view Defence Minister, Charles Hernu, was not over exploited by the Greens. Part of the reason for this was no doubt to be found in the apparent latent support within much of public opinion for the action of the French Secret Service. The public outcry to be heard in many a European country was conspicuous by its absence in France.

This is perhaps not surprising given the traditional weakness of 'civil society' in France in the face of the State (Hoffman 1974, Ch. 5). The Greens are, of course, affected by the dominant political culture as much as any other group, with the result that, just like other minority political movements in France, they face an uphill task in making themselves heard within a political culture, based on central *state* integration, which largely ignores them. The French political system inherited from the Revolution of 1789 and subsequent Napoleonic modifications leaves little or no room for political 'outsiders', that is movements or parties that are not represented within the state apparatus. Such movements or parties have extreme difficulty in exerting influence on the political process in France.

The second event of note was the nuclear accident at Chernobyl in the USSR in 1986. Here again the French Greens were not the protesting pivot one might have expected under the circumstances. There is a dual explanation for this. Firstly, the French public, Greens included, were subject to one of the most successful state exercises in misinformation in Western Europe. The accident happened on 26 April 1986 and ten days later the Ministry of Agriculture published a press release which began: 'Given the distance, the French territory has been totally unaffected by radioactivity resulting from the accident at Chernobyl'.[8] Subsequently, on 12 May, the daily paper, *Libération*, was able to headline:

'The Radioactive Lie (the radioactive cloud did indeed pass over France)'.

For two weeks, official sources of information about levels of radioactivity in the environment maintained exactly the opposite, thus confirming many an ecologist's opinion that there exists a major problem of information in the French nuclear field. Secondly, the anti-nuclear movement of the 1970s had finally lost its battle with the nuclear industry when the Left arrived in power in 1981. Mitterrand had promised to slow down the nuclear programme and to organize a meaningful parliamentary debate. He did neither, but the faith placed in him was such that by that time the movement had lost much of its steam. When the accident many ecologists feared actually happened, it almost seemed as if the anti-nuclear movement had lost its voice, having cried wolf so many times.

The third event was the wave of social protest which took France by surprise at the end of 1986. The students, schoolchildren, primary school teachers and railway workers all put the right-wing Chirac government to the test, yet this movement barely evoked any response from the green movement and took little or no part in it.

The Greens were, however, very active on the electoral front. The Presidential elections in May were the highlight of 1988. A. Waechter, the Green candidate, gained virtually the same number of votes as B. Lalonde in 1981, a result which was considered a relative success in that it indicated a certain electoral stability (see Table 1).

The French electoral tradition is for first-round candidates to 'advise' their supporters on how to vote in the second round. Ecologist candidates have always refused to do this, maintaining that their supporters are adult enough to decide for themselves even if their individual sympathies lean more to the left/centre-left than to the right (R. Dumont, B. Lalonde).

Table 1 Green candidates in Presidential elections.

	Number of Votes	Share of the Votes (%)
1974 Rene Dumont	337 800	1.3
1981 Brice Lalonde	1 126 282	3.9
1988 Antoine Waechter	1 149 642	3.8

Source: Nullmeier et al. 1983, p. 61, p. 66; Wright 1989, p. 369.

1989 perhaps saw the definitive emergence of the Greens onto the political stage in France. Their results in the municipal elections surprised even the most seasoned political commentator. These elections are, of course, different from legislative or presidential ones which have no measure of proportional representation. Nevertheless the Greens almost doubled their score compared with the 1983 municipal elections, which were held under the same system. In the first round they won 287 seats and, more surprising still, in those towns where the ecologist lists decided to follow the national decision and maintain their presence independently in the second round, their share of the vote often increased: in the 16 towns of over 30 000 inhabitants[9], for example, the Green vote rose by an average of 3.67 per cent (first round 12.63 per cent, second round 16.3 per cent). The total number of seats won in both rounds was 1369. The European elections in June of the same year confirmed this breakthrough, with 10.59 per cent of the total vote the French Greens sent nine MPs to the European Parliament and became the fourth largest force in French politics.

Green Activists

The activists are the people who, in any social movement, play the key role in defining the movement's policies, strategies and campaigning priorities. We have therefore undertaken three surveys[10] over the last five years to try to determine who these people are, what their socio-economic status is, from what generation they come, what their social and political background, their attitudes to politics, to the established political parties and to elections in general are. We believe that the results of these surveys not only help to explain some of the choices made by the movement in terms of ideology and organizational structure, but also help us to understand the basis for some of the divisions within the movement which have already been mentioned in the preceding section. The future direction of the movement depends, to a considerable degree, on the results of these internal struggles and, more specifically, on which groups and individuals emerge victorious.

A Social Elite?

It is first of all clear that a very high proportion (nearly 90 per cent) of activists work in the tertiary sector, with education and the so-called intermediary professions[11] being especially well represented (see Table 2). It is equally clear that they are generally highly educated and that very few of them come from either the farming community or the manual working class.[12]

The most significant aspect of these results is certainly the large majority of people engaged in education and particularly the sphere of higher education. Twenty-five people in secondary and primary education and twenty-one in higher education amount to an overall percentage of 46.5: the number of what might be called 'professional intellectuals' is considerable, reflecting a long national tradition of intellectual sway in the formation and direction of social and political movements.

Comparing these results with those obtained in 1983, we discover that this tendency has become more marked since then. In 1983, 30.5 per cent were working in primary, secondary or higher education as teachers, researchers or students. By 1987-8, the figure had risen to 42.5 per cent. A number of explanations for the predominance of the educated middle

Table 2 Occupation background of green activists

Occupation group	National survey 1987	Regional survey 1988	Total	Percentage
Professionals	17	7	24	22.4
(of which employed in higher education)	(10)	(4)	(14)	(13.1)
Intermediary professions	22	20	42	39.3
(of which employed in education)	(12)	(13)	(25)	(23.4)
Farmers	1	1	2	1.9
Shopkeepers and self-employed	3	4	7	6.5
Students	4	3	7	6.5
Clerical workers	10	7	17	15.9
Manual workers (semi-unskilled)	2	1	3	2.8
Housewives	0	1	1	0.9
Unspecified	2	2	4	3.7
Total	61	46	107	99.9[a]

[a] Because of rounding, the figures do not add up to 100.

classes, and particularly of the so-called 'intermediary' professions, among green movement activists have been advanced. Firstly, the intermediary professions constitute one sector of the working population that has grown particularly rapidly in recent years. Secondly, they do not belong to the traditional manual working class, nor to the managerial class, nor are they involved in production, trade or credit. Some have a safe job as they are employed by the state or local authorities; others, although often sufficiently well-qualified to obtain permanent, well-paid posts, deliberately choose to work either part-time or on short-term contracts, to give themselves greater freedom of control over their time. They do not therefore relate to the world of work in the same way as other groups of workers. Their dissatisfaction with the socio-economic system is thus less likely to be expressed through demands for better pay or greater job security. Nor is the nature of their work likely to lead to objective alienation in the way that Taylorist working practices do. Rather, their concerns are associated with post-materialist values (see Inglehart 1977) and relate to the quality of life, leading for example to demands for increased work autonomy or a

Table 3 Age of green activists

Age Group	National survey 1987	Regional survey 1988	Total 1987–8	Percentage	Percentage 1983 survey
18-30	13	12	25	22	31
31-40	27	18	45	40	41
41-50	11	8	19	17	16
51-60	9	3	12	11	6
60+	5	6	11	10	6
Total	65	47	112	100	100

greater say in the decision-making process of the firm or service in which they work. They are the product either of a comfortable socio-economic position, in which basic material needs have been satisfied, or a less stable position which is the result of a deliberate choice by people who value freedom and autonomy above material well-being.

An Ageing Movement?

It is perhaps not surprising, given what we said above about the importance of May 1968 as a point of reference, to discover that the average age of activists in 1987-8 was around 39 years old, corresponding to an average age of 20 in 1968, and that 40 per cent of activists in 1987-8 came from the 31-40 age group (see Table 3).

The poor showing of the Greens in elections after the Socialist government came to power in 1981 led some commentators to suggest that the movement might be in decline.[13] However, this hypothesis appears to be refuted by the membership figures which show a slow but steady increase in membership during this period (see Table 4), and by the findings of the 1983 survey, which showed that the movement was continuing to attract young members as nearly a third of activists were in the age group 18-30. The movement therefore continue to be relatively successful in turning the latent support for the green movement among young people, as evidenced by opinion polls, into active commitment.

The more recent 1987-8 survey appears to pose a question mark over this finding since it indicates an apparent decline in the percentage of young activists in the movement. As the 1983 survey showed, many (nearly one-third) of activists had already been active in the anti-nuclear movement or in other grassroots environmental groups and had come to the green movement by this route. Could it be that the decline of the anti-nuclear movement and the decision to turn the Greens into a political party, with the move towards a more hierarchical structure and the

Table 4 Green Party membership, 1984–9

Year	Ongoing members Total (%)	Lapsed members rejoining Total (%)	New members Total(%)	Total
1984	513 (48)	0 (0)	559 (52)	1072
1985	628 (54)	0 (0)	536 (46)	1164
1986	718 (59)	55 (5)	443 (36)	1216
1987	808 (62)	111 (9)	376 (29)	1295
1988	914 (48)	131 (7)	874 (46)	1919
1989	1301 (30)	174 (4)	2849 (66)	4324

Source: Data from Les Verts, AGM, Marseilles 1989.

increased emphasis on fighting elections that this transformation implies,[14] had discouraged younger activists from becoming involved in the movement, at least up until the elections of 1988 and 1989? In any case it is difficult to make any definitive statement with regard to this question because Les Verts are a party with an extremely high turnover of new members as Table 4 shows.

Since the election successes of 1989, and therefore after our surveys were completed, there has been a major influx of new activists into the movement. According to a survey of readers of the Green weekly bulletin, Vert Contact, carried out in June 1989 (4000 questionnaires, 1348 responses, 33.7%), the new members are predominantly recruited from younger cohorts: 29% of those who joined in 1988-9 are below 30, 47% between 31 and 45; the average age of these most recent members is 37.8 as opposed to 41 years for the older members (i.e. those who joined between 1984-1987).[15]

It is clear that Les Verts themselves attach considerable importance to younger members within their organization since a youth section was created in 1987 which, judging by the report delivered at the Annual General Meeting (AGM) of 1989, seems to be functioning satisfactorily.

The results of the 1989 Municipal and European elections suggest that there continues to be a reservoir of support for the green movement, particularly among younger voters (see Boy 1989). The ability or otherwise of the movement to continue to capitalize on this support and turn it into active commitment will, as the movement itself appears to recognize, be an important factor affecting its future development.

Political Background and Attitudes

The decision by the French Greens in favour of an autonomous movement, rather than a broadly based alliance with other groups, is not surprising in the light of the responses to the questions about political background

Table 5 Links to other political organizations

To which political organization/movement do you feel closest?
(More than one response possible)

Organization/ Movement	National survey 1987	Regional survey 1988	Total	Percentage
None	23	14	37	21
Regionalists	19	14	33	19
PSU	15	16	31	17
Miscellaneous left	41	25	66	37
Miscellaneous right	3	3	6	3
Other	5	0	5	3
Total	106	72	178	100

and attitudes. In answer to a question about which existing political party activists felt closest to nearly half replied the PSU, a minor left-wing party which at the time was very much in decline (and has since dissolved itself), while over a third did not reply, thus indicating no preference. This desire to see the Greens as an independent force was further underlined by the responses to the question about what ecologist candidates should do when they are forced to withdraw in the second round of an election. Activists were asked whether they should drop out in favour of a candidate of the left or right and an overwhelming majority (82 per cent) replied that they should do neither: no *consigne de vote* (advice for the second round vote) should be given, suggesting a clear perception of the ecology movement as a non-aligned, autonomous political force.[16] Furthermore, the vast majority of activists, in the earlier survey as in the more recent one, had never belonged to any other political party, nor had they previously been involved in political activity: in 1987-88, only 15% declared they had been a member of another political organization.

The decline in the number of activists in the 1987-8 survey (compared with 1983) that named the PSU as the party to which they feel closest is undoubtedly due to the aforementioned decline of the PSU as a political movement during the 1980s. A significant minority nevertheless continued. to name either the PSU or the regionalist movement as the political grouping to which they feel closest (see Table 5). We also asked whether the socio-political vision of the Greens and that of the Alternative Left are compatible. The results make it abundantly clear that most activists prefer to see the Greens as a non-aligned, autonomous political force; 82 per cent of respondents in the 1987-8 survey rejected any compatibility between the two visions.

Another important feature of green activists is their union membership. Both the 1983 and 1987-8 surveys found that about one-third of activists are members of a union, which is relatively high considering the generally low level (about one in ten of the workforce) of unionization in France. Of those who are unionized approximately four out of five belong to the independent left trade union, the *Confédération Française Démocratique du Travail* (CFDT). Before its change of direction and adoption of a strategy of *recentrage*, this union used to be considered the most sympathetic to green issues, largely because of the central role it played in the anti-nuclear movement in the 1970s. It was in this context that one early study saw the anti-nuclear movement, and the political ecology movement that accompanied it, as a 'pre-social movement' which, as the old social movements characteristic of industrial society increasingly became exhausted or were sucked into the system as instruments of control or management, would emerge as a forerunner of the social movements of post-industrial society (Touraine *et al.* 1980). For the transformation from pre-social movement to social movement successfully to be realized, it was suggested that the best strategy for the movement to adopt would be to ally itself with those groups, such as the CFDT, which were fighting the same adversary. In post-industrial society this was no longer the capitalist class of factory owners but rather the technocratic elite who are not only in a position to determine the collective destiny of society, but also have the power to impose their decisions. The CFDT was seen as a natural partner of the political ecology movement because:

> In spite of the advances it has made in, amongst others, the metal industry, it is above all a trade unionism of the modern sectors of the economy, that is, those sectors where the machine operators and technicians can … organise a new social movement by fighting against the appropriation of knowledge by management and by co-operating with consumers against the latter.[17]

With the transformation of the 'pre-social movement' into a political party in January 1984, the abandonment of the strategy of alliance and the loss of the close links which existed between the ecologists and the CFDT during the 1970s, it would appear that the movement's political role has been reinforced at the expense of its social one. What we mean by this is that, at the time of these links, the French green movement came as close as it ever has hitherto to establishing a genuine social base, and that the loss of links with other groups within civil society which could be considered broadly sympathetic to the green movement's aims appears to have precluded the establishment of such a social base at least for the time being. Furthermore the 1970s was a period of 'social experimentation', a feature which we consider indispensable to the formation of a distinctive political culture (cf. Rosanvallon and Viveret 1977) and without which a new social movement is unlikely to emerge. It seems to us that this type of experimentation in the field of daily personal and political life was stronger in France during the 1970s; to take but one example, in the region of Britanny this was certainly the period during which the green movement in its different manifestations was closest to the Breton regionalist movement. The anti-nuclear struggles of Plogoff and Le Pellerin bear witness to this hypothesis.[18] Subsequent to François Mitterrand's presidential victory in 1981, the political arm of the movement became the dominant partner and energies were shifted from activity principally at the level of civil society to that of political institutions.

The long march across the institutions had begun. As we indicate below, the adoption of an autonomous political strategy was probably, at the time, the only realistic choice open to the movement, given the national political context in which it has emerged. However it may be that the adoption of this strategy, even if unavoidable in the short term, will prove to be a source of weakness rather than strength in the long term if, as we have suggested, the movement's implantation within civil society has weakened in favour of its political role. We shall return to this question in the concluding section.

Ideology

'Ni gauche, ni droite, mais devant' ('Neither right, nor left, but in front')
The ideology of the ecologist movement is an extremely diffuse affair, reaching from the extreme right to the extreme left of the political philosophy spectrum. Indeed it is so diffuse that ecologists themselves often have considerable problems in presenting a coherent vision of their belief system. This difficulty is understandable for at least two reasons. Firstly the ecologist movement is, as we have shown, a relatively recent phenomenon which is still in the process of defining its ideology. The second reason is perhaps more fundamental, however, in that the green movement claims that the dominant ideologies of Left and Right are part of the problem, not only in their content but also in their form. At times one even wonders whether political ecology does not wish to be the first social and political movement to dispense with the tools of ideology.[19]

> We rely on an extraordinary eclectic political and philosophical ancestry. To try to weld this into some easily articulated ideology really would be a waste of time – and would completely miss the point. Ideologies are by definition both reductionist and divisive.[20]

There seems to be little doubt that the green movement adopts the pejorative interpretation of ideology, using it as an inherent criticism of other people's belief systems. Certain activists speak of '*courants de pensée originaux*', (currents of original thought) as opposed to '*idéologies*', (ideologies) of the right and left (M. Carré/M. Perrigueax/G. Masquelier/B. and G. Massip, Paris, AGM, 1986). Others, such as the present leader of the Greens (A. Waechter), use the term '*pensée écologiste*' (ecological thought) in opposition to the concept of '*références idéologiques*' (ideological references).[21] Even in internal debate, the term is most often used in this derogatory sense.

However, we should perhaps draw a line between the use of ideology as a political tool, and ideological content as it is presented in a belief system. Every social movement must have what Heberle (1951) terms a set of 'constitutive ideas' in order to hold people together. These beliefs are not always immediately apparent and it is therefore necessary to analyse what lies behind the discourse, beyond the façade of apparent social reality, in order to 'debunk' (Berger and Kellner 1981, p. 11) the green movement's beliefs and find out their origins and import. Some indication of this ideological diversity may also be gleaned from the answers to the question 'Which areas of concern should the Greens concentrate on?', which are summarized in Table 6.

In our view four distinct currents, or sources of reference, may be identified in the discourse of the French green movement:

(1) conservationist,
(2) personalist/humanist,
(3) modernist,
(4) utopian.

These sources often overlap but each has been present at one time or another in the green movement and has contributed therefore to ecologist ideology. They present a picture of a belief system which is synergetic.

Conservationist

Perhaps the most widely held image of ecologists is that of the straw-hat brigade whose principal life-support is carrot juice and who live in communes illuminated by candles. This image stems from the romantic naturalist and conservationist tendencies which have existed and still exist in the ecology movement: from J.- J. Rousseau complaining that trees should be made to stand to attention in French gardens[22] through to an advertisement for ecological holidays in 1988:

> With local people, living in a farmhouse cottage, taking long walks in the country, horse-riding, ski-ing, in transhumance with the shepherds, following in the tracks of Jean Giono, savouring good country cooking, your head in the stars and your feet in a field of ammonite...[23]

The theme of a romanticized clean country life away from the insalubrious 'nature' of town life is one which lies at the heart of the ecological collective (un)conscious and is, indeed,the starting block for the

Table 6 Areas of green concern

Which areas of concern should the Greens concentrate on?
(Respondents were asked to give four areas of concern in order of preference.)

Area of concern	Preference				
	1st total (%)	2nd total (%)	3rd total (%)	4th total (%)	Total %
Natural					
Environment					
pollution etc.	31 (28)	16 (18)	17 (20	13 (20)	77 (22)
Energy (incl.					
Nuclear Power)	22 (20)	16 (18)	8 (10)	4 (6)	50 (14)
Social					
Social/economic					
problems	9 (17)	26 (29)	16 (19)	0 (0)	61 (17)
Social Solidarity					
anti-racism,democracy	9 (8)	14 (15)	8 (10)	16 (25)	47 (13)
Others					
Holistic ecology,					
defence of life	23 (21)	0 (0)	0 (0)	0 (0)	23 (7)
Other areas	7 (6)	19 (21)	35 (42)	31 (48)	92 (26)
Total	111(100)	91(101[a])	84(101[a])	64(100)	350(99[a])

[a] Because of rounding, figures do not add up to 100.

present-day green movement via the different nature conservation groups that accompanied industrialization in France.[24] These conservationist groups are, in many ways, the forerunners of the present environmentalist majority within the French Greens, to the extent that, although ecologist thinking has gone well past the simple protection of nature, the latter still seems to be the overriding concern of the activists encountered in our survey. As we show below, Table 6, in answer to the question 'Which areas of concern should the Greens concentrate on?' The majority identified both 'natural' and 'social' concerns, but 21 per cent refused to split up their answer, preferring to reply that all concerns were interrelated and should be treated holistically.

The conservationist element within the wider ecology movement is a phenomenon which can be traced back to the beginnings of ecological awareness and is reflected in one of the directions taken by the movement, especially in the early days, which consisted in stirring people's consciences with forecasts of doom. The movement came into the public eye on a wave of potential catastrophes and this form of message was politicized following the MIT (Massachusetts Institute of Technology) report in 1971-2, 'The Limits to Growth', based on the work of the Club of Rome. One of the most widely publicized reactions to this report was the English ecologists' 'Blueprint for Survival' (E. Goldsmith et al.) which appeared in 1972. This work was quickly translated and indeed was a direct source of inspiration for the movement's very first electoral campaign in Mulhouse (Alsace, 1973).[25] The authors used the scientifically-based predictions in the MIT report of natural resource scarcity to construct an ecological alternative: the only one possible in terms of the survival of the human species. This idea of a forthcoming apocalypse in the absence of the 'right' social and political policies is an old hobbyhorse of the political right-wing and, although it may have been tactically useful in the constitution of the green movement by stimulating awareness, its long-term effectiveness as a platform for political and social change is perhaps limited in that it could simply lead to a form of fatalism less than conducive to long-term commitment. We might also add that such a 'blue-print' future brings us, paradoxically, full-circle back to the very criticism ecologists make of traditional ideologies: that of being determinist.

Humanist/Personalist

In France, the Personalist school of thought dates back to the philosopher, C. Renouvier (1815-1903), who first presented the term in his work Le Personnalisme (1902).

Renouvier considered the person to be the centre of a philosophical 'lay' religion (religion laïque), the principal task of which would be to solve the problem of evil in society. During the 1930s, the term Personalist was readopted by the philosopher E. Mounier who aimed to create a movement, based on a doctrine of social and moral humanism, which would herald a new civilization. Such a form of revolutionary humanism, in Mounier's opinion, was necessary in the face of a rampant materialism (East and West) that had the effect of producing either an individualistic form of Social Darwinism or a faceless bureaucratic collectivism. Mounier's was a fight to unite this 'pernicious dualism' (Encyclopedia Universalis France 1985, p. 715) (spiritualism/materialism) within a radical social and political movement.

The importance of spiritualism in all human endeavour[26] was underlined for Mounier by the Wall Street crash of 1929. This indicated the need to reestablish spiritual values amidst the marasmus of materialism, a form of 'catastrophism' similar to that which was, as we have shown, characteristic of the ecology movement in its early stages.

Furthermore the idea of the primacy of the Person over material necessity is an implicit criticism of what are considered the excesses of Marxist materialism. The ecologist critique of Marxism stems from similar concerns and indeed its avowed objective is 'the painless birth of a new civilisation which respects the human person and the biosphere'.[27]

Personalism was also contrasted with bourgeois individualism. This was, for Mounier, the basis of bourgeois capitalism, the ethics of which he loathed: 'the first priority of individualism is to centre the individual on her/himself, while the first priority of personalism is to decentre the individual so as to establish her/him in the open perspective of the complete person' (cf. Mounier 1985).

This respect for the individual in the midst of bureaucratic consumerist anonymity is a recurring theme of the French green movement which proposes a 'new orientation towards respect for, and the promotion of, the development of the whole person, (and) of human relations'.[28]

The articulation of freedom and autonomy is a theme common to both personalism and ecologist theory. The individual unit, be it an individual, a community or a region, is conceived as a free entity within a superior whole of which it is an integral and necessary part. Just as the person only really exists in relation to another, so autonomy as a personalist and ecologist concept is translated politically by independence from the political power blocks. This is reflected in the autonomous political strategy of *Les Verts*. The green movement has, since the late 1970s, consistently distanced itself from the traditional political blocks in an attempt to create for itself a distinctive political and ideological identity. 'Neither right nor left, but in front' was first heard in West Germany and has now become a frequently heard slogan of the movement. In this view there exists an underlying consensus between the Right and Left over the major decisions affecting society in general and with regard to economic growth in particular, hence the global rejection of the different political blocks and their accompanying ideologies.

> Question (D. Souchet): Do you see any difference between Mitterrand, Barre and Chirac for the moment?
>
> Reply (A. Waechter, Ecologist presidential candidate 1988) : For the moment, no.[29]

Finally, Mounier was also dismayed by the incapacity of the institutionalized Left to imagine anything other than the utilitarian, consumerist tools of capitalism as a model for a future socialist society. In this respect, the Greens of today have adopted certain ideas which have a fifty-year-old history:

> The main challenge facing the twentieth century will doubtless be whether it is able to avoid the dictatorship of the technocrats who, whether of the right or left, forget man beneath the organisation (Mounier 1985, p. 115).

These words reflect the Personalists' concern over the direction which Western industrial society has taken through a form of social mechanization and 'disempowerment' of the individual. This process was held responsible for the *depersonalization* of Western society and led to a form of individualistic atomization. It was not a question of refusing technological progress, just as is not the case with the Greens, but rather of opposing its excesses and some of its consequences. It is perhaps at this point that the Personalist movement of the 1930s resembles most strongly the Greens of today.

Modernist

Amidst the wealth of green movement literature there is a strand of thought lying just beneath the surface that we might call 'modernist' or 'futurist'. This current conceives of a better ecological future by means of modern technology:

> Ecologism does not therefore refuse technical progress, as it is too often believed. Quite the contrary, the most radical current in the movement, represented by Murray Bookchin, is perhaps over-optimistic in believing that technological possibilities are limitless and that the most sophisticated techniques, the astonishing products of the coming together of biology and computer science, could be harnessed to serve human beings and make human work less burdensome.[30]

It sometimes appears to represent more a latent temptation than a concrete proposition. It is nevertheless present and is characterized by references to post-industrialism and to the increasing importance of the tertiary sector which is, as we have seen, the sector employing the vast majority of ecologist activists and voters.

There is little doubt that the social and professional make-up of Western industrial society is under profound transformation and that the traditional 'role' of the 'proletariat' in social change is rapidly diminishing (Gorz 1980). The role played by technocracy in the Greens' belief system is not dissimilar to that played by the capitalist class in the ideology of socialism; just as the latter was the arch enemy of the labour movement, so technocracy (*le pouvoir technocratique*) is often cited as the ecologists' main adversary.[31] The question is, will this new society be technologically 'liberating' and ecologically acceptable or will it be a (potentially) perfected form of social and political domination? Therein lies the crux of the hope in the new technologies: that they will be conducive to the kind of convivial society which the Greens aspire to. This 'hope' is placed in different sectors. For example the development of the *Télématique* sector[32] in France has opened up possibilities of individual and collective communication that inspire some elements of the French green movement:

> The promotion of a more direct form of democracy which depends less on the election of representatives, such as the popular initiative referendum (RIP). *Les Verts* propose that the possibilities offered by télématique[32] in this field should be explored.[33]

and leave others cold:

The popular initiative referendum is a good idea because it is democratic. However it only has any real significance insofar as the resulting vote is the product of genuine and serious debate. If this is not the case, then the result is a grotesque manipulation, and Le Pen[34] in particular has fully understood the advantage to be derived from such manipulation, for example with regard to immigrants and the death penalty. When you think that some Greens want to study the possibilities of télématique in this context, you begin to wonder if you are not dreaming! Where will real confrontation of ideas take place?[35]

The fear here is that information technology can be simply another means of social control.

This modernist futurist trend is a further example of the oppositions we have so often found in the Greens' belief system. On the one hand there is the inference that the technique in itself may be liberating and on the other the realization that it could be if social relationships allow it to be (cf. Dickson 1981).

Utopian

This strand is perhaps the one which has caused most problems to the ecologist movement in that it is the one which most clearly overlaps with other political movements. Several of the most basic tenets of the ideology of the French green movement (autonomy, decentralization, direct democracy, socially useful production) have a long history in political theory. Outside the dominant centralist tradition in socialism, a decentralist, self-managing current also exists which has its origins in the nineteenth century utopian socialist movement. Themes such as labour-intensive rather than capital-intensive work, non-alienating socially useful production, the redistribution of wealth, political and economic decentralization, a small human-scale economy and work-sharing are all themes which anarchists, democratic socialists and political ecologists would adhere to. This historical and philosophical link between anarchism, democratic socialism and political ecology has, with regard to the green movement, been referred to at various points during the movement's short lifespan. Whether it is emphasized or not depends on the period in question: during the 1970s, one of the two principal green movement papers (La Gueule Ouverte) boasted its anarchism: 'The disappearance of political parties, of the vote, of the delegation of power and of hierarchies, and thus of the State' (La Gueule Ouverte no. 80, 10 November 1986) and one of its principal theorists (D. de Rougement) describes himself as being 'completely Bakunian' (Allan-Michaud 1979, p. 850). Others, such as D. Simmonet and P. Lebreton, consider that the green movement has given a new lease of life to ideas which had gone out of fashion:

The old federalist and libertarian ambition, so abused by history, has

found its second wind with ecologism (Simmonet 1979, p. 83).
... are not the ecologists rediscovering, a century later, what it has become traditional to call the generous utopias of the early socialists? (Lebreton 1978, quoted in Allan-Michaud 1979, p. 851).
Allan-Michaud (1979, p. 851) speaks of federalism's revenge over centralism and Bakunin's over Marx by quoting M. Bookchin, one of the green movement's extremely popular American (eco-anarchist) theoretical references during the first half of the 1970s.

Within the wider vein of anarchist/democratic socialist thought, the writings of P. Proudhon (1809-1865) on federalism, of R. Owen (1771-1858) and C. Fourier (1772-1837) on utopian cooperatives [36] and of W. Morris (1834-1896) on the adverse effects of industrialization are precursors of the ecologists' belief system.[37]

In its overwhelming desire to forge its own political identity, the green movement in the 1980s made much less reference to the anarchist/ democratic socialist ideals of its predecessors. However one potential problem with such a manoeuvre is the creation of a form of historical amnesia[38] leading to a desire to 'rediscover' the world through green eyes. The limits of such a vision are recognized at the highest levels: 'Let us stop starting from scratch and constantly rebuilding the world, it's one of the reasons for our lack of progress'.[39]

One of the consequences of this tendency to 'start from scratch' is the millenarist phenomenon which has always been latent within the French green movement and which has become more visible over the recent past. Millenarism, in social movement theory, is a term which has been applied to those movements, principally religious, that await ultimate collective and total salvation with the coming of the saviour, be it Christ as in the revelations of St John and in Jewish apocalyptic literature, or a boat full of European goods (cf. Wilson 1973).

This is not to say, of course, that the green movement awaits a saviour. It is, however, to suggest that the movement periodically harks back to its early 'catastrophic' period of a 'new-age dawning' vision of social reality. R. Dumont's campaign in 1974 was based on an apocalyptic vision of the future in the absence of ecologist measures being adopted. Similarly, instances of the inevitability of the 'ecologist coming' (if activists are prepared to wait long enough) are to be found in more recent literature, coinciding with this urgent desire to forge an independent political identity based on an alternative political culture:

> Time and events are working for us if we remain faithful to our identity and stop wasting our time and effort on electoral politics.[40]

This is an example of an unswerving faith in the face of what is seen as global opposition (based on ignorance) to the green movement's theory and practice. Faith of this nature can also perhaps be seen as serving the function of group cohesion, reinforcing the desire for independence and precluding the necessity for broader alliances.

The utopian tradition in the movement is, therefore, one which raises its head periodically. It is one which was most visible during the period 1974-81, which saw the wider green movement at its strongest. In the more recent period (1981-8), it was a lot less often referred to as the more institutionalized arm of the movement (the political party, Les Verts) attempted to carve out its own political niche. This aspiration to create an autonomous political movement is supported by a majority of activists, as our survey has shown.

Part of the problem for the green movement is that, on the one hand, it rejects the dominant ideologies of both left and right, while on the other it is suspicious of the very concept of ideology itself. Yet it is clear that ideology is always present in a social movement in some form, and if the term hurts too much we can call it a belief system. The belief system of the French green movement is one which is extremely heterogeneous and synergetic, differing, in this respect, from what greens would consider more rigid and monolithic ideologies, such as Marxism. It is this heterogeneous nature of its belief system that produces the oppositions between reactionary/ utopian, anarchist-socialist and modernist/reactionary tendencies within the movement.

To return once again to our survey, it would seem that the dominant tendency in the green movement at present is what we have called the 'naturalist' one. This is not, of course, to say that the majority of the present-day Verts are simply interested in protecting the natural environment: it does, however, suggest that the overriding concern of the activists who replied to our questionnaire is to be found in this domain. It seems to us that the political ecology movement has been divided over the emphasis to give to 'social' and ' natural' issues since its inception and that this division is to be found in the present-day Verts. This has been illustrated at each AGM since A. Waechter, who is seen as being the leader of the naturalist tendency (Le Monde, 19 November 1989), gained control of the Greens in 1986. As examples of this one can point to the votes obtained by the different motions put forward or signed on the one hand by A. Waechter and on the other by his principal opponents (Y. Cochet/J. Briere/D. Anger). The titles of motions are in italics and the percentages are those of final round votes:

1986
A. Waechter et al., Ecology is not looking for a marriage: 68 per cent
Y. Cochet et al., Construct: 32 per cent.
1987
E Tête et al. (Waechter tendency): 62.4 per cent

Y. Cochet et al., *Let's get involved in politics*: 13.3 per cent.
1988
Waechter et al., 66.6 per cent (no opposing motion as such, three complementary ones)
1989
A. Waechter et al., '... *Harness your plough to a star* ...' 54.3 per cent
G.. Hascouet et al., 24.2 per cent
J. Brière et al. (Y. Cochet among others): 10.9 per cent.

Without entering into the significance of the percentage drop in A. Waechter's support at the 1989 AGM of the Greens in Marseilles, it is quite clear that the majority of activists remain faithful to his conception of political ecology. This is, we believe, confirmation of the division between the *natural* and *social* tendencies within the movement, as shown in the survey of 1987. It could also be significant in explaining the transformation from what we consider to have been an embryonic social movement in the 1970s to a fully fledged political party with principally environmentalist concerns. The latter would seem at present to have *replaced* the former, rather than becoming simply an indispensable political arm of a broader social movement.

Conclusion

The green movement finally emerged as a significant actor on the French political stage, as we have shown, following its successes in the Municipal and European elections of March and June 1989. Its long-term significance and durability have yet to be measured, of course, but it remains the case that, compared with some of its European counterparts, particularly Germany, the movement's electoral success has been a long time coming and it is still some distance from making the transition to a social movement. This requires explanation.

One possible form of answer may lie in the articulation of the opposition between *structural* and *cultural* explanations of social change. The opposition between these two approaches to the explanation of social change is best illustrated in the continuing conflict between Marxist and Weberian interpretations of social history. Put in its most basic form the question is: do values create structures or the reverse? In the case of the French Green Movement, the question is thus whether it is the unfavourable external institutional and cultural setting which explains their lack of success hitherto, or whether it is their own political culture, and the internal ideology and practices which are a part of it, that have been the principal cause of their lack of progress.

There is no doubt that the electoral system of the French Fifth Republic

Table 7 Perceived reasons for the Greens' lack of impact

Why have the Greens failed to make progress in France?
(Open question, 112 replies, 256 reasons offered).

	Total	Percentage
Exogenous factors		
Institutions/state	40	16
Media/image	34	13
Political tradition	25	10
Absence of alternative movement		
and social base	22	9
French culture	21	8
Finances	12	5
All exogenous factors	154	60
Endogenous factors		
Internal practices (lack of conviviality,		
internal conflict, gap theory-practice,		
strategy, sectarianism, leaders,		
ideological diversity, etc.)	77	30
Insufficient number of activists	12	5
Overpoliticized	2	1
All endogenous factors	91	36
Miscellaneous	11	4
Total	256	100

constitutes a major obstacle to institutional representation for the French green movement as national level. The Presidential elections are mainly a tribune to air views for minority parties and the 12.5 per cent hurdle of the Legislative elections has proved, up to now, to be too high. The more local elections, particularly those at Regional and Municipal level, and the European elections, with their system of proportional representation, therefore currently offer the best hope of electoral success for the movement. This institutional environment, combined with problems of visibility in the French media (Allan-Michaud 1989) has, we are convinced, made it more difficult for ecologists to progress: from institutional recognition comes greater credibility, which in turn leads to greater visibility in the public eye; greater visibility in turn offers increased hopes of electoral success and greater institutional recognition.

It is also clear that, if we compare France and Germany, a similar electoral percentage has vastly different ramifications in the two countries:

> With 13.9% of the vote in Rennes, *Les Verts* only win four seats on the municipal council while in Frankfurt, with 10% of the vote, they can force the Social Democrats into negotiating to form a coalition and are in a position to obtain several posts as vice-chairs of committees ... (De Bresson 1989).

Is this structural explanation the only reason? Of the activists themselves, 16 per cent believe that institutional reasons are the major cause of the Greens' difficulties and a further 13 per cent attribute the Greens' lack of protest to the media and problems of image (see Table 7).

It is certainly the case that, in general, the institutional framework of the Fifty Republic has not facilitated the task of the green movement in establishing itself in France. Equally the political culture of the Fifth Republic has not made the Greens' task any easier. The French centralist tradition, to which the Fifth Republic has returned,[41] is one which tends to disempower the individual. She/he believes her/himself to be powerless in face of an all-powerful and increasingly bureaucratic state. The French have a term for this: *déresponsabilisation de l'individu*. One consequence of this is to accentuate a certain form of French individualism and, secondly, to create a less than favourable environment for the development of one of the principal ecologist tenets: autonomy.

A word of explanation may be necessary here in order to clarify this point. The tradition of central state power in France seems to us to have had the effect of rendering the individual both largely powerless in the face of, yet at the same time dependent on, central authority. This feeling of powerlessness appears in turn to have a negative effect on long-term collective solidarity within French society. The individualism which is a characteristic of all capitalist, consumerist societies is, it would appear, accentuated in the French context by the unequal relationship between the State and the citizen, even if what Gramsci called *civil society* - a whole range of structures and activities like trade unions, schools, the churches and the family[42] – is perhaps not sufficiently autonomous from political and administrative institutions.[43] This lack of autonomy may in turn help to explain the enormous difficulties encountered by minority political formations in asserting themselves in the political arena. It could also go a long way to explaining the formidable power of *state integration*. Two recent examples of this are the personal trajectories of F. Mitterrand and B. Lalonde, both of whom were longstanding critics of the Fifth Republic before being painlessly integrated into its institutional structure.

Furthermore the national cultural context seems especially hostile to ecologist analyses. Established ideological, cultural and philosophical traditions have combined to create an environment which is less than congenial to many ecology themes such as feminism, non-violence and a certain form of spiritualism incorporating the power of intuition. In this context one could perhaps argue that the French tradition of rationalism has hindered the progress of the movement in France.

The French Greens' own political culture could also perhaps go some way to explaining its difficulties. This may be approached from two different angles: externally and internally. Externally, there would seem to be a considerable amount of overlap between the political culture and the green movement and that of the alternative left. Certainly, at the level of practices, there is often little to distinguish them and they have frequently cooperated together in both local and national actions.[44] Furthermore there are several areas of convergence, in ideological terms, between the two movements and the refusal of many Greens to recognize this has contributed, as we have shown, to a certain a-historical world-view, as illustrated by the millenarist tendency visible in some ecologist literature. This apparent practical convergence can be a source of confusion for external sympathizers who are not aware of the state of internal ideological debate between the two groups.

Internally, there would seem to be some distance between acclaimedly novel political practices and those visible to the observer. Different instances of this have been noted and we will give just two as illustrations. The ecologist movement world-wide stresses that a new form of political practice, more participatory and open with less mutual distrust and suspicion, is necessary if the ecologist movement is to make headway. These laudable sentiments are not always immediately obvious to the observer. The AGMs and CNIRs[45] of Les Verts frequently do not constitute the political expression of conviviality which ecologists in principle favour and, on the level of form alone, there is very often little to distinguish a meeting of Les Verts from those of other organizations: personal attacks, power struggles and political manoeuvring are all prevalent. Activists themselves are aware of this.

> We must understand that if we continue to be as unconvivial in our meetings, if we continue to squabble amongst ourselves in the newspapers, if we continue to maintain that we are the only ones who ever get it right then we will never bring together people other than dogmatic idealists or dreamers.[46]

Such a distance between proclaimed theory and observable practices can be both internally and externally damaging. A comparison with the internal practices of the Green Party in Britain is revealing in this respect. At the beginning of each party meeting the British Greens hold what they term a 'tuning-in' session, i.e. a short moment of silence allowing participants to divest themselves of any potential aggression, thereby paving the way for an exchange based on conviviality. At the European Green

Congress at Dover in 1985, the reaction of a section of the French Greens to this was that of benign amusement. It was considered to be a vestige of a mystical green past, the type of experience they had been through and given up fifteen years ago and which was, therefore, dépassé.

This desire to put into practice ecologist theories that lay claim to an alternative political practice specific to ecologists is reflected in the reply to the question 'What explains the French ecologists' lack of success?' 30 per cent suggested that the (negative) image of internal practices projected to the outside world went a long way to explaining this lack of progress and contributes to the hypothesis that the political culture of the French Greens may be, as yet, insufficiently developed. By this we mean that the osmosis between the different elements of ideology (Rosanvallon and Viveret 1977, p 62) does not yet seem to have come about. This is perhaps inevitable given the youthfulness of the movement, but nevertheless constitutes an obstacle to the development of what some activists and commentators would like the movement to become: a fully fledged social movement.

To continue with this last point a social movement is not, we believe, synonymous with a political organization, the latter being but a manifestation, albeit an indispensable one, of the former. We therefore wonder whether the French green movement has not invested too much energy into the development of its political arm, Les Verts, at the expense of the broader social movement. Given that 30.5 per cent of activists (not necessarily the same ones, admittedly) believe that the lack of progress of the Greens can be attributed to structural factors, one may wonder why, if the French state is guilty of such obstruction, so much energy has been invested into building up the political organization in order to contest elections, at the expense of the wider social movement. The answer to this question probably lies, as we have indicated, in the traditional weakness of 'civil society' in relation to the state in France, and the consequent pressure on the Green movement, as on any minority political group or social movement in France, to organize itself into a political party and take part in the political process with the eventual aim of gaining a stake in power at the level of the state.

The creation of Les Verts in 1984 means that the links between the political organization and the broader social movement do not seem to be as strong, or even as obvious, as they might be expected to be. Is it the case, for example, that conservationist associations sympathize with, and vote for, Les Verts?[47] Or that members of organic food coops vote Green? This in turn raises the question: what constitutes an ecologist social base? Does it exist and, if so, how solid is it? The answer to these questions may be two-fold.

Firstly it does not seem to be the case that Les Verts are the natural political expression of the broader social movement. It is difficult to be in any way categorical on this point but the research being carried out at the present time in this aspect (Prendiville, forthcoming) suggests that the Greens are now always in touch with what could have constituted a *social base* of support. What one might think of as the 'natural' support has been present for some time but the identification of other groups within society which are 'objective' ideological partners of the ecologists[48] with the political expression that the Greens represent has not been made. Nor, it seems, do these groups wish to make it, for fear of losing their identity and efficiency. As such and apart from the activists themselves, there seems to be an insufficient amount of group consciousness among groups which could be considered natural 'ideological bedfellows'. Secondly, many people question the idea that the green movement has any recognizable social base. We believe it may have but that it is one which is in a constant state of flux and is, as such, perhaps a contradiction in terms. That is to say that the somewhat traditional concept of a social base as being easily identifiable and forming a relatively stable platform for a social movement – as was the case for example with the working class and the socialist movement – may no longer be as useful a concept with regard to the green movement. We have seen that the social classes which provide electoral support and make up the Greens are principally those of the intellectual and tertiary sector. This is a potential factor of cohesion. However, at the same time, the political profile of the voters and activists is vastly different. The former's sympathies, as we have seen, tend to lean to the left.[49] The latter's are principally centred on concerns for the protection of the environment, as the surveys reveal. Whether these two directions will converge as the Greens gain greater institutional credibility remains to be seen.

There is, no doubt, a play-off between the importance of structure and values in the explanation of social activity in general, and the green movement's difficulties in particular. In answer to the question, '*Why have the Greens failed to make progress in France?*', both structural and cultural reasons were given. What is perhaps revealing as to the state of thinking within the movement is that around two-thirds (61 per cent) of replies were of the opinion that the causes for the relative lack of progress were *exogenous*, which could be taken as suggesting that the Greens themselves can do little to change the situation as they are victims of an unfavourable structural and cultural environment. Such an analysis may not be conducive to making changes within the movement.

Finally we must address the question of political autonomy. Are the Greens an autonomous political movement? Certainly the political organization *Les Verts*, has insisted on remaining independent from the left and right in elections. It has also been at great pains to distance itself, as we have seen, from any institutional convergence with the alternative left, hoping thereby to avoid any confusion in the public eye. This is, of course, with a view to creating an independent political identity. The 1989

Municipal election results certainly seem to give support to this strategy but the Legislative elections will be a lot less favourable to ecologist candidates. We believe the Greens have gone a long way to forging of a, necessarily independent organization. We are less convinced that this organization is the centre of a social and political movement based on a distinctive political culture which integrates to a sufficient extent the vital elements of continuity, participation, constitutive beliefs and group consciousness (see among others, Banks 1972; Heberle 1951; Oberschall 1973; Smelser 1962; Touraine 1978; Turner and Killian 1972; Wilkinson 1971; Wilson 1973). The overwhelming impression which remains from the results of the activists' survey is one of an organization split between a majority desire to develop principally environmentalist themes and a minority which wishes to integrate social themes to a larger extent than at present.[50] Such an internal desire seems to reinforce the external environment image projected by the media and also brings us back to our 1981 comment regarding the victory of the 'ecologists over the environmentalists' within the French green movement (Prendiville 1981). The data from our surveys suggest that this assertion may have been premature. Are the 'environmentalists' in the movement now taking their revenge and gaining the upper hand? The conflict between the two tendencies remains and is far from having been definitively resolved by the victory of the Waechtar tendency at the Assemblée Générale of Les Verts in November 1989 (see Le Monde, 21 November and 12 December 1989). In any case it appears that the environmentalists are, for the time being, in the ascendant within the movement. Should their victory prove definitive, this would tend to corroborate D. Allan-Michaud's 1979 forecast of a possible environmental trade unionism with respect to the then ecology discourse, and could prove damaging in the long term for a movement with aspirations to become a lasting, autonomous social movement.

Editor's note: I am extremely grateful to Dr James Mitchell for his unselfish and essential help in editing the final version of this chapter.

NOTES

1 This split was already evident at the ecologists' first national gathering at Bazoches in June 1974, at which no agreement was reached on proposals for a national structure. Despite this the Mouvement Ecologique was set up later that year, although it was attacked by many ecologist groups for claiming to speak on behalf of the entire ecologist movement.

2 He stood for election in Paris on a green ticket in a by-election in November 1976 and at both the 1977 Municipal and 1978 Parliamentary elections. He then stood as Presidential candidate for the Greens in 1981, gaining over 1.1 million votes in the first round. In 1984 he headed, together with François Doubin and Olivier Stirn, an independent green list, Entente Radicale Ecologiste (ERE), which was opposed by the official

green list headed by Didier Anger. At the 1986 Parliamentary elections he stood against Charles Hernu, former Socialist Minister of Defence, in protest at the sinking of the Greenpeace ship *Rainbow Warrior*, and was again a candidate at the 1988 parliamentary elections when he stood unsuccessfully for election of Melun (Seine-et-Marne) with the support of the Socialist Party. He is currently (1990) Minister for the Environment in Michel Rocard's government.

3 The Lip factory in Besançon, threatened with closure by its owners, was taken over by the workers in 1973 and eventually reopened in 1974.

4 The PSU is a small left-wing party. It was created during the Algerian crisis and was active in the anti-nuclear movement in the 1970s and early 1980s.

5 Larzac was the proposed site for an army training area. Groups were formed throughout France to fight the project, which was eventually abandoned by President Mitterrand after his victory in the 1981 Presidential elections.

6 Malville is the site of France's first commercial fast-breeder nuclear reactor. It became the focus for opposition to the French nuclear programme and was the scene of violent demonstrations, at which one person was killed in 1977.

7 The problem of self-identification has still to be resolved in that there remain differences in analysis as to the 'nature' of political ecology between the two main tendencies (natural/social division in the movement, see Table 6.

8 Communiqué de Presse, Ministère de l'Agriculture, 6 May 1986. All French quotations only appear in English translations in the main text, all translations are ours.

9 Saint Brieuc, Besançon, Quimper, Cholet, Vannes, Lorient, Strasbourg, Colmar, Mulhouse, Caluire, Saint Priest, Paris XIV, Montauban, Poitiers, Limoges, Nanterre.

10 The data on French Green Party activists reported in this paper are based on the following three surveys. (a) 1983 national survey: 102 questionnaires filled out by activists throughout France in 1983, 60 of these were contacted at the 1983 Annual General Meeting (AGM) at Besançon and the remaining 42 were contacted through local Ecology groups throughout France. (The full results of this survey are discussed in Chafer 1984.) (b) 1987 national survey: 160 questionnaires were distributed at the November 1987 AGM in Paris; response rate: 65 (40.6 per cent). The full results of this survey are reported in Prendiville, forthcoming. (c) 1988 regional survey: Brittany. The same questionnaire was mailed to 172 activists from January to April 1988. Addresses were obtained from one Green Party activist, response rate: 49 (28.5 per cent).

11 The social classes referred to are those of the French statistical institute, INSEE (Institut National de Statistique et des Etudes Economiques). It must be pointed out that the category 'Farmers' in the French context does not encompass the same professional field as in Britain. The persons cited as farmers used the term 'paysan' to describe themselves. In British terms this should be taken to mean small farmers. The *intermediary* groups are those skilled social categories which include: primary school teachers, social workers and the 'new' youth group leaders, speech therapists and psychotherapists. Clerical workers are the loose equivalent of the British semi-skilled/unskilled category of the Registrar General's Social Categories. They include such professions as office personnel (public and private), police and military personnel and shop assistants.

12 The same is true of ecologist voters, cf. Boy 1980; 1989.

13 See for example 'La plongée des écolos', Le Monde, 6 March 1986.
14 French people have traditionally been reluctant to join political parties, while nevertheless being prepared, on occasion, to become active in social movements at the level of civil society. The student movements of 1968 and 1986 are examples of this. Some commentators have also pointed to a general political demobilization within France since the election of François Mitterrand to the Presidency in 1981.
15 Source: Les Verts, Paris, January 1990.
16 Electoral surveys have nevertheless shown that approximately two-thirds of ecologist voters transfer to a candidate of the left in the second round of voting if no ecologist candidate is present. This percentage dropped to 62 per cent in a survey taken by Le Monde-Sofres at the 1989 AGM in Marseilles. See Le Monde, 28 November 1989.
17. Touraine et al. 1980, p. 320; we may add that the CFDT remains uppermost in the minds of activists: see the survey in Le Monde, 28 November 1989.
18 See Prendiville 1980; Plogoff and Le Pellerin were two major anti-nuclear struggles of the 1970s. The former is of particular importance in being the only example of the French state withdrawing its plans for a new nuclear installation in the face of public opposition.
19 Significantly, no mention of ideology is to be found in the index of F. Capra's The Turning Point (1983). Equally, the word is absent in the index of Bunyard and Morgan-Grenville (1987).
20 Porritt (1984, p. 200); we might add that this form of eclecticism can, of course, have its advantages in that people of apparently different social and political horizons can come together under the ecologist banner. It can also have its disadvantages when the contradictions in perspective between these different horizons become clearer. J. Porritt's work has also been criticized as representing an 'end to ideology' vision of political ecology (see Weston 1986).
21 cf. The speeches of leading activists at the Paris AGM 1986.
22 From La Nouvelle Héloïse, cited in Simmonet (1979, p. 100).
23 Association Plein Air Nature in the brochure of the Salon Vivre et Travailler AUTREMENT, Paris, 19-27 March 1988. This exhibition is the first of its kind, wishing to publicize the French 'Alternative' under its many different guises and not solely, therefore, a manifestation of the green movement.
24 The first of these groups, la Société impériale zoologique d'acclimation now la Société Nationale de Protection de la Nature was created around 1854. More recently, Allan-Michaud (1979) traced the contemporary green movement back to the actions of J. Pignero, founder of the Association contre le Danger Radiologique (ACDR) in 1957, which became the more well-known Association pour la Protection contre les Rayonnements Ionisants (APRI) in 1966 and P. Pellerin, journalist for La Vie des Bêtes, 1958-60 and later founder of Bêtes et Nature, which he cites as an early example of the politicization of ecology themes.
25 This pioneer status of ecology actions in the region of Alsace was fully exploited by A. Waechter, himself from Alsace, when he gained control of the Greens in 1986.
26 The phrase used by Mounier, 'La révolution sera spirituelle ou elle ne sera pas', bears a striking resemblance to one of the movement's political slogans, 'L'Europe sera verte ou elle ne sera pas', first used in the 1979 European elections and subsequently rejected as implying an authoritarian approach. Spiritualism here is not simply religious but a reflection of human values, the latter being the basis for action.

27 Les Verts, leaflet, Besançon 1983.
28 Le Pouvoir de Vivre, Montargis, Aujourd'hui Ecologie, 1981.
29 France-Inter, 4 March 1988 (Radio broadcast).
30 Simmonet 1979, p. 17; cf. Toffler 1970, p. 443. The author himself prefers the term 'super-industrialism'.
31 See Touraine et al. (1980), who first theorized this idea with regard to what he considered to be the movement's vanguard, the anti-nuclear movement.
32 Télématique: a hybrid term for the linking up of audiovisual and computing capabilities. The best example of this in France is the 'Minitel' system, a form of electronic telephone attached to a screen and terminal complete with nationwide data base information.
33 Référendum d'Initiative Populaire (RIP): at present the internal system of consultation of the French Greens (a motion supported by 10 per cent of members is open to consultation). The Greens propose this as a nationwide method. This statement is taken from Y. Cocher's motion, Construire, to the AGM of Les Verts, Paris, 1986.
34 Leader of the extreme right-wing French National Front.
35 A. Fournier, Reflections, AGM, Les Verts, Paris, 1986.
36 Fournier called them phalanges or phalansteres although he never managed to set any up. R. Owen, on the other hand, experimented with such an ideal community, albeit short-lived, in Indiana, USA.
37 This anarchist/democratic socialist thought tradition within political ecology has been well documented, for example by Williams (n.d.) and by Allan-Michaud (1979).
38 Cohn-Bendit, one-time member, was the first to point out this worrying tendency within Les Verts at the unofficial inaugural meeting of Arc-en-Ciel when he spoke of their 'ahistorical' tendency, 18 January 1987, Charonne, Paris.
39 G. Marimot, Secretaire, Rapport d'Activité, AGM, Paris 1987.
40 M.-T. Pagel, Les Verts, AGM, Paris 1986.
41 This may be changing with the process of decentralization instigated by Mitterrand, although some criticism of its insufficiency has begun to appear.
42 cf. Boggs (1976), in the context of contemporary France we would add the sector of vie associative (associations).
43 A point made by P. Viveret in his contribution to the Forum for the creation of a new political culture organized by Arc-En-Ciel (Paris 19-20 March 1988) in which he talked about the process of decision making from the Ministry down to civil society.
44 For example, Réseau pour un avenir sans nucléaire which brought together the LCR (Trotskyist), PSU, FGA, Fédération Anarchiste and Les Verts to organize the anti-nuclear demonstration a year after Chernobyl.
45 Conseil National Interrégional; ruling body of Les Verts.
46 P. Parraux, AGM, Paris 1980.
47 This was not found to be the case by Gilles Guyomard in his DEA (Diplôme d'Etudes Approfondies) thesis (1978).
48 Third World activists, organic farmers/consumers, regionalists, environmentalists, alternative left.
49 In the 1988 Presidential election, of those who voted for Antoine Waechter in the first round, 70 per cent, when forced to make a choice, said they would go for Mitterrand in preference to Chirac in the second round; see Boy (1989). However, when it came to the actual vote, Mitterrand obtained the votes of only 50 per cent of those who had voted for Waechter in the first round, while another 30 per cent abstained; see

Paris-Match, 6 May 1988. The difference in emphasis between activists' and voters' concerns was further underlined in the survey of *Le Monde* and *Sofres* (*Le Monde*, 28 November 1989) carried out at the AGM in Marseilles. In answer to the question, '*In your opinion what are the priorities for France in the next few years?*' 73 per cent of activists gave '*Protecting the environment*' first priority and 54 per cent put '*Reducing social inequality*' in second place. In answer to the same question in September 1989, 77 per cent of ecologist *voters* cited '*Creating jobs*' as their most important aim and '*Protecting the environment*' came second, supported by 70 per cent.

50 It is important, however, to note that a sizeable minority (23 first choice replies = 20.5%) refused to separate social from natural issues. This 'holistic' approach could, we believe, have considerable future significance in terms of an autonomous ecologist political culture.

REFERENCES

Allan-Michaud, D. (1979). *Discours écologique*. Bordeaux: Université de Bordeaux, International Certificate of Human Ecology.

Allan-Michaud D. (1989), 'Le mouvement écologique français, Problèmes de visibilité et de lisibilité', paper presented at the Joint Sessions of the European Consortium for Political Research, Paris.

Banks, J. A. (1972). *The Sociology of Social Movements*. London: Macmillan.

Berger, P. and Kellner H. (1981). *Sociology Reinterpreted*. New York: Penguin.

Bidou, C. (1983) ,'Les aventuriers du quotidien', *Politique Aujourd'hui*, No. 1 pp. 11-24.

Boggs, C. (1976). *Gramsci's Marxism*. London: Pluto Press.

Boy D. (1980). 'L'électorat écologiste en 1978', paper presented at the Association Française de Science Politique, September.

Boy, D. (1989) 'L'Ecologisme en France', paper presented at the Joint Sessions of the European Consortium for Political Research, Paris.

Bresson De, H. (1989) 'Les Soutiers de la marée verte', *Le Monde*, 16 March.

Bunyard, P. and Morgan-Grenville, F. (1987). *The Green Alternative: Guide to Good Living*. London: Methuen.

Capra, F. (1983). *The Turning Point*. London: Fontana.

Chafer, T. (1984). 'The Greens in France: an emerging social movement?' *Journal of Area Studies*, No. 10, Autumn, pp. 36-44.

Dickson, D. (1981). *Alternative Technology*. London: Fontana/Collins.

Gorz, A. (1980). *Adieux au prolétariat*. Paris: Galilee (English translation: *Farewell to the Proletariat*. London: Pluto Press, 1982).

Guyomard, G. (1978). *Les Associations et la Transformation du Champ Politique Local* (*Fonctions d'agrégation et de médiation des associations de protection de l'environnement du littoral du Nord-Finistère*). Thése de DEA, Université de Rennes 1, UER de Sciences Juridiques.

Heberle, R. (1951). *Social Movements: An Introduction to Political Sociology*. New York: Appleton-Century-Croft.

Hoffman, S. (1974). *Essais sur la France*. Paris: Seuil.

Inglehart, R. (1977). *The Silent Revolution: Changing Values and Political Styles among Western Publics*. Princeton, NJ: Princeton University Press.

Lebreton, P. (1978). *L'Ex-Croissance - les chemins de l'écologisme*. Paris: Ed. Denoël.

Mounier, E. (1985). *Le Personnalisme*. Paris: Presses Universitaires de France.

Nullmeier, F.; Rubart, F. and Schultz, H. (eds.) (1983) *Umweltbewegungen und Parteiensystem: Umweltgruppen und Umweltparteien in Frankreich und Schweden* (Berlin: Quorum).

Oberschall, A. (1973). *Social Conflict and Social Movements*. Englewood Cliffs, NJ: Prentice Hall.

Porritt, J. (1984). *Seeing Green*. Oxford: Basil Blackwell.

Prendiville, B (1980). *Aspects du nucléaire et l'experience Bretonne*. Unpublished M.A. thesis, Université de Haute-Bretagne, Rennes.

Prendiville, B. (1981). Review of Touraine et al., *La prophétie anti-nucléaire*, in *Journal of Area Studies*, No. 4, p. 38.

Prendiville, B. (forthcoming). *The Political Ecology Movement in France*. PhD Reading University.

Rosanvallon, P. and Viveret, P. (1977). *Pour une nouvelle culture politique*. Paris: Seuil.

Simmonet, D. (1979). *L'Ecologisme*. Paris: Presses Universitaires de France.

Smelser, N. (1962). *The Theory of Collective Behaviour*. London: Routledge and Kegan Paul.

Toffler, A. (1970). *Future Shock*. London: Pan Books.

Touraine, A. (1978). *La Voix et le Regard*. Paris: Seuil (English translation: *The Voice and the Eye*. Cambridge: Cambridge University Press, 1981)

Touraine, A. Hegedus, Z., Dubet, F. and Wieviorka, M. (1980). *La prophétie anti-nucléaire*. Paris: Seuil (English translation: *Anti-Nuclear Protest: The Opposition to Nuclear energy in France*. Cambridge: Cambridge University Press 1983).

Turner, R. and Killian, L. (eds) (1972). *Collective Behaviour*, 2nd ed. Englewood Cliffs, NJ: Prentice Hall.

Weston, J. (ed.) (1986). *Red and Green: The New Politics of the Environment*. London: Pluto Press.

Wilkinson,.P. (1971). *Social Movement*. London: Pall Mall Press.

Williams, R. (n.d.). *Socialism and Ecology*. London: Socialist Environment and Resources Association.

Wilson, J. (1973). *Introduction to Social Movements*. New York: Basic Books.

Wright, V. (1989). *The Government and Politics of France*, 3rd. ed. London: Unwin Hyman.

Mirror, Mirror on the Wall:
Who's the Greenest of Us All?

ALISTAIR McCULLOCH

School of Administration and Law

Robert Gordon's Institute of Technology, Aberdeen, UK

John Button, *A Dictionary of Green Ideas*. London: Routledge, 1988.

John Elkington and Tom Burke, *The Green Capitalists: How to Make Money and Protect the Environment*. London: Victor Gollancz, 1989.

Sandy Irvine and Alec Ponton, *A Green Manifesto: Policies for a Green Future*, London: Optima, 1988.

Jonathon Porritt *Seeing Green: The Politics of Ecology Explained*. Oxford: Basil Blackwell, 1984.

Jonathon Porritt and David Winner, *The Coming of the Greens*. London: Fontana, 1988.

Martin Ryle, *Ecology and Socialism*. London: Radius 1988.

Elkington and Burke inform us in a postscript in the second edition of *The Green Capitalists* that 'one thing is clear: the 1990s will be the Green Decade' (p. 239). Whatever the truth of this prediction, 1989 has certainly been the 'Green Year'. In Britain, we have seen the conversion of Mrs Thatcher, the promotion of the verdant Chris Patten (the newly appointed Secretary of State for the Environment) and the corresponding demotion of the non-green Nicholas Ridley, the European elections, rise of green advertising, and the making of green media personalities such as Jonathon Porritt and Sara Parkin. If we were to go back to 1979, although the year saw a 1000 per cent growth in the membership of the Ecology Party (from about 500 to about 5000 as a result of the party's decision to field more than 50 candidates in that year's general election and thus become eligible for the party election television and radio broadcast) it is difficult, if not impossible, to recall any single item of news that could be deemed to carry an explicitly green message. From a decade away, that year brings to mind images which emphasize the problems of an industrialized, urbanized society, in which the wider, natural, environment was largely seen to be irrelevant to either the problem or the solution. From a decade away, that perspective seems to be not only short-sighted, but quite simply wrong. Since 1979, the green message has gradually spread wider in a manner which is (paradoxically) not unlike that of the despoiling oil slick as it, slowly at first but ever more quickly, spreads over the face of the ocean. Like the oil slick, the green message has, as it has spread, stuck to more and more of the things it has touched and, again like the oil slick, it has spread, it has had a tendency to become more and more diffuse. Finally, as with oils, there are many different types of green, and the books included in this review represent some of the more important of these different shades of green.

None of the books, it must be said at the outset, was designed to be an academic volume, and, as popular writings, they have themselves contributed to the development and spreading of green politics. Indeed, Porritt's *Seeing Green*, which was first published in 1984 and which stood for a long period on its own as the basic green text, is now approaching its tenth reprinting. The book stands firmly in the contemporary Liberal tradition and offers an easily read outline and discussion of what seemed in 1984 to be very radical ideas, but which have since permeated the manifestos of the major political parties in both the English-speaking world and continental Europe. Porritt stands on record as being pleased that his forecast that 'the likelihood of greening such stalwarts of industrialism as Norman Tebbit, Geoffrey Howe, Nigel Lawson and Mrs Thatcher herself is remote indeed' (p. 230) has proved (at least superficially) wrong. It is also instructive to see the way in which two of the books under consideration illustrate in a passive way the development of a specifically British green presence. Porritt's 1984 book contains a foreword by (at the time) the best-known Green in Britain, Petra Kelly, whereas by 1988 when Sandy Irvine and Alec Ponton's contribution to the debate was published, Porritt himself was invited to contribute the foreword. Given Porritt's central position during the 1980s as leading member of first the Ecology Party and then Friends of the Earth, it is fitting that John Button in *A Dictionary of Green Ideas*, after defining 'green' as 'a set of beliefs and a concomitant lifestyle that stresses the importance of respect for the earth and all its inhabitants, using only what resources are necessary and appropriate, acknowledging the rights of all forms of life, and recognising that all that exists is part of one interconnected whole', goes on to cite Porritt's extensive list which gives 'the minimum criteria for being green'.

The presence of a dictionary in a review of books regarding a developing social and political movement is unusual to say the least. The fact that this volume both can and should be included in such a review is indicative of the extent to which individuals in the green movement (or green movements depending on the degree of coherence the commentator grants the entity) view their ideas as being sufficiently new and different from those used in more traditional political discourse is to merit a new vocabulary. This is expressed in Button's hope that the volume 'will be an early step on the way to creating a green vocabulary that will help us to speak to each other, and will help people who are new to green thinking to understand us' (p. x). The language used in this quotation is reminiscent of much green writing with its suggestion that the cogniscenti should aim to improve the communication within their extant and correctly oriented group, while at the same time inviting the uninitiated to enter the debate once they are aware of the terms in which the discourse is being conducted. Given the aim (and the extent of the redefinition which is implied by the aim), the book includes much more than a strictly academic understanding of the concept 'ideas' would suggest, and upon investigation we quickly discover that what we have to hand is an excellent reference book which gives a green perspective on, or green definition of, many concepts and phenomena as well as defining the various elements of 'greenspeak' which confront the student of political ecology. It performs both of these tasks by an admirable combination of straightforward definition, discussion, and quotation from both the better and less well-known writing on whatever is the subject under consideration. Whether readers consider themselves to be greens or not, for the individual who intends either to teach or study the politics of the environment or environmental politics this dictionary is a very important tool.

As befits a book which was intended to appeal to more than the already converted, following some introductory words concerning the state of the green debate in 1984, Seeing Green provides a three-fold discussion in the traditional form of diagnosis, prescription and prognosis. As would be expected from books which approach the question of the environment from different perspectives, Porritt's Seeing Green, Elkington and Burke's The Green Capitalists, Irvine and Ponton's A Green Manifesto, and Ryle's Ecology and Socialism, all offer different analyses of the situation. For Porritt, the problem lies in the nature of industrial society. Thus he states that 'we have indeed seen extraordinary progress since the time of the Industrial Revolution, but not without incurring very considerable ecological debts which we are now having to pay off ... As a result, we have ended up in a right old mess' (p. 110). The nature of the pressures on the ecosystem ('the complex web of interactions within and between a community and its environment': Button) which Porritt describes will be familiar to anyone who has more than a passing acquaintance with green politics: population, topsoil loss, disappearing forests, oil-based energy, agriculture, acid rain and the greenhouse effect.

Irvine and Ponton prefer to discuss the basis of the problem in less specific terms. They say that too many demands have been placed upon both planet and people, and that these demands are a consequence of

> Human numbers ... Human technologies and the extent and inten-
> sity of their systems ... Human institutions, especially economies
> that are dependent on the overconsumption of physical space and

natural resources ... a culture which fragments reality, devaluing all that cannot be precisely measured and quantified ... What is so deadly, however is (these factors') interaction, and the way in which they multiply each others' effects. (p. 9).

In *Ecology and Socialism*, Ryle is attempting to claim the real green politics for socialism 'a label which covers many differing perspectives, but which has at its heart the belief that an egalitarian and humane society must ensure that the most important resources of that society are controlled by the community as a whole, and not by private capitalist entrepreneurs' (Button), and begins forcefully (although incorrectly) with the statement that 'energy is at the centre of the debate about our ecological future', before going on to argue that 'pollution is inextricably linked with energy consumption' (pp. 2 and 5), and challenging the view that ecology can form the basis for a new politics because the diversity of nature means that we can find within it examples to support almost any type of social relationship or human practice if we choose to look hard enough. This last line of criticism is not unique to Ryle, but its strength against those who would use examples from nature to demonstrate that a green society must of necessity be a friendly and cooperative society is both self-evident and worth repeating. Ryle prefers to attempt to ground green politics as the product of 'a long tradition of progressive thought and struggle – liberal and libertarian and socialist' (p. 12). The seat of the problem, as might be expected from the title of the book, is seen as lying in private ownership and the markets which private ownership generates.

In *The Green Capitalists*, Elkington and Burke appear at first sight to rely rather more on description than do the other authors who are under consideration here. This, however, is an illusion which disappears once the assumptions and implications underpinning the discussion are brought to the fore. Having traced the relationship between human beings and their environment from prehistoric time to the present, and having pointed out the range and pace of the changes which are taking place (as well as providing a very succinct history of the worst of the industrially caused environmental disasters), the two writers (who it appears worked mainly on separate sections of the book) then discuss the reasons for the development of an environmental consciousness at this particular time, pointing out that 'historically, a period of high unemployment, economic uncertainty and intensifying international tension signal the onset of political conservatism' (p. 61). This, of course, is to beg the question of whether or not green politics is essentially conservative in its nature. They state that the development of an environmental consciousness has occurred because there is a generation 'born since 1945 ... now on the verge of power (which together with) its successors form(s) an emergent majority ... Three experiences, wholly new to mankind, have marked their lives:

the threat of nuclear war, the magnitude of global poverty and the degradation of the environment' (p. 62). Unfortunately, Elkington and Burke then rather spoil the force of their argument by citing the Band Aid concert as their sole evidence of the 'vigour of the political impulse to which these experiences have given birth'. However, they do say that of the three movements which 'most reflect the emerging voice of the post-war generation, the environmental movement is pivotal. Intellectually, it integrates the other experiences.'

Given these differences in diagnosis, it is no surprise that we are also given divergent prescriptions. For Porritt, the answer is a rejection of growth, the development of a new economics which would take into account the externalities which classical economics neglects, nuclear disarmament, and the introduction of sustainability – a word of Latin derivation first used in this sense in 1971 meaning 'the capacity of a system to maintain a continuous flow of whatever each part of that system needs for a healthy existence' (Button) – as the principle which would underpin development. Porritt also includes in the prescriptive section of the book a chapter on the way in which green politics replaces the spirituality – 'the acknowledgement and direct experience of a dimension to existence beyond the material and the directly tangible' (Button) – which industrial society has lost. In this, he introduces us to the Gaia – 'an appropriate name for the complex, sensate, living "being" of the earth's biosphere' (Button) – hypothesis, feminism – 'the belief that discrimination against women is intolerable and must be ended' (Button) – and Christianity (not included in Button's work although we are given the benefit of his views on various aspects of spirituality). This is one of Porritt's weakest chapters because he has to try to fit a relativist approach to religion – 'a spirituality which incorporates a belief in the power of god or a similar universal spirit' – (Button) in which all roads seem to lead to the godhead (although for much of the debate the godhead seems to be taken to be female) into a self-confessed Christianity. As a self-confessed Christian myself, I find it impossible to combine a belief in the Creator and in Jesus Christ with a belief in the relativism which permeates much of the green movement's spirituality.

Irvine and Ponton give no space to the spiritual aspects which have such importance for Porritt (he also discusses the issue in the book he co-authored with David Winner, The Coming of the Greens), but say that 'social change cannot be left solely to individual actions. It must be part of a concerted political programme which seeks to change both our institutions and the values they embody' (p. 10). A Green Manifesto is their preferred political programme. The prescription they offer is based on four fundamental assumptions. These are that:

Life on Earth should continue.

Human life on Earth should continue.

Natural justice should be done.

There is a quality of life worth pursuing independent of material well-being.

From these fundamental assumptions they drive, first, 'working principles, to guide both individual and collective action' and then ways in which 'governments might begin to move towards this (green) goal, and away from the present slide into ecological and social chaos' (pp. 14 and 16). For them, the fundamental problem is overpopulation and they cite (as do Elkington and Burke) Garrett Hardin's seminal essay 'The Tragedy of the Commons' in support of their cases. Unfortunately, the acceptance of this famous allegory by any writer also necessarily means the acceptance by them of the view of human nature upon which the logic of Hardin's case rests. The fact that Hardin accepts an essentially Hobbesian view of human nature in which greed (or rational self-interest as the economists would have it) is the major human motivating force, makes it impossible for greens who accept Hardin's thesis to apply, as do Irvine and Ponton, the working principle that 'good ends can only come about by good means' (p. 16). Elkington and Burke are on somewhat safer territory in their use of the argument about the commons given that they are arguing from a capitalist perspective which accepts this more pessimistic view of human nature.

A Green Manifesto spends some time discussing the desirability of sustainable supplies, and the inevitability of this approach to natural resources given the problems associated with the cornucopian vision – a 'view of the future in which, despite all the signs to the contrary, the earth can continue to supply ever-increasing amounts of whatever human beings might desire' (Button) – and, with regards to the problem of pollution, says that 'technological gadgets merely shift the problem around, often at the expense of more energy and material inputs and therefore more pollution' (p. 36). Irvine and Ponton argue that the problems must be attacked at source and that prevention of pollution together with the conservation of all resources will be the most realistic approach. These aims are supported by Elkington and Burke, but they see the more realistic way forward as being the development of an alliance between the environmentalists and big business. They cite David Bellamy who stated that, 'the only way to beat them is to join them. We have got to become the developers' (p. 150), before going on to discuss the various international actors in the multi-faceted environmental-lobby corporate relationship. Unlike the other green propagandists,they draw back from a whole-hearted adoption of sustainable development as popularized by Professor Pearce, saying instead that the concept is a 'compass point rather than a route map, offering a rallying point around which new alliances can form' (p. 171).

The capitalist solution to the pollution problem is that which is rejected by the Greens Irvine and Ponton, that is the application of more of the thing which caused the problem in the first place: technology and, in particular, new forms of technology such as that involved in genetic engineering, biotechnology – 'those areas of technology concerned with the use of living organisms in industrial and agricultural processes' (Button). Elkingon and Burke accept that there are reservations concerning these (and other sunrise) developments, but state that:

> the prospects of a green sunrise are higher this time than they were at the dawn of the Industrial Revolution. For one thing today's emerging technologies are typically considerably cleaner and more resource-efficient than those they will replace. For another, they will be developed and deployed in a climate in which environmental concerns are increasingly important. (p. 201)

It is hard to be as optimistic as these writers, given that these emerging technologies are dependent upon a continuing growth economy with a concomitant impact upon resources irrespective of how resource efficient they are, and that they are likely to follow older industries which have shown a tendency to cross national boundaries to take advantage of any lax environmental regulations.

Ryle rejects the capitalist prescription, and urges greater autonomy, while accepting the need for a coordinating and redistributive mechanism (which is lacking in Porritt's *Seeing Green*) to ensure that gross inequalities do not arise under the eco-socialism which he proposes as the solution to the current crisis. He suggests that the state 'should act as the protector of the general interest' (p. 61) and that state intervention is a necessary part of an ecologically sound future. He argues from the British experience of the Second World War to suggest that people would accept the necessary level of intervention and regulation, but seems to forget that even the most interventionist Greens see the planet's problems being solved in the long rather than the short term, and that following a mere six years of war and a further six years of regulation the population of Britain seemed unwilling to accept further regulation.

The four books give differing prognoses, with Porritt's 1984 volume being the most pessimistic. He comments that:

> Our real fear is not that we shall run out of oil or clean water or other vital resources, but that we shall run out of time ... There should be no illusions about the urgency of this: as more and more people are driven into positions of political extremism, the threat posed to democracy today is as great as the threat to the biosphere ... The longer we resist the inevitability of change, the less chance is there that we shall achieve it democratically. (pp. 220–1)

This pessimism reflects, in part, the prevailing sociopolitical conditions of the time when the book was written and is not reflected to the same extent in the later The Coming of the Greens, where, in the concluding paragraph, the authors state 'categorically that green thinking has already had a considerable impact on the way we live, and that the advance of green ideas has been astonishingly rapid' (p. 268).

If one thing above all else can unite the many varied types of Greens, then it is their attitude to the Labour Party and to attempts to graft an eco-prefix onto the socialist body. This is the case with both of the books with which Porritt is involved and also A Green Manifesto. Irvine and Ponton call eco-socialism 'a condition in terms', saying that 'left wing ideology has not disputed the size and ingredients of the economic cake, arguing merely over how it should be sliced up. It shows no sign of recognising that our problems start with the quantity and quality of the productive forces themselves' (pp. 141–2). This is in direct contravention to the position taken by Ryle who issues that by now familiar call, first issued by the then Liberal leader Jo Grimond some quarter of a century ago, for a realignment of the left, because 'it is within the terms of socialism ... that the ecological challenge can best be understood and met' (p. 100).

The Green Capitalists, on the other hand, makes the bold statement that 'socialism as an economic theory, though not as a moral crusade, is dead' (p. 252), despite the obvious definitional problems of contemplating a socialism without its fundamental economic dimension. Elkington and Burke go on to say that the 'argument now is about what kind of capitalism we want ... (and that must be green capitalism) if there is to be a planet worth having for our children to inherit'. However, the reaction of greens (or even radical liberals and socialists) to Elkington and Burke's examples of the ways in which 'environmental fund-raising organizations, for example, are working up new approaches for helping companies tap into the green marketplace', is hardly likely to be enthusiastic. The writers describe the link-up between Kleenex and the World Wide Fund for Nature, under which Kleenex boosted their sales of disposable tissues by 76 per cent with the development of 'Wildlife Tissues', and the offer made by Fiat the car manufacturers to donate '£1 for every telephone call in support of its campaign to protect Madagascar's wildlife' (p. 221). These examples would seem to put the environment (and the movement which champions its cause) into the same position as the cartoon character who sits calmly on the end of a branch of a tree talking to another character while that second character saws away at the same branch which is our hero's only support.

All six books are worthy to be read, and the five polemical books are also worthy of criticism. For example, Ryle never addresses the basic question of the definition of green, and is highly eclectic in his choice of 'green' writers, working his way through Porritt, Murray Bookchin, Paul

Ekins, André Gorz and the 1987 Green Party Manifesto without considering the very great differences between them. Each of the books reviewed here has a different message to deliver, and is aimed at a different audience, although whether that message is well received will depend upon the ideological stance of the reader and the degree of prior knowledge which the reader possesses. Seeing Green is for the novice who wants to know what are the basic arguments in favour of the green position. The Coming of the Greens is to my mind the best read and offers a very useful discussion of the diffusion of green ideas, although, as with Seeing Green, an updated version would be useful given the developments since 1988. The Green Capitalists will appeal to those who want a concrete example of the way in which the system incorporates, makes harmless, and then makes a profit out of movements and ideas which seek to challenge it by selling the idea back to the activist in the form of one or more commodities. A Green Manifesto looks to spell out a programme for a green government and does this in a compelling way, although, while the authors are aware of the incorporating tendency mentioned above, I am not convinced that their proposals have the force to overcome this danger. Ecology and Socialism also demonstrates Ryle's awareness of this danger, but his discussion (which is aimed at the more politically aware reader than any of the other books) fails to convince at least this reader of the practicality of his proposals for the realignment of the left in Britain (and presumably throughout the rest of the developed world). Finally, to remove any possible doubt as to the meaning which these representatives of the various tendencies in green politics are trying to get across, I would suggest that each book is read with a copy of A Dictionary of Green Ideas close to hand. As a final thought for the student of green politics who enjoys a challenge, I would recommend that he or she takes the three days necessary and applies Button's dictionary to the definition of green given in F. Capra and C. Spretnak's Green Politics (London: Paladin, 1985, pp. xvi-xvii.) Perhaps John Button could be persuaded to give a prize for the best effort.

Book Reviews

Anna Bramwell, *Ecology in the Twentieth Century: A History.*
New Haven, CT: Yale University Press, 1989.
It is clear that green politics did not spring, fully formed, from the head of any one ideologist, and that green ideas have a history. However, since we are still debating whether there is anything distinctive that can be called a green ideology, any history of green ideas is also inevitably a contribution to the very definition of green politics. The more usual histories search for isolated themes such as decentralization or anti-industrialism which only become green at the particular moment when a diverse range of ideas from anti-consumerism to feminism are moulded together in the green melting pot. For instance, David Pepper's valuable *The History of Modern Environmentalism*, stresses a continuity in political values as the principal means of identifying the green element within environmentalism. This is not the approach favoured by Anna Bramwell. By ignoring the political values of contemporary greens she aims to alter radically the debate about green ideology. Drawing on thinkers usually ignored elsewhere, including leading Nazis, she argues that political ecology already has a hundred year history in which the green parties play only a small and, for her, largely counter-productive role.

This apparently broader perspective depends on restoring to the centre of the green debate a stress on two scientific ideas, the biological holism of Haeckel, Driesch and other early ecologists, and the energy economics of the diverse range of theorists concerned with resource depletion. But, besides the intellectual history of scientific ecology, Bramwell also provides a more political definition of the true ecologist, a defence of some aspects of the pre-war eco-Nazi and High Tory traditions and a vituperative critique of contemporary green politics. This makes for a rather confusing journey, combining studies of maverick individuals whose politics were largely ignored in the 1930s as well as today, such as the pro-fascist novelists Knut Hamsun and Henry Williamson, with useful summaries of her previous work on the ecological themes in broader movements, including Nazism, and her attack on the left-wing character of contemporary green parties.

However, Bramwell's case, that there is a narrative of ecology as a movement that has both right and left wings, united by a common underground ecological tradition, cannot be sustained by her own definition of political ecology. She attempt to establish a relation between diverse individuals and political forces based on a broad recognition of the political significance of humanity's dependence on nature and a sense of loss at the damage caused by industrial society. But, she arbitrarily rejects the influence of important left-wing currents, from early utopian socialism, to Morris and the New Left, and with equal assurance ignores histories, such as Martin Wiener's *English Culture and the Decline of the Industrial Spirit*, which attempts a more structural explanation of the emergence of anti-industrial sentiments.

The real problem with her definition of political ecology is that by defending the idea that there is a politics which can be drawn directly from nature (p. 236), and which reflects 'natural values', Bramwell tries to go beyond identifying ecology as a theme which can be articulated in contradictory form by left and right, to an attempt to herself articulate a true ecology, based on a 'true reading' of nature, an ecology which is clearly of the right. However, if her project is of the right, it stems from that part of the British New Right which places a particular emphasis on the nation. In itself, her useful information on High Tory, fascist and Nazi ecology, could provide the starting point for an analysis of the openness of ideas about the natural world to use as a tool for contradictory political mobilizations but, unfortunately, Bramwell's commitment to the idea of immutable natural law means that she herself is not in a position to pursue this idea.

In attacking the green parties, she seems to contradict her own earlier claim that political ecology is a broad movement, with left and right wings. The 'red entryism' which had corrupted green parties 'show[s] that ecologism has already lost its way'. While she says 'Their policies have little to do with real green values' (p. 235), it is not clear how the Nordic nationalism, which united British and German eco-fascists (ideas which are not directly criticized by Bramwell) are any more legitimately connected to real green values. The fact that leading Nazis such as Himmler, Hess and Darré, shared an interest in rural self-sufficiency and homeopathy is important, but cannot be separated from their use of nature, as bloody and masculine, to legitimate other elements in Nazism, including the belief in Aryan superiority. Bramwell condemns Nazi atrocities, but does not seem to recognize the role played in them by the belief that there is a politics which follows directly from nature. For her, if the green parties are betraying an earlier ecological tradition, it seems that their error is in large part a failure to recognize the importance of national culture. The green parties' critique of Western exploitation of the Third World is described as 'scapegoating' and even 'racialist' (p. 130). She sees them as advocating 'the abandonment of treasure and knowledge to tribes and nations in foreign lands who pose no threat to us. Consciously, or otherwise, this is a death-wish' (p. 248). This internationalism is seen as a characteristic linking the 1920s and 1990s Greens:

> The craving for the Other identity of the Protestant North middleclass ... which led in the 1920s to a yearning for the non-national pan-Aryan, leads today with equal ease to a longing to merge with the masses of the Far East. (p. 29)

It is the non-exclusive internationalism of the contemporary Greens which is seen as most dangerous. The Greens naively argue that 'aid to the Third World, or at least that dwindling part of it still unaffected by prosperity... must increase' (p. 240) but since aid has 'disappeared into arms purchases and gold taps' (p. 235) this innocent strategy is likely to undermine the West's economic competitiveness:

> The question is whether, if ecologism returned to being a non-party matter, Western man could restore his sense of values, while surviving in a world dominated by anti-ecological ideology and potentially dominated by the expanding economies of nations like Japan and Indonesia, Brazil and Korea, who do not share the culture-specific ecological concerns of the West. (p. 236)

It is unfortunate that her political project obscures the more useful coverage elsewhere in the book of the common political themes including self-sufficiency, opposition to trade and decentralization, which have influenced both left and right ecologists. Despite the problems with her definition of political ecology, her exhaustive research on the pre-war ecologists makes the book useful for specialists, though perhaps rather misleading for the general reader. In essence it cannot really be read as a history of ecology; it is more accurately an attempt to rearticulate a lost right-wing ecological tradition in opposition to 'all the remnants of a callous disregard for human and natural values which characterised post war collectivism'.

Brian Doherty
Department of Government
University of Manchester

Timothy W. Luke, *Screens of Power: Ideology,
Domination and Resistance in Informational Society,*
Urbana, IL: University of Illinois Press 1989.

Computer screens, digital watches, cable television, even the cash regis-
ters that ring in these products as we buy them, stand as testimony to a
changed society. In an era of 'postmodernism', 'postindustrialism', 'silent
revolutions', 'hyper-reality', and just plain old 'New Times', defining our
environment has become an analytical industry in itself. Timothy Leary has
gone from extolling us to 'turn on, tune in and drop out' to telling us to
'turn on, boot up and print out'. The information society seems to have
established itself in our lives with a particular vengeance. Through the fu-
sion of critical theory with a semiotic approach, Timothy Luke, in his book
Screens of Power, tries to draw some sort of map that defines this technological
modernity that we have come to know.

Eloquently arguing for an approach that decodes the symbolism
inherent within a society in order to uncover the underlying truth, Luke
decodes the messages relayed on the 'screens of power' to find that
capitalism has changed in a substantial way to ensure its longevity. By using
examples such as the US media coverage of the 1984 D-Day celebrations
and the Chernobyl incident, Luke emphasizes the continuity of capitalism
through an informational mode of production. Rather than reifying the
post-war industrialism into a granite-carved context for social study by
seeing everything as an adjunct in industrialism, he describes informational
society as a 'complex new order whose social and political structures are
dominated increasingly by the development, elaboration, and expression
of formalized discourses and scientific disciplines' (p. 10). New capacities
for communicative and informational abilities means, for Luke, new
capacities for ecological destruction and new capacities for the legitimization
of that destruction.

'Informationalism' represents the need to move away from notions of
post-industrialism that tie the changes to previous forms of production.
Looking around us provides evidence enough that the industrial process
is losing ground. With informationalism Luke is suggesting that the
dominant ideas of industrialism come to permeate culture, society and
politics in much deeper ways than was previously possible. Communication
technologies and their place in the 'global village' extend the reach while
downsizing the message of informational capital. Scientism and the market
become so embedded in thought and ideas as to be taken out of discussion.
The computer and television screens that comprise so much of our lives
become the screens of power behind which hide the ritualistic obeisance
of the deity of scientific and technological progress.

If this new form of society is characterized by the production, dissemination and distribution of information through the new medias, through new communicative capacities and through new technologies in general, then an approach which emphasizes the symbolic and decodes the mystical becomes apt even for the social scientist. It has particular connotations for those studying the social movements. This is why the new social movements lie at the core of politics in an informational society. At the same time as the emergence of an informational form of production a number of new social movements have emerged that seem to say that all is not well. Movements such as the green movement offer some of the few new challenges to this new form of modernity. It is therefore possible to understand something, more about informational politics if we understand the current wave of environmental interest that has brought into vogue some ideas that were previously peripheral.

Using Luke's framework for analysis, ideologies become stylistic representations of the deep cleavage in informational society. As such we can understand the green movement as transnational symbolism of revolt against the environmental destruction in informational society. Being green becomes a style. I am green because I perceive myself to be so. I can be green because I drive steel stakes into trees ear-marked for felling or because I choose to take a CFC-free aerosol at my local supermarket. Housewives, activists and extremists become part of a single phenomenon. In consumer society consumer politics take their place alongside more traditional modes of political action.

The diversity in membership and composition of the green movement becomes muted as it is expressed through ideology. There is no need to adhere to the set texts of 'green' theory. To be seen to be 'green' is enough. It implies a simple starting point which can be interpreted in a variety of radically differing ways. However, this is not to deny its value or its importance. Indeed it is a crucial component of green strength. In informational society, forms of resistance are naturally phrased in terms that reflect the society they are resisting. One-dimensional society implies a one-dimensional form of resistance. The style of being 'green' stands as a counterpoint to the Gordon Gecko 'greed is good' (or perhaps 'growth is good') lifestyle of the informationalized market system.

In Britain a recent advertisement for a make of nappies used a picture of its product on a young child with the slogan 'Green peace'. When the name of one of the most prominent environmental groups become so vogue as to be marketable to a mass audience as a synonym for all that is positive, rather than being defined out of the arena of political discourse, it must point to some profound shift in the terrain of ideological discourse. What Luke succeeds in doing is to push the analysis of society, politics and culture onwards and into the lines of change that already characterize our society. *Screens of Power* begins to do what is so much needed in social analysis. It addresses the new as indeed novel and not merely as an adjunct to the old with which we are so much more familiar. It is far from being a detailed map, but it shows clearly that critical approaches are very useful points of departure if we are to understand this bewildering modernity. For that alone this book is worthwhile. However, by providing us with an incisive and witty guidebook to informational society, Screens of Power gives us useful directions for understanding the changed role and nature of ideology, and hence moves social analysis on with the moving society that it seeks to analyse.

Paul Taggart
Department of Political Science
University of Pittsburgh

Koula Mellos, Perspectives on Ecology: A Critical Essay.
London: Macmillan Press, 1988.

It is of some interest that academia has until quite recently remained studiously silent concerning the social and political ideas of the environmental and latterly green movement. Since the mid 1960s, and growing with the movement, there has been a steady accumulation of ideas to which we might conveniently append the title 'political ecology'.

While there has been some academic analysis of the social and ideological origins of the movement it is only very recently that the ideas of the political ecologists themselves have been acknowledged at all (and it is worth adding that some important writers, notably Edward Goldsmith, remain to be 'discovered').

There is no doubt that academia is discomforted by these ideas which cannot easily be fitted into conventional analytical frameworks. The radical ecologists are only acknowledged at all by Marxists, and overwhelmingly analysts adopt a dismissive tone. Although new, in so far as it looks in some detail at the social and political ideas of the political ecologists, Koula Mellos's book nevertheless fits comfortably into the conventional mould.

Mellos creates a clear framework which categorizes political ecology into three kinds of theory. The first encompasses both the neo-Malthusian and expansionist writings of the 1970s that focused primarily on the 'global environmental problematic'. The second encompasses 'eco-development' ideas that have been pursued by some of the international development agencies as a response to the failure of conventional development strategies in rural Africa and Asia. The third encompasses the 'radical ecologists', focusing specifically on Murray Bookchin, André Gorz and William Leiss.

The basic of the categorization – which is also the main message of the book – is concerned with the attitude to 'human nature' termed 'anthropological assumption', which Mellos imputes to the various writings. The neo-Malthusians and expansionists are seen as writing from a liberal individualist perspective. While this is explicit in the writing of Ophuls and can easily be deduced in the writing of Garrett Hardin and the expansionists (Herman Kahn, John Maddox and Wilfred Beckerman), it is beginning to stretch matters when this is extended to 'The Limits to Growth' study. While it might be assumed that because the members of the Club of Rome are basically *haute bourgeois*, that they will therefore inevitably subscribe to 'possessive individualism', it is noteworthy that 'Limits' steered carefully clear of any social or political prescription.

Mellos sees eco-development as being underpinned by an 'anthropology of individual self-sufficiency'. At face value this is odd, given that three theories – and practice, in so far as this has been developed – of eco-development are of organization and decision making. Mellos justifies this categorization by stating that the eco-development theorists fail to confront adequately private property or capitalist relations as these operate at the community level.

That is really like saying that if your theory isn't 200 per cent antiindividualist according to my criteria then it must, by definition, be individualist. Certainly, for all the criticism that might be levelled at the eco-developmentalists, there is little indication that Mellos has any notion of the complexities of cultural and political contexts which they are attempting to confront.

Mellos's process of categorization is stretched to breaking point when it comes to the radical ecologists. These are defined as subscribing to a 'petit bourgeois anthropology of asocial individualist self-sufficiency'. Although a lot of argument is expended on justifying such a stance, it is necessary to disregard vital elements of, and in the end append a flagrantly contradictory label to, the work of these writers.

All of the radical ecologists analysed (and it is anomalous that Mellos failed to include Bahro and perhaps other German writers) have evolved out of Marxist origins. They have all moved in their several directions through a process of intellectual effort, and often praxis as well, that attempts to render relevant aspects of Marxism coherent to the actual problems of our day.

My own thoughts on Gorz are that he has been ensnared by French dualist philosophical traditions into denying the possibility of any truly holistic socio-ecological solution to the human condition. This is a very long way from being a petit bourgeois anthropology of asocial individual self-sufficiency especially in view of the major role which Gorz sees for the state in his utopia! Certainly, Gorz's critique of Marxism has much to teach us about a politics relevant to our predicament.

Bookchin, too, might be accused of finding difficulty ultimately escaping from his national philosophical traditions, namely American individualism. Nevertheless, his complex and subtle argument, particularly as presented in Chapter 12 of his *The Ecology of Freedom*, sums to among the best attempts so far to work through Marx's notions of the achievement of communist society, taking account of the social and technological problems and possibilities facing us today.

Only in the last chapter of Mellos's book are we confronted with the simplistic 'correct' approach to the sociopolitical resolution of the environmental problematic. In a word, 'the crucial point' is that:

ecological restoration in our own social formation is necessarily tied to the working class struggle for liberation from capitalist productive relations.

While acknowledging that there is no solution to our predicament that does not take the working class with it, Gorz and Bookchin have concluded that we will destroy the world long before the working class leads us to the promised land and that therefore we must seek other routes to human emancipation.

Mellos's scholastic labelling exercise does absolutely nothing to help us toward an effective theory let alone praxis, that will rescue the world from ecological catastrophe. I suspect this is one of those situations to which Marx was heard to remark: 'if that's Marxism, then I'm no Marxist!'.

Adrian Atkinson
Development Planning Unit
University College London

Notes on Contributors

Anthony DeSales Affigne teaches in the Department of Political Science at Brown University. He is currently working on a book about the Exxon Valdez oil spill. His other research interests include European and American elections, environmental politics and comparative social policy.

Adrian Atkinson lectures in the Development Planning Unit of University College London. He received his Ph.D in Geography from the London School of Economics and Political Science in 1988 and is currently preparing a book entitled *Principles of Political Ecology*.

Susan Baker is Lecturer in European Business Studies at the University of Ulster. Her research, at the European University Institute, Florence, Italy, concerned ideology and industrialisation in Ireland. Her present research interests include the relations between industry, the policy making structures and interest groups and, in particular, environmental issues. Dr Baker has published the results of her research in several activities and chapters in books and is currently preparing a book on the emergence and evolution of Irish environmental movements.

Tony Chafer is Senior Lecturer in French Studies at Portsmouth Polytechnic. He has written a number of articles on the French anti-nuclear and Green movements.

Mario Diani is Lecturer in Sociology at the Bocconi University, Milan, Italy, and Honorary Research Fellow, Department of Government, University of Strathclyde. He received his Ph.D. from the University of Milan in 1987. Dr Diani is the author of several books and articles on new social movements and green parties and is currently preparing a book on networks of ecological groups in Italy.

Brian Doherty is a postgraduate research student at the Department of Government, University of Manchester.

E. Gene Frankland is Professor of Political Science at Ball State University in Muncie, Indiana USA. He received his Ph.D. from the University of Iowa in 1973. His special areas of interest are comparative politics and environmental policy. He has written several articles on Green parties, parliamentary recruitment, and political socialization and is currently co-authoring (with Donald Schoonmaker) a book on the West German Greens 1980-90.

Herbert Kitschelt is Associate Professor of Political Science at Duke University. He has published several books on energy technology policy, new social movements, and changes of party systems in Western democracy. His most recent books are The Logics of Party Formation. Ecological Politics in Belgium and West Germany (Cornell University Press, 1989) and Beyond the European Left. Ideology and Political Action in the Belgian Ecology Parties (Duke University Press, 1990). His articles have appeared in Comparative Politics, Comparative Political Studies, International Organization, Political Studies, World Politics, and a number of other journals and edited volumes.

Alistair McCulloch is a Lecturer in the School of Administration and Law at Robert Gordon's Institute of Technology, Aberdeen. He received his Ph.D. in Politics from Exeter University in 1986, and is the author of several journal articles on green political theory and green politics in Britain.

Thomas Poguntke is a Lecturer in Political Science at the University of Mannheim. He received his Ph.D. from the European University Institute in Florence and has published several articles in journals and edited volumes on Green Parties and the New Politics. He is currently involved in a cross-national research project on organizational change of political parties in Western democracies.

Brendan Prendiville graduated at Portsmouth Polytechnic in 1978 in French Studies. He completed a History MA (University of Rennes 2/ France) on the Breton Anti-Nuclear Movement in 1980 and is currently engaged in Ph.D research (University of Reading) into the French political ecology movement with particular emphasis on the situation in Brittany. He is also teaching in the Sociology Department of Rennes University 2.

Paul Taggart is a postgraduate research student at the Department of Political Science, University of Pittsburgh.

The Editor

Wolfgang Rüdig is Senior Lecturer in the Department of Government at Strathclyde University. After graduating in political science at the Free University Berlin, he received his Ph.D. from the University of Manchester. He is author or co-author of Energiediskussion in Europa (3rd. ed., Neckar Verlag 1981), Anti-nuclear Movements: A World Survey of Opposition to Nuclear Energy (Longman, 1990), and The Green Wave: A Comparative Analysis of Ecological Parties (Polity Press, forthcoming 1991). He is also editor of the book series Environment, Politics and Society (Edinburgh University Press). Currently, he is engaged in research on comparative water policy and the British Green Party.

Index